Top zone numbers: 5 6 7 8 9 10 11 12 13 14 15 16

ARCTIC OCEAN

ZEML'A FRANCA-IOSIFA

SPITSBERGEN (Nor.)

GREENLAND (Den.)

Greenland Sea

NOVAJA ZEML'A

Thule

Baffin Bay

VICTORIA ISLAND

BAFFIN ISLAND

Godhavn
Godthåb

ICELAND
Reykjavik

JAN MAYEN (Nor.)

Hammerfest

Barents Sea

Murmansk

13

NORTH

Yellowknife

Hudson Bay

Churchill

KAP FARVEL

FAEROE ISLANDS (Den.)

Oslo

SWEDEN NORWAY FINLAND

14

Archangel'sk

LENINGRAD

U.S.S.R.

75°

60°

8

Days Strait

CANADA

Edmonton

AMERICA

Calgary Winnipeg Quebec

Minneapolis Ottawa

City UNITED

CHICAGO DETROIT NEW YORK

St. Louis

STATES Washington Philadelphia

Phoenix Dallas New Orleans

Goose Bay

NEWFOUNDLAND

Montréal

8½

ATLANTIC

AZORES (Port.)

OCEAN

UNITED KINGDOM

IRELAND

LONDON

PARIS
FRANCE

Lisbon
SPAIN Rome

North Sea DEN.
NETH.
BEL.
SWITZ. AUS. HUNG.
ITALY YUGO.

Stockholm
MOSCOW

Gorky

EUROPE

Volgograd

BERLIN POL.
GER. Warsaw
CZECH.
ROM.
BUL.

Black Sea

Ankara

15

45°

Mexico

Gulf of Mexico

MEXICO CITY

LIPPERTON (Fr. Poly.)

Miami

BAHAMAS

CUBA
JAM.
BELIZE (U.K.)
GUAT.
EL SAL. HOND.
NIC. HAITI

COSTA RICA PANAMA

BERMUDA (U.K.)

DOM. REP.
PUERTO RICO (U.S.)

9

Tropic of Cancer

CAPE VERDE

CANARY IS. (Sp.)

MOROCCO

Casablanca
Rabat

Algiers

Tripoli

SAHARA

MAURI-
TANIA MALI NIGER CHAD

SENEGAL
GAMBIA
GUINEA-BISS.
SIERRA LEONE GUI.
LIBERIA I.C.

PORT.
GREECE TURKEY

Mediterranean Sea

ALGERIA LIBYA

TUN.
Bengazi

CAIRO
EGYPT

Khartoum

SUDAN

Addis Ababa

SYRIA IRAQ
LEB.
ISR. JOR.

SAUDI
ARABIA

IRAN
AFG.

KUWAIT PAK.
U.A.E.

OMAN

15½

YEM. P.D.R. OF YEM.

ETH.

15°

ECUADOR

ARCHIPIÉLAGO DE COLÓN
GALAPAGOS ISLANDS (Ec.)

VEN.
Bogotá GUYANA
SURINAM
COL. FR. GUIANA

PERU Surinam Zone 8 + 30 min.

SOUTH

BRAZIL

Lima

Belém

Equator

GHANA NIGERIA CAM.
EQUAT. GUI.
GABON CONGO
ZAIRE

CEN. AFR. REP.

UG. KENYA

RW.
BDI. TANZANIA

SOMALIA

0°

Antofagasta

AMERICA

PARA.

Asunción

Recife

Brasília

Salvador

RIO DE JANEIRO

Tropic of Capricorn

ATLANTIC

OCEAN

ANGOLA

ZAMBIA
RH. MOZ.

BOTS.

S.W. AFR. (S. Afr. Admin.)

Johannesburg

SOUTH AFRICA
Cape Town

SWAZ.
LESO.

MADAG.

INDIAN

OCEAN

17

15°

30°

Santiago

CHILE ARGENTINA

URUGUAY
Montevideo
BUENOS AIRES

45°

Graphic Linear Scale

Punta Arenas

FALKLAND ISLANDS (U.K.)

CABO DE HORNOS
CAPE HORN

SOUTH GEORGIA (Falk. Is.)

SOUTH ORKNEY ISLANDS (B.A.T.)

0 100 200 300 400 500 600 700 800 900 1000
Statute Miles
Miller Cylindrical Projection

0°
15°
30°
45°
60°
75°

60°

Circle

Bellingshausen Sea

Weddell Sea

ANTARCTICA

ENDERBY LAND

75°

Phila Hach's
United Nations
Cookbook

Edited by
Dianne Moore
Book House, Inc.

Recipes Collected
From UN Ambassadors
After Their Visit To
Tennessee 1976

Published by Book House, Inc.
P.O. Box 34542
Bartlett, Tennessee 38134

Library of Congress Number — 81-50666

International Standard Book Number — 0-918544-72-6

Printed in the United States of America

WIMMER BROTHERS FINE PRINTING & LITHOGRAPHY
MEMPHIS, TN 38118
"Cookbooks of Distinction".TM

Dear Friends,

Several years ago I received this beautiful thought through the mail. I hope it will free your mind and lift your spirit and encourage you to learn more about the fascinating and interesting people that inhabit our world. It is my hope that one day we may all seek to understand each other and live in harmony without sacrificing the differences which make each nation unique.

Love and best wishes to each of you.

Phila R. Hach

Phila R. Hach

Let it be declared, announced, and hereby celebrated . . .
That all people everywhere are dependent upon one another.
That everyone needs everyone else for freedom, life, love, and happiness.
That all things in the natural order are dependent upon everything else.
That our little planet and all the planets and stars in all the solar systems are in a state of mutual dependence upon one another.
That this universally shared dependence comes from God and is of God.
And that each individual part of this great relationship has its own part to play — its own destiny to fulfill in God's plan.

ABOUT THE AUTHOR

Phila Rawlings Hach received her degree in music from Ward-Belmont College and later her degree in foods and nutrition from Vanderbilt University and Peabody College for Teachers.

After graduation from college, Phila joined American Airlines as a stewardess and later became a Supervisor of Training for the company. She did special research in holding foods at high altitudes and compiled an in-flight food manual for the airline industry. While with American, she collected recipes from country homes around the world.

In the early 1950's she joined the staff of WSM-TV and for years conducted a very popular homemakers' show, "Kitchen Kollege". She was the recipient of The National Zenith Television Award for outstanding contributions to public service programming and was twice selected Cook-of-the-Month by "The Chicago Tri-

bune". She is listed in the first edition of "Who's Who of Living American Women".

Phila is the author of three previous cookbooks, "Kitchen Kollege" (which won the Southern Graphic Arts Award), "From Phila With Love", an intimate handwritten collection of her favorite recipes, thoughts and prayers, and "Kountry Kooking", one of the most celebrated books of fine Southern cuisine. She makes her home in Clarksville, Tennessee, where she and her husband, Adolf, and son, Joe, own and operate a delightful Country Inn, "Hachland Hill".

Phila says of all the honors bestowed on her, that of serving the entire delegation of the United Nations was her most memorable. This United Nations Cookbook has been 4 years in the making and has endeared her to those who made it possible.

"I would like to dedicate this book to the United Nations and what it has meant to the world through its endeavors to promote love and understanding, health and prosperity and above all to unite the great peoples of our earth."

Phila

POSTAL ADDRESS · ADRESSE POSTALE · UNITED NATIONS, N.Y. 10017
CABLE ADDRESS—ADRESSE TELEGRAPHIQUE · UNATIONS NEWYORK

EXECUTIVE OFFICE OF THE SECRETARY-GENERAL
CABINET DU SECRETAIRE GENERAL

17 June 1976

Dear Mrs. Hach,

On behalf of the Secretary-General I would like to thank you for the important part which you played in the United Nations visit to Tennessee by organizing the delicious food on this occasion.

Both at the State dinner and at the luncheon on the grounds at the Parthenon, the food was a most striking example of the delights of country cooking. The dishes were of a truly wide variety, and all of us who were present enjoyed them thoroughly. Under the attractive tents and within the setting of the Parthenon, the lunch proved indeed to be a most pleasant event.

I would appreciate it if you could convey our gratitude to all those who helped in preparing these excellent meals.

With kind regards,

Yours sincerely,

Kurt Herndl
Deputy Executive Assistant
to the Secretary-General

Mrs. Phila R. Hach
Hachland Hill
Clarksville, Tennessee 37040

VI

United Nations Association of the United States of America

300 East 42nd Street, New York, NY 10017
212•697•3232   Cable: UNASAMER

President
Robert M. Ratner

Founding Chairman
Robert S. Benjamin
1909-1979

Honorary Chairmen
Arthur J. Goldberg
Henry Cabot Lodge
Charles W. Yost

National Chairman, UN Day 1980
*(By appointment of
the President of the U.S.A.)*
Charles L. Brown, Chairman
American Telephone and Telegraph Company

August 19, 1980

The publication of Phila Hach's United Nations Cookbook is a pleasing reminder of the June, 1976 United Nations visit to Tennessee. On that occasion, at the invitation of the Governor and a committee of leading Tennessee citizens, and with the full cooperation of the United Nations Association, representatives of over one hundred member nations, the Secretary-General of the UN and numerous senior UN officials visited Tennessee.

During their day in Nashville, there were many highlights, including a Forum at Vanderbilt University, at which UN Secretary-General Kurt Waldheim received the Cordell Hull Peace Award, and a special performance of Nashville's famed Grand Ole Opry. However, unquestionably the most pleasant interlude in the crowded day was the traditional Southern "dinner on the grounds"--the grounds in this case being Nashville's beautiful Centennial Park--a meal conceived and executed by Phila Hach.

This book of recipes from all corners of the world is, in a sense, a "thank you" from those dignitaries who participated in the UN visit to Tennessee. The diversity that is the United Nations can be seen in the many selections in the book.

UNA-USA--whose goal is to educate and inform the American people about all aspects of the UN System--considered it particularly appropriate that the 1976 UN visit was to Nashville. The Nashville chapter of UNA was the first in the Association, beginning operations in 1945 prior to the signing of the UN Charter in San Francisco. Chapters in Memphis, Knoxville, Chattanooga, and Oak Ridge also participated in the 1976 UN visit.

The Association is pleased that a portion of the royalties from the United Nations Cookbook will be used to support the educational programs of UNA-USA. We are pleased to join with Phila Hach in this publication which should give many years of continuing pleasure to its readers. Bon appetite!

Robert M. Ratner
President

Country Cooking Goes
Worldwide ... and the Favorite
Recipes of the World Come Home
to Tennessee

On June 7, 1976, more than 100 of the Permanent Representatives at the United Nations visited Nashville as guests of the Governor and the people of Tennessee — an unprecedented and historic event.

That visit, which Secretary of State Henry Kissenger called "an innovation in diplomacy" brought the world to Tennessee and showcased Tennessee to the world.

Their excellencies and spouses, led by Secretary-General Kurt Waldheim, were honored at a forum at Vanderbilt University, treated to an old fashion "Luncheon on the Grounds" at the Parthenon, relaxed at Opryland and attended a special performance of the Grand Ole Opry.

It was the overwhelming response to that delightful luncheon that brought this cookbook into being.

From the onset Phila and Adolf Hach became a moving force in the success of the UN Visit. They planned and catered the elegant State Dinner honoring Secretary-General and Mrs. Waldheim and the leading Tennessee businessmen who financed the visit.

Their total commitment to the UN project was responsible for bringing together a group of Clarksville and Middle Tennessee businessmen who underwrote the cost of the luncheon. The luncheon, typical of Tennessee hospitality, was served with great elan under a colorful tent setting in Centennial Park.

A personally inscribed copy of Phila's **Kountry Kooking** Cookbook was included among the official Tennessee mementoes presented to the Ambassadors.

That cookbook went home with each of the visitors, and evoked great interest as it contained many of the recipes served at the luncheon. Phila received many letters from those impressed with the foods of Tennessee, among which was one from Baron Rudiger von Wechmar of West Germany who praised "the marvelous food served us."

From these responses was born the idea of Phila's United Nations Cookbook. She subsequently requested the favorite national recipes of the Ambassadors; they responded enthusiastically and sent recipes to Clarksville for inclusion in the book.

Phila's culinary abilities have set standards in the South. She has served the Vice-President and Senators, Wall Street Bankers, celebrities of this country and European, South American and African Heads of State.

Her cookery played a major role in Secretary-General Waldheim's statement, "In Tennessee, we came to understand in full measure the meaning of Southern hospitality."

You will delight in Betty Waldheim's Sachertorte Mit Schlag and in the Callaloo and Saltfish Accra as offered by Ambassador Abdullah of Trinidad and Tobago.

From Swaziland comes a traditional recipe for Swazi Cornmeal Dumplings and from "down under" Australian Ambassador Harry offers a Party Meringue.

Mrs. Chaim Herzog of Israel sends her recipe for Eggplant A La Medi.

South Africa is represented with "Lekker Poeding" and Bobotie Loaf. Spanish Ambassador de Pinies includes his special recipes for Gazpacho Andaluz and Tocino del Cielo. And from the Greek Isles come Madam Papoulias' dessert recipes for Baklava and Fenikia, which are not to be outdone by Governor Scranton's own Deep Dish Pennsylvania Blueberry Pie.

You will relish Curry from Burma, Spinach Turnovers from Cyprus, Argentine Empanadas, Cloudberries Parfait from Finland and other recipes from Ireland, Malta, Mexico and the rest of the world.

And now savor the hospitality of the world and its Ambassadors when the UN comes **home** to Tennessee.

> Brooks Parker
> Project Director
> UN Visits Tennessee

July 7, 1980

Preamble
The Permanent Representatives
to the United Nations

We the people of the United Nations determined

To Save succeeding generations from the scourge of war, which twice in our lifetime has brought untold sorrow to mankind, and . . .

To Reaffirm faith in fundamental human rights, in the dignity and worth of the human person, in the equal rights of men and women and of nations large and small, and . . .

To Establish conditions under which justice and respect for the obligations arising from treaties and other sources of international law can be maintained, and . . .

To Promote social progress and better standards of life in larger freedom, . . .

And for these ends

To Practice tolerance and live together in peace with one another as good neighbours, and . . .

To Unite our strength to maintain international peace and security and . . .

To Ensure, by the acceptance of principles and the institution of methods, that armed force shall not be used, save in the common interest, and . . .

To Employ international machinery for the promotion of the economic and social advancement of all peoples . . .

Have resolved to combine our efforts to accomplish these aims.

Accordingly, our respective Government, through representatives assembled in the city of San Francisco, who have exhibited their full powers found to be in good and due form, have agreed to the present Charter of the United Nations and do hereby establish an international organization to be known as the United Nations.

San Francisco June 24, 1945

My personal thanks to the following members of the United Nations and their staffs for the help rendered in making this book possible.

Phila R. Hach

Phila R Hach

Afghanistan
H.E.M. Abdullah Malikyar and Madame Malikyar

Albania
H.E.M. Rako Naco

Algeria
H.E.M. Abdellatif Rahal and Madame Rahal

Argentina
H.E. Dr. Carlos Ortiz de Rozas and Señora de Ortiz de Rozas

Australia
H.E. Mr. Ralph L. Harry, C.B.E., and Mrs. Harry

Austria
H.E. Mr. Peter Jankowitsch and Mrs. Jankowitsch

Bahamas
H.E. Mr. Livingston Basil Johnson and Mrs. Johnson

Bahrain
H.E. Dr. Salman Mohamed Al Saffar and Mrs. Al Saffar

Bangladesh
H.E. Mr. Khwaja Mohammed Kaiser and Mrs. Kaiser

Barbados
H.E. The Hon. J. Cameron Tudor, C.M.G.

Belgium
H.E.M. Edouard Longerstaey and Madame Longerstaey

Benin
H.E.M. Thomas S. Boya

Bhutan
H.E. Mr. Dago Tshering and Mrs. Tshering

Bolivia
H.E. Dr. Mario R. Gutierrez and Señora de Gutierrez

Botswana
H.E. Mr. Thebe David Mogami and Mrs. Mogami

Brazil
H.E.M. Sérgio Correa da Costa and Madame Correa da Costa

Bulgaria
H.E. Mr. Guero Grozev and Mrs. Grozev

Burma
H.E.U Myint Maung and Mrs. Myint Maung

Burundi
H.E.M. Joseph Ndabaniwe and Madame Ndabaniwe

Byelorussian Soviet Socialist Republic
H.E. Mr. Guerodot G. Tchermouchtchenko and Mrs. Tchernouchtchenko

Canada
H.E. Dr. Saul F. Rae and Mrs. Rae

Central African Republic
H.E.M. Jean-Arthur Bandio and Madame Bandio

Chad
H.E.M. Beadengar Dessande and Madame Dessande

Chile
H.E. Vice Admiral Ismael Huerta and Señora de Huerta

China
H.E. Mr. Huang Hua and Mrs. Ho Li-liang

Colombia
H.E. Dr. Germán Zea and Señora de Zea

Congo
H.E.M. Nicolas Mondjo and Madame Mondjo

Costa Rica
H.E. Lic. Fernando Salazar and Señora de Salazar

Cuba
H.E. Dr. Ricardo Alarcon de Quesada and Señora de Alarcon Quesada

Cyprus
H.E. Mr. Zenon Rossides and Mrs. Rossides

Czechoslovakia
H.E. Dr. Ladislav Šmíd and Mrs. Šmíd

Democratic Yemen
H.E. Mr. Abdalla Saleh Ashtal and Mrs. Ashtal

Denmark
H.E. Mr. Henning Hjorth-Nielsen and Mrs. Hjorth-Nielsen

Dominican Republic
H.E. Dr. Alfonso Moreno-Martinez and Señora de Moreno

Ecuador
The Chargé d'Affaires Dr. Mario Alemán and Señora de Alemán

Egypt
H.E. Dr. Ahmed Esmat Abdel Meguid and Mrs. Abdel Meguid

El Salvador
H.E. Dr. Reynaldo Galindo Pohl and Señora de Galindo Pohl

Equatorial Guinea
H.E. Sr. Benjamin Ecua Miko and Señora de Ecua Miko

Ethiopia
H.E. Mr. Mohamed Hamid Ibrahim

Fiji
H.E. Mr. Semesa K. Sikivou, C.B.E., and Mrs. Sikivou

Finland
H.E. Mr. Aarno Karhilo and Mrs. Karhilo

France
H.E.M. Louis de Guiringaud and Madame de Guiringaud

Gabon
H.E.M. Jean-Baptiste Essonghe and Madame Essonghe

German Democratic Republic
H.E. Mr. Peter Florin and Mrs. Florin

Germany, Federal Republic of
H.E. Baron Rüdiger von Wechmar and Baroness von Wechmar

Ghana
H.E. Mr. Frank Edmund Boaten and Mrs. Boaten

Greece
H.E.M. George Papoulias and Madame Papoulias

Grenada
H.E. Mrs. Marie-Jo McIntyre

Guatemala
H.E. Lic. Juan Luis Orantes-Luna and Señora de Orantes

Guinea
H.E. Madame Jeanne Martin Cisse

Guinea-Bissau
H.E.M. Gil Fernandes

Guyana
H.E. Mr. Rashleigh Esmond Jackson and Mrs. Jackson

Haiti
H.E.M. Raoul Siclait and Madame Siclait

Honduras
H.E. Ing. Roberto Martinez Ordoñez and Señora de Martinez Ordoñez

Hungary
H.E. Mr. Imre Hollai and Mrs. Hollai

Iceland
H.E. Mr. Ingvi S. Ingvarsson and Mrs. Ingvarsson

India
H.E. Mr. Rikhi Jaipal and Mrs. Jaipal

Indonesia
H.E. Mr. Chaidir Anwar Sani and Mrs. Anwar Sani

Iran
H.E.M. Fereydoun Hoveyda and Madame Hoveyda

Iraq
H.E. Dr. Abdul Karim Al-Shaikhly and Mrs. Al-Shaikhly

Ireland
H.E. Dr. Eamonn Kennedy and Mrs. Kennedy

Israel
H.E. Mr. Chaim Herzog and Mrs. Herzog

Italy
H.E.M. Piero Vinci and Madam Vinci

Ivory Coast
H.E.M. Siméon Akke and Madame Akke

Jamaica
H.E. Mr. Donald O. Mills and Mrs. Mills

Japan
H.E. Mr. Isao Abe and Mrs. Abe

Jordan
H.E. Sherif Abdul Hamid Sharaf and Mrs.
Sharaf

Kenya
H.E. Mr. Charles Gatere Maina and Mrs. Maina

Kuwait
H.E. Mr. Abdalla Yaccoub Bishara and Mrs.
Bishara

Lao People's Democratic Republic
H.E. Dr. Vithaya Sourinho and Madame
Sourinho

Lebanon
H.E.M. Edouard Ghorra and Madame Ghorra

Lesotho
H.E. Mr. David Ketso 'Noto and Mrs. 'Noto

Liberia
H.E. Mrs. Angie Brooks-Randolph and Mr. Isaac
M. Randolph

Libyan Arab Republic
H.E. Mr. Mansur Rashid Kikhia

Luxembourg
H.E.M. Jean Rettel and Madame Rettel

Madagascar
H.E.M. Blaise Rabetafika and Madame
Rabetafika

Malawi
H.E. Mr. T.J.X. Muwamba and Mrs. Muwamba

Malaysia
The Chargé d'Affaires Mr. Ajit Singh and Mrs.
Singh

Mali
H.E.M. Mamadou Boubacar Kante and Madame
Kante

Malta
H.E. Mr. Joseph Attard Kingswell and Mrs.
Attard Kingswell

Mauritania
H.E.M. Moulaye El Hassen and Madame El
Hassen

Mauritius
H.E. Mr. Radha Krishna Ramphul and Mrs.
Ramphul

Mexico
H.E. Sr. Roberto de Rosenzweig-Diaz and Señora
de Rosenzweig-Diaz

Mongolia
H.E. Mr. Tsevegzhavyn Puntsagnorov and Mrs.
Puntsagnorov

Morocco
H.E.M. Driss Slaoui and Madame Slaoui

Mozambique
H.E. Mr. José Carlos Lobo

Nepal
H.E. Mr. Shailendra Kumar Upadhyay and Mrs.
Upadhyay

Netherland
H.E. Dr. Johan Kaufmann and Mrs. Kaufmann

New Zealand
H.E. Mr. Malcolm J.C. Templeton and Mrs.
Templeton

Nicaragua
H.E. Dr. Guillermo Sevilla-Sacasa and Señora de
Sevilla-Sacasa

Niger
H.E.M. Illa Salifou and Madame Salifou

Nigeria
H.E. Mr. Leslie O. Harriman and Mrs. Harriman

Norway
H.E. Mr. Ole Algard and Mrs. Algard

Oman
H.E. Dr. Kamal M. Hagras and Mrs. Hagras

Pakistan
H.E. Mr. Iqbal A. Akhund and Mrs. Akhund

Panama
H.E. Dr. Jorge Illueca and Señora de Illueca

Papua New Guinea
H.E. Mr. Paulias Nguna Matane and Mrs. Matane

Paraguay
H.E. Dr. Francisco M. Barreiro and Señora de Barreiro

Peru
H.E. Sr. Carlos T. Alzamora and Señora de Alzamora

Philippines
H.E. Mr. Narciso G. Reyes and Mrs. Reyes

Poland
H.E. Mr. Henryk Jaroszek and Mrs. Jaroszek

Portugal
H.E.M. José Manuel Galvão Teles and Madame Galvão Teles

Qatar
H.E. Mr. Jasim Yousif Jamal

Romania
H.E.M. Ion Datcu and Madame Datcu

Rwanda
H.E.M. Callixte Habamenshi and Madame Habamenshi

Saudi Arabia
H.E. Mr. Jamil M. Baroody and Mrs. Baroody

Senegal
H.E.M. Medoune Fall

Sierra Leone
H.E. Dr. Edward Wilmot Blyden III and Mrs. Blyden

Singapore
H.E. Mr. T.T.B. Koh and Mrs. Koh

Somalia
H.E. Mr. Abdirizak Haji Hussen and Mrs. Hussen

South Africa
H.E. Mr. Roelof F. Botha and Mrs. Botha

Spain
H.E. Sr. Don Jaime de Piniés and Señora de Piniés

Sri Lanka
H.E. Mr. Hamilton Shirley Amerasinghe

Sudan
H.E. Mr. Mustafa Medani and Mrs. Medani

Surinam
H.E. Mr. Henricus A.F. Heidweiller and Mrs. Heidweiller

Swaziland
H.E. Mr. N.M. Malinga and Mrs. Malinga

Sweden
H.E. Mr. Olof Rydbeck and Mrs. Rydbeck

Syrian Arab Republic
H.E.M. Mowaffak Allaf and Madame Allaf

Thailand
H.E. Dr. Pracha Guna-Kasem and Mrs. Guna-Kasem

Togo
H.E.M. Dabra Togbe and Madame Togbe

Trinidad and Tobago
H.E. Mr. Frank Owen Abdulah

Tunisia
H.E.M. Rachid Driss and Madame Driss

Turkey
H.E. Mr. Ilter Türkmen and Mrs. Türkmen

Uganda
H.E. Mr. Khalid Younis Kinene and Mrs. Kinene

Ukrainian Soviet Socialist Republic
H.E. Mr. Vladimir N. Martynenko and Mrs. Martynenko

Union of Soviet Socialist Republic
H.E. Mr. Yakov Aleksandrovich Malik and Mrs. Malik

United Arab Emirates
H.E. Dr. Ali Humaidan and Mrs. Humaidan

United Kingdom of Great Britain and Northern Ireland
H.E. Mr. Ivor Richard, Q.C., and Mrs. Richard

United Republic of Cameroon
H.E.M. Ferdinand Léopold Oyono and Madame Oyono

United Republic of Tanzania
H.E. Mr. Salim Ahmed Salim and Mrs. Salim

United States of America
H.E. Mr. William W. Scranton and Mrs. Scranton

Upper Volta
H.E.M. Télesphore Yaguibou and Madame Yaguibou

Uruguay
H.E. Dr. Carlos Giambruno and Señora de Giambruno

Venezuela
H.E. Dr. Simón Alberto Consalvi and Señora de Consalvi

Yemen
H.E. Mr. Mohamed A. Sallam and Mrs. Sallam

Yugoslavia
H.E. Mr. Jakša Petrić and Mrs. Petrić

Zaire
H.E.M. Mutuale Tshikankie and Madame Mutuale

Zambia
H.E. Mr. Dunstan Weston Kamana and Mrs. Kamana

Roster of the United Nations

The 151 members of the United Nations, with the years in which they became members.

Member	Year	Member	Year	Member	Year
Afghanistan	1946	Ghana	1957	Pakistan	1947
Albania	1955	Greece	1945	Panama	1945
Algeria	1962	Grenada	1974	Papua New Guinea	1975
Angola	1976	Guatemala	1945	Paraguay	1945
Argentina	1945	Guinea	1958	Peru	1945
Australia	1945	Guinea-Bissau	1974	Philippines	1945
Austria	1955	Guyana	1966	Poland	1945
Bahamas	1973	Haiti	1945	Portugal	1955
Bahrain	1971	Honduras	1945	Qatar	1971
Bangladesh	1974	Hungary	1955	Romania	1955
Barbados	1966	Iceland	1946	Rwanda	1962
Belgium	1945	India	1945	Saint Lucia	1979
Benin	1960	Indonesia	1950	Samoa (Western)	1976
Bhutan	1971	Iran	1945	Sao Tome e Principe	1975
Bolivia	1945	Iraq	1945	Saudi Arabia	1945
Botswana	1966	Ireland	1955	Senegal	1960
Brazil	1945	Israel	1949	Seychelles	1976
Bulgaria	1955	Italy	1955	Sierra Leone	1961
Burma	1948	Ivory Coast	1960	Singapore	1965
Burundi	1962	Jamaica	1962	Solomon Islands	1978
Byelorussia	1945	Japan	1956	Somalia	1960
Cameroon	1960	Jordan	1955	South Africa	1945
Canada	1945	Kampuchea (Cambodia)	1955	Spain	1955
Cape Verde	1975	Kenya	1963	Sri Lanka	1955
Central Afr. Emp.	1960	Kuwait	1963	Sudan	1956
Chad	1960	Laos	1955	Surinam	1975
Chile	1945	Lebanon	1945	Swaziland	1968
China[4]	1945	Lesotho	1966	Sweden	1946
Colombia	1945	Liberia	1945	Syria	1945
Comoros	1975	Libya	1955	Tanzania	1961
Congo	1960	Luxembourg	1945	Thailand	1946
Costa Rica	1945	Madagascar (Malagasy)	1960	Togo	1960
Cuba	1945	Malawi	1964	Trinidad and Tobago	1962
Cyprus	1960	Malaysia	1957	Tunisia	1956
Czechoslovakia	1945	Maldives	1965	Turkey	1945
Denmark	1945	Mali	1960	Uganda	1962
Djibouti	1977	Malta	1964	Ukraine	1945
Dominica	1978	Mauritania	1961	Union of Soviet Soc.	
Dominican Rep.	1945	Mauritius	1968	Repubs.	1945
Ecuador	1945	Mexico	1945	United Arab Emirates	1971
Egypt	1945	Mongolia	1961	United Kingdom	1945
El Salvador	1945	Morocco	1956	United States	1945
Equatorial Guinea	1968	Mozambique	1975	Upper Volta	1960
Ethiopia	1945	Nepal	1955	Uruguay	1945
Fiji	1970	Netherlands	1945	Venezuela	1945
Finland	1955	New Zealand	1945	Vietnam	1977
France	1945	Nicaragua	1945	Yemen	1947
Gabon	1960	Niger	1960	Yugoslavia	1945
Gambia	1965	Nigeria	1960	Zaire	1960
Germany, East	1973	Norway	1945	Zambia	1964
Germany, West	1973	Oman	1971		

FLAGS OF THE UNITED NATIONS

AFGHANISTAN

BAHAMAS

ALBANIA

BAHRAIN

ALGERIA

BANGLADESH

ANGOLA

BARBADOS

ARGENTINA

BELGIUM

AUSTRALIA

BENIN

AUSTRIA

BHUTAN

Mutton, rice and fruit are the staple diet in Afghanistan. Bread, the basic food of all people, is quite different from our western concept of bread. In Afghanistan, it doubles as a plate; some meats are eaten on it. The bread folds up around the meat and is picked up with the fingers. The bread is baked in big round mud ovens.

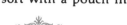

2 cakes yeast
1 1/2 cups lukewarm water
3 cups sifted whole wheat flour

1 teaspoon salt
2 tablespoons oil (for softer bread)

KHUBZ or PITTA BREAD
(Typical Bread of the Near East)

Soften yeast in water, add 1 cup flour. Let stand 30 minutes in warm place. Then mix in rest of flour and salt. Let stand 3 hours again in a warm place. Divide dough into 8 pieces. Knead and pat the dough for 1/2 hour, flipping and patting the dough into a large flat round loaf. Lay on a shallow, greased pan. Let rise 30 minutes. Bake in moderate oven at 350 degrees until brown, approximately 10 minutes. Sprinkle with cold water as it bakes to prevent it from getting too brown. It should be soft with a pouch inside.

1 quart canned grape leaves (about 100) drained and soaked 45 minutes in cold water
1 1/2 lbs. ground lean lamb
3/4 cup rice, uncooked

4 tablespoons butter
1 teaspoon allspice
Salt to taste
4-6 lbs. hot water

STUFFED GRAPE LEAVES WITH LAMB
(Serves 10)

Mix lamb, rice, allspice, salt and water thoroughly. Place grape leaves rib side up on work surface. Put 1 1/2 teaspoons of filling in middle of each leaf. From stem end roll up half way, fold in sides to form packet and continue to roll up. Place in a heavy stainless steel pan in layers. Sprinkle each layer with chopped fresh garlic, mint leaves, salt and thin sliced lemons. Cover with broth made from lamb bones and weight down and simmer over very low heat for 2 hours or until done. Serve with yogurt.

Proverbs:
"Pleasant words are like honeycomb, sweetner to the soul and health to the body."

PULE ME DROP
(Sweet Stuffed Chicken)

EMATUR
(Typical Dessert Cake)

Albania is a lovely, mountainous country about the size of Maryland, located on the Adriatic Sea. The main staples are cornbread, olives and goat's milk. The Albanians don't use many flavorings.

1 4-lb. roasting chicken
2 cups dry bread crumbs
1/2 cup melted butter
1/4 cup seedless raisins or currants

1/4 cup mixed nuts, chopped
1/2 cup sugar
6 tablespoons chicken stock
3/4 teaspoon cinnamon

Mix bread crumbs with butter, add other ingredients; moisten with chicken stock. Stuff into chicken. Roast in pan, uncovered, in 325 degree oven for 3 hours. I prefer to put crumb mixture under chicken and bake as directed.

1 cup water
1 cup butter, melted
1 cup sugar

2 cups flour
1/4 cup blanched almonds
(I use a little almond flavoring)

Bring water to a boil, add sugar and butter, and boil 3 minutes. Slowly add flour, stirring until it forms a smooth paste. Continue to stir for 5 minutes with a wooden spoon. Spread out on greased cookie sheet. Cut into diamond shapes. Place almond on top. Bake 15 minutes at 450 degrees; reduce heat to 300, and bake until brown.

Cooking vessels are mostly of copper, lined with tin and are usually much larger than we are accustomed to. Almost every kitchen has a mortar and pestle to crush their spices and nuts. The western custom of drinking kraut juice may have started in Albania. One of these favorite appetizers is called orme (a pickled cabbage juice).

Chopped cucumbers in yogurt is often served in bowls as a cold soup for lunch.

Breakfast usually consists of cheese, bread or light pastry and coffee. The evening meal consists of vegetable, pilaf, ripe olives, black coffee and pastires.

Cooking fats of the Middle East:
Alya — rendered fat from sheeps tail.
Samna — butter from buffalo milk usually melted and clarified.
Ghee — a type of Indian butter.

Algeria is a country about three times the size of Texas in North West Africa bordering on the Mediterranean Sea, and south to the Sahara Desert. The Tell, a fertile plain, is 50-100 miles wide with moderate climate. Chief crops are wine grapes, artichoke, flax, olives, pomegranates, figs, and dates. The waters of the Mediterranean supply wonderful fish.

THETCHOUKA

4 tomatoes, skinned and reduced to pulp in 2 tablespoons butter, with 2 cloves of garlic. To this, add thin strips of red bell peppers, or pimentos. Sauté until done.
Just before serving:
Beat 6 eggs until light. Pour over mixture and cook until set. I like to do this in a heavy skillet.

CUTTLEFISH OR SOLE

Soak fish in salted water. Then steam with a sprinkling of mixed herbs (tarragon, chervil, and basil). Place in casserole, sprinkle with white wine, sliced mushrooms, parsley and dabs of butter. Run under broiler until mushrooms are done. Serve with lemon and cracked pepper. Serve with Algerian Couscous, made from freshly ground millet.

LEMON SQUARES

1/2 cup butter	1 cup flour
1/4 cup powdered sugar	pinch salt

Cream together. Put into 8 x 8-inch pan. Bake 350 degrees 15 minutes, do not brown. Mix 2 eggs, 1 cup sugar, 2 tablespoons flour, 2 tablespoons fresh lemon — pour over hot crust as soon as taken from oven. Bake 20 minutes or until completely set. Cool — sprinkle with powdered sugar, cut in small squares.

Where there's room in the heart, there's room in the house.

3

Angola stretches about 1,000 miles along the southwest coast of Africa. Its land area is about twice the size of Texas. Its major crops are coffee, corn, sugar, palm oil, cotton, wheat, tobacco, cocoa, sisal, wax, fish and fishmeal. It was founded by the Portuguese in 1491. Besides its wealth of food products, it exports iron, diamonds, cotton goods and soap.

GREEN TOMATO AND APRICOT CHUTNEY

1 gallon green tomatoes
1/2 gallon sliced onions
5 cups dried apricots
7 cups of brown sugar
2 tablespoons celery seed

1/2 teaspoon whole cloves
1 quart vinegar
4 tablespoons mustard seed
1 tablespoon turmeric

Slice tomatoes and onions and leave in brine for 1 1/2 hours. (Make brine with 1 cup salt to 4 quarts of water). Put vinegar and other ingredients in a deep pan and boil 10 minutes. Drain tomatoes and onions and add to the boiling mixture. Simmer for about 1 hour until very tender and dark. Makes about 8 pints.

YELLOW RICE

4 tablespoons butter, melted
1 cup long grain rice
3 cups boiling water
1 stick cinnamon
1/2 teaspoon turmeric, ground

pinch of saffron
1 teaspoon salt
1 cup seedless raisins
sugar

Combine melted butter in heavy saucepan with rice. Stir until coated with butter. Add boiling water and rest of ingredients. Simmer covered for 20-30 minutes until all water is absorbed. Turn out on serving platter. Sprinkle with sugar and serve.

GOLDEN EGG CAKE

9 to 14 egg yolks
1/2 cup cold water
1/4 teaspoon salt
1/2 teaspoon cream of tartar

1 cup sugar
1 cup sifted cake flour
1/2 teaspoon baking powder
1 teaspoon vanilla

Beat egg yolks, water and salt for 20 minutes in electric mixer, until thick. When foamy, add cream of tartar and continue to beat. Sift the sugar five times and sift the flour once. Sift the flour four more times, each time with 1/4 cup of the sugar and the baking powder. Add remaining 3/4 cup sugar to the yolk mixture, folding in 2 tablespoons at a time. Fold in the vanilla. Sift in a small amount of the flour mixture at a time. Bake in an ungreased angel food pan at 275 degrees for the first 30 minutes, and then at 325 degrees for the next 30 minutes. The cake should bake for 1 hour or more. Invert pan until cake is cool.

A mountainous country about four times the size of Texas, Argentina is known for the fine beef raised there. Sugar, peanuts and fruits grow abundantly. This is one of the most prosperous, educated and industrialized Latin American nations.

EMPANADA

Dough:
1/2 lb. cold salt butter or margarine
6 1/2 cups flour

3/4 to 1 cup cold water
1 teaspoon salt

Beef Filling:
1/2 cup vegetable oil
4 medium onions, peeled and
  chopped
1 1/2 lb. ground chuck
2 sweet roasted pimentos, drained
  and chopped
1/2 cup dark seedless raisins

1 1/2 teaspoons oregano
1 teaspoon sweet paprika
Pinch of black pepper
1 tablespoon salt
4 large eggs, hard cooked, peeled
  and chopped
24 small green pitted olives

Dough: Cut butter into pieces, using electric mixer, mix with flour and salt. Gradually add 3/4 cup water. Mix for 6 minutes. Dough should form a ball. Pat into round shape. Place dough in plastic bag and keep at room temperature for 20 to 30 minutes. Divide dough in half and knead for 2 minutes. Roll out on lightly floured surface to a thickness of 1/8-inch and 5 1/2 inches in diameter. Should make enough for 24 circles.

Beef Filling: Heat oil in skillet and sauté onion until bright yellow. Add beef, stirring until beef loses its red color. Stir in pimento, raisins, oregano, paprika, and salt and continue sautéing for 2 minutes. Drain off excess oil; chill in refrigerator for 1 hour. Stir in chopped eggs just before filling the dough. Reserve olives to add to each empanada.

Preparing the Empanada: Preheat oven to 450 degrees. Place 4 tablespoons of filling on each circle of dough. Insert 1 olive into each mound of filling. If dough is dry, moisten with cold water. Fold dough in half. Press down firmly just below the mound of filling. Turn edge over, pressing down firmly. Then working from left to right, crimp and pleat in points to seal edges. Brush each empanada with a glaze made of 1 egg, beaten with 1/2 teaspoon sugar. Place empanadas 1 inch apart on an ungreased baking sheet and bake for 20 minutes or until golden brown. Left over baked empanadas can be stored in the refrigerator and reheated for 10 minutes at 350 degrees. Yield: About 24.

Australia is almost as large as the continental United States, and is located southeast of Asia. The Indian Ocean is to the west and the Pacific Ocean to the east. Its nearest island neighbor is Indonesia. The northeast section of the country has thick jungles with heavy rains, while the northwest part is desert.

STEAK AND KIDNEY PIE

2 small beef kidneys	3 tablespoons parsley
Flour	3 tablespoons celery tops
3/4 lb. cubed beef steak	Salt and pepper
1/2 cup suet or fat	1 cup mushrooms
1 large onion, chopped	1 cup carrots, diced
Hot water	Rich biscuit dough
1 bay leaf	

Soak kidneys in salt water overnight. Cut steak and kidneys in 2-inch squares and dredge in flour. Brown steak, kidney and chopped onion in suet. Add hot water to cover. Add bay leaf, parsley, celery, salt, pepper, mushrooms, carrots and simmer gently for 1 hour. Pour into a deep baking dish and top with rich pastry rolled thin. Bake at 400 degrees until crust is brown.

PARTY MERINGUE

(A Favorite of the Australians!)

4 egg whites	8 tablespoons sugar
1/2 teaspoon vanilla	2 teaspoons white vinegar

Remove eggs from refrigerator a while before using. Put the egg whites in a large bowl, beat at high speed of mixer until stiff, but not dry. Then fold in sugar, vinegar and vanilla, gradually. Grease cookie sheet with butter and sprinkle with sugar. Place mixture on sheet in round shapes. Put in oven at 250 degrees for 1 to 1 1/2 hours. Remove from oven onto plate to cool away from drafts. To serve, top with whipped cream, strawberries, or grated bitter chocolate.

KIWI SHERBERT

1 cup water	Juice of 1 lemon
1 cup sugar	2 egg whites, stiffly beaten
6 very ripe kiwis	

Bring sugar and water to a boil and cook for 5 minutes. Cool to room temperature. Peel the kiwi and purée in blender. Add to lemon juice and water, sugar mixture. Freeze until mushy. Beat the egg whites until stiff and stir into the partially frozen kiwi mixture. Return to freezer. Serve in orange shells or peach halves or melon!

The cream is skimmed from scalded milk, so that the albumin is coagulated with it. It is warmed over a slow heat not to exceed 150 degrees. (This generally takes about 3 hrs. in a double boiler) — discard the crust which forms on top. Chill cream. It is delicious over berries and with preserved ginger!

DEVONSHIRE CREAM or CLOTTED CREAM

---

2 pieces day old bread
1 tablespoon butter
Salt and ground nutmeg

Chopped parsley
1 beaten egg

BREAD DUMPLINGS

Cut bread in small pieces. Dampen with hot soup. Cream butter. Add seasonings, parsley, egg and dampened bread. Blend well. Form into balls. Drop in hot soup and cook for 5 minutes.

---

1 6-lb Beef Tenderloin,
  roasted rare
Make forcemeat using
  1/4 cup each of Onion
  Butter
  Mushrooms
  Cognac
  Cooked Veal
  Cooked Pork
  Cream
  Chicken Liver
  Mix well

Season with 1/2 tsp. each of
  Parsley
  Basil
  Thyme
  Rosemary
  Allspice
  Pepper

BEEF WELLINGTON

Blend with 1 whole egg and mix thoroughly. Pat on cooked tenderloin. Cover with a rich pastry and bake in hot oven 425 degrees until brown. Slice and serve.

1/4 cup boiling water
1 stick butter

1 1/2 cups pastry flour
1/4 teaspoon salt

BUTTER HOT WATER PASTRY

Melt butter in hot water. Gradually stir in flour. Add salt. Mix quickly, chill and roll out thin and shape over Beef Wellington. Brush top with butter before baking.

It is better to bend than to break.

Austria is a primarily mountainous country, slightly smaller than Maine, located in eastern Europe. At one time the powerful Austrian empire ruled large portions of the continent. Many people think of the Danube River and the Strauss waltz of the same name when Austria is mentioned. Austrians are fine cooks, and specialize in extremely rich, highly-caloric pastries.

SACHER-TORTE MIT SCHLAG

5 ounces Baker's German sweet chocolate
5 ounces very fine sugar
5 ounces sweet butter or margarine
6 egg yolks

6 egg whites
5 ounces cake flour
1/4 teaspoon baking powder
Apricot marmalade

Preheat oven to 350 degrees. Grease and flour springform pan. Soften chocolate in top of double boiler. Beat sugar, butter and egg yolks until mixture is fluffy. Beat egg whites until stiff. Combine flour and baking powder. Alternately fold egg whites and flour into chocolate mixture. Spoon batter into pan. Lower oven to 300 degrees and bake 40 minutes, or until cake springs back. Turn off heat, open oven door and leave cake in oven for ten minutes. Remove from oven and cool for 20 minutes. Remove from pan and cool on plate for several hours. Cut cake horizontally, fill with marmalade and reassemble, using bottom of cake for top layer. Glaze top and sides of cake with thin layer of marmalade.

ICING:
6 ounces Baker's German sweet chocolate
3 1/2 ounces sifted confectioner's sugar

Juice of 1/2 lemon, strained and boiled
Few drops boiling water

Melt chocolate in top of double boiler and stirring with wire whisk, add sugar. Add hot lemon juice and boiling water, little by little, stirring constantly. Hold cake with left hand, pour icing on center of cake and turn cake, tilting it so that the icing runs down the sides evenly. Do not smooth with knife, should be thick and still running. Serve with slightly sweetened whipped cream.

SALZBURGER NOCKERL

2 egg yolks
3/4 teaspoon grated lemon rind
1 teaspoon vanilla
1 tablespoon flour

4 egg whites
Pinch of salt
2 tablespoons sugar
Powdered sugar

Preheat oven to 350 degrees. In a medium mixing bowl, stir egg yolks with a fork, then add lemon rind and vanilla and mix lightly. Sprinkle the flour over the top. Set aside a few minutes, while you beat egg whites with a wire whisk or electric mixer. Add salt and beat until mixture clings to beater. Add sugar, continue beating until egg whites form stiff peaks. Use a rubber spatula to fold a spoonful of the egg whites into the yolk mixture lightly. Then fold yolk mixture into the egg white bowl. Fold briefly, but do not mix. In a well-buttered 8 x 10-inch casserole or baking dish (should be 2 inches high) make three mounds of the egg mixture (the mounds are the "nockerl") and then bake 10 to 12 minutes. It is ready when lightly brown on the outside, but soft inside. Sprinkle with powdered sugar and serve immediately. Serves 6. (Note: Unlike a soufflé, a nockerl is supposed to have peaks and valleys — like a moonscape.)

8 veal cutlets	Flour
English mustard	Beaten egg
Worchestershire Sauce	Cracker crumbs
Salt and pepper	

Rub mustard on veal cutlets. Sprinkle with Worchestershire sauce. Sprinkle with salt and pepper. Dip in flour, beaten egg and then cracker crumbs. Fry in skillet until tender. Serve with following sauce.

Sauce:

1 small can tomato paste (if desired)	Pinch thyme
	1 teaspoon celery salt
1 bay leaf	1 cup white sauce
	1/2 teaspoon onion salt

Add all ingredients to white sauce. Remove bay leaf after simmering for 5 minutes. Salt and pepper to taste. Serve over meat.

Sift gether in large bowl:	Add:
1 cup sifted enriched Best Flour	2/3 cup hazelnuts, walnuts or pecans, ground
1/3 cup sugar	Blend in:
	1/2 cup soft butter or margarine using spoon or pastry blender

Chill 1 or 2 hours. Roll out on floured pastry cloth or board to 1/8-inch thickness. Cut into rounds with floured 2 1/4-inch cutter. Place on ungreased baking sheet and bake in 375 degree oven for 7 to 10 minutes until light golden brown. These cookies are delicious plain; or make sandwich cookies with chocolate buttercream centers. The traditional Austrian manner is to spread the top of each sandwich thinly with jam, then with chocolate frosting. Sprinkle with slivered nuts.

Christopher Columbus' first stop in the New World was on San Salvador in the Bahamas. There are nearly 700 islands which comprise the Bahaman group, with total area slightly smaller than the state of Connecticut. The islands are an international banking and investment management center. Other chief industries include tourism and rum.

SUCKLING PIG

1 suckling pig (10 lbs., prepared for roasting)	1 clove garlic, cut
	Rum
Vinegar	Butter or oil
Salt and pepper	1 1/4 cups water

Wash pig and wipe out with cloth wrung out in vinegar. Rub all over with salt, pepper and garlic. Then brush with rum inside and out.

Stuffing:	1 tablespoon pepper
1 1/4 lbs. soft bread crumbs	2 teaspoons chopped thyme
4 tablespoons rum	Pinch of nutmeg
4 tablespoons bacon drippings	Grated rind of 1 lime
1 onion, minced	1 ounce raisins
1 clove garlic, minced	1 tablespoon Worcestershire Sauce
1 tablespoon powdered ginger	1 egg, lightly beaten
1 1/2 teaspoons salt	

Stuff the pig loosely and sew up with trussing needle and thread. Prop the mouth open with a piece of wood. Tie two front legs together and the hind legs under the belly. Wipe once again with vinegar cloth and brush with oil. Score back in several places and cover the ears with foil to prevent burning. Add 1 1/2 cups water. Roast at 350 degrees for 3½ hours, basting frequently with the fat and pan drippings. Cover with foil, if pig gets too brown. Allow 20 minutes per pound, plus 30 extra minutes. To serve — take prop out of pig's mouth and insert apple. For gravy — after removing pig from pan; pour off excess grease; add 1 pint hot water to pan drippings, salt and pepper, thicken with cornstarch and serve with pig.

CANDIED CITRUS PEEL

3 grapefruit shells or	3 cups sugar
6 orange shells	1 cup water
1 tablespoon salt	

Wash fruit shells and remove loose membrane. Cut peel into strips 1/4-inch wide from stem to blossom end. Add salt and cover with cold water. Boil 15 minutes. Pour off water and add fresh water and boil 20 minutes. Drain water again, add fresh water and boil another 20 minutes. Drain thoroughly and cover with 2 1/2 cups sugar and the cup of water. Simmer, stirring until remaining syrup has boiled away. Place on waxed paper and roll in remaining sugar.

Bahrain is an independent Arab Shiekdom in the Persian Gulf. Pearls, shrimp, fruit and vegetables along with oil are the mainstays of the economy.

KIBBEE SINEEA
(Ground lamb with borghul and Pinenuts)

1 cup borghul (cracked wheat) washed and allowed to stand 15 minutes
1 1/2 lbs. ground lamb (leg or shoulder)
Cracked pepper to taste
1 tablespoon salt
1/8 teaspoon allspice
1/8 teaspoon clove
1 tablespoon dried mint leaves
5 tablespoons pinenuts lightly browned in butter
4 medium sized onions minced and browned in butter
1/4 cup melted butter
(Bowl of ice water to dip hands in)

Combine lamb, moistened cracked wheat, salt, pepper and spices and knead until very easy to handle, dipping hands often in ice water — spread half of the meat mixture in baking pan — spread with mixture of pinenuts and onions — smooth over top, use spatula to form a small ridge for absorption of butter; cut into diamond shapes — spread with butter. Bake for 25 minutes at 400 degrees.

YOGURT CHEESE
(Labna)

Pour 4 cups yogurt into a large sieve lined with a double thickness of dampened cheesecloth and set over a bowl. Let the yogurt stand for 8 hours, or until the whey has drained off and the curds are firm. Season the cheese with salt to taste. Makes about 2 cups.

YOGURT CREAM CHEESE

In a bowl combine 2 cups yogurt and 1 cup heavy cream. Pour the mixture into a sieve lined with a double thickness of dampened cheesecloth and set over a bowl. Let the mixture drain for 8 hours, or until the whey has drained off and the curds are firm. Makes about 1 1/2 cups. Serve with Summer fruits.

Memory is the mother of all wisdom.

East Pakistan has very heavy monsoon rains. Small, fertile farms produce most of the world's jute, used in twine and sacks. Most of the people are Moslem and Bengolis.

LAMB CHOPS COOKED IN A PAPER SACK

(Note: Do not use recycled paper)

2 lbs. lamb chops, cut 1/2-inch thick	1/4 teaspoon pepper
2 tablespoons butter	1 tablespoon minced parsley
1 teaspoon salt	1 tablespoon minced marjoram
	Lemon slices

Sprinkle each chop with seasoning and herbs. Dot with butter and lemon slices. Place in big brown grocery sack, tied loosely. Place in shallow baking pan and bake about 1 hour at 350 degrees. *Fish may be cooked in this manner. Bake fish only 30 minutes!

DRIED APRICOT CONFECTION

1 cup dried apricots, ground	1 cup ground almonds
4 cups shredded coconut	1 teaspoon cinnamon
1 can Eagle Brand Sweetened Condensed Milk	Powdered sugar

Grind all together, mix with Eagle Brand Milk. Shape into small balls. Roll in powdered sugar.

CUCUMBER AND YOGURT SALAD

In a bowl beat 2 cups yogurt until it is smooth and season it with salt and pepper to taste. Add 2 cucumbers, peeled, seeded, and chopped, and 1 green hot pepper, seeded and chopped, and combine the mixture well. Add 1 tablespoon coarsely chopped fresh coriander, if desired, and chill the salad for at least 4 hours.

Genesis 3-18:
"And thou shall eat the herbs of the field."

Barbados lies alone in the Atlantic; its 106 square miles are almost completely surrounded by coral reefs. It is the farthest eastern island of the West Indies group. In addition to crops of sugar and cotton, Barbados also has a thriving rum industry.

WEST INDIAN SEAFOOD SAUCE

2 cups slightly cooked shrimp (soaked in lime juice for 10 minutes)
1/3 cup lime juice
4 ounces butter
1 medium onion, chopped
1/2 cup thinly sliced, peeled tomatoes
2 tablespoons chopped parsley
2 cloves garlic, crushed

1/4 teaspoon pepper
2 teaspoons celery salt
1 1/2 cups fish stock made by simmering bones and fish heads in water for 4 hours; seasoned with celery tops, a parsnip, bay leaf, and 1 spring onion
2 eggs
2 tablespoons vinegar

Heat butter in saucepan. Fry onion, tomatoes, parsley and garlic until golden and season with pepper and celery salt. Add stock. Beat the eggs, blend with the vinegar and stir into the sauce. Do not boil. Add shrimp and heat thoroughly. Serve over rice!

PEANUT SAUCE FOR RICE or BAKED BANANAS

2 tablespoons grated onion
2 tablespoons olive oil
1 ounce dark brown sugar
Juice of 1 lime

2 tablespoons peanut butter
1/2 pint coconut milk
Salt

Lightly fry onion in oil. Add sugar, lime juice and peanut butter. Blend thoroughly. Slowly add the coconut milk, stirring all the time. Cook slowly, until thick.

BAKED PAPAYA

2 lbs. underripe papaya
1 stick butter
1/4 teaspoon nutmeg

Dash salt
1/4 cup water

Peel, seed and quarter the papaya. Place in baking dish, slice butter over them, add nutmeg, salt and water. Cover and bake 45 minutes in 300 degree oven. Delicious!

Praise a fool and you make him useful.

Tiny Belgium is only slightly larger than the state of Maryland, but is a flourishing industrial country. Forty percent of its industrial production is exported. Belgium produces steel and fine glassware, and is also a center for diamond-cutting. In northern Belgium the chief language spoken is Flemish (Dutch) while southern Belgians speak French.

CARBONNADE FLAMANDE
(Beef in Beer)

3 lbs. chuck beef, cut in 1-inch cubes	Parsley sprig, celery tops, 1 bay leaf,
Flour by dredging	1 teaspoon thyme, and 4 peppercorns, crushed
Salt and pepper	
4 tablespoons oil	2 cups beef broth
4 large onions, sliced	2 cups dark beer
4 cloves garlic, minced	1 tablespoon brown sugar
Bouquet garni (tie in cheesecloth)	1 tablespoon wine vinegar

Wipe the meat; dredge in flour, salt and pepper. Brown in oil in a heavy skillet or stew pot. Brown a little at a time, adding more oil if needed. Return meat to pot and add onion slices, crushed garlic, bouquet garni, broth and beer. Use just enough broth and beer to cover meat. Simmer, covered for 3 hours on top of stove over low heat or in 300 degree oven. When meat is tender, remove garni. Add sugar and vinegar. Simmer 10 more minutes. Serve with boiled potatoes!

BELGIUM WAFFLES

2 1/4 cups cake flour	1/2 teaspoon salt
3/4 cups white sugar	2 tablespoons butter
4 whole eggs	1 ounce powdered sugar
1 cake fresh yeast	1 pint whipping cream
1 teaspoon vanilla	1 teaspoon almond extract
1 cup lukewarm milk	1 pint fresh strawberries

Mix yeast with 1 cup lukewarm milk and 4 eggs. Place dry ingredients in big bowl; make a well in center and add egg and yeast mixture. Add melted butter. With hands, work into a smooth batter. Cook on a well-greased, hot waffle iron until done. Sprinkle with powdered sugar. Top with whipped cream, flavored and sweetened to taste; serve with fresh, sliced, sweetened strawberries!

WHIPPED BUTTER

1 lb. sweet or salted butter at room temperature	1 egg
	1/4 cup heavy cream, cold

Combine butter and egg and beat at high speed of electric mixer about 5 minutes. Add cream and beat an additional 10-15 minutes until light and fluffy. Fill two 1-pound airtight containers and store in the refrigerator. This is also excellent combined with herbs and seasonings or cinnamon and sugar.

Benin is a country on the Gulf of Guinea on the west coast of Africa. It has dense vegetation with mostly hot and humid weather. Its main crops consist of kapok, palm products, peanuts, coffee, and tobacco. The official language is French. Under the name Dahomey the country became independent in 1960. The name was changed in 1975 during a coup. A socialist state with a Marxist-Lenninist philosophy exists.

STUFFED FIGS

1/2 cup miniature dot chocolate
1/2 cup pecan pieces
1/2 cup mixed candied orange and

Lemon peel soaked overnight in 2
   tablespoons rum
Dried figs

Open figs and stuff with mixture of all the above ingredients. Shape in rounds allowing filling to be seen. Store in cool place and serve with tea or coffee.

MARINATED PINEAPPLE FRITTERS

1 ripe pineapple sliced 1/3-inch
   thick (core removed), sprinkle with
   sugar and dark rum, let stand
   overnight.

Make batter using
   2 eggs, separated

1/3 cup sugar
1/2 cup flour
1 cup milk
1 teaspoon vanilla
1/2 cup finely chopped peanuts

Combine egg yolks with sugar. Beat smooth and stiff. Add milk alternately with flour. Fold in stiffly beaten egg whites, vanilla and peanuts. Dip dried pineapple slices in batter and fry until golden brown. Sprinkle with powdered sugar.

TANGERINE JAM

2 lbs. tangerines
4 cups sugar

Cut tangerines in half and squeeze out juice. Set aside. Remove the pulp in each tangerine and cook the tangerines in water until soft, about 10 minutes. Drain well. Cover with fresh water and let soak overnight, changing the water several times to get rid of the bitterness. Now drain the peel and grind through the coarse blade of your food chopper. Put the reserved tangerine juice in saucepan. Add the sugar and ground tangerines. Simmer until peels are thick about 30 minutes. Serve over ice cream or on buttered toast.

Bhutan is a tiny kingdon in the Eastern Himalayas, adjoining Tibet and India. It is 190 miles long and 90 miles wide, and is mostly mountainous jungles. The people are Buddhist and Hindus of Napolese descent. Most of our cardamon seeds come from this region.

INJON
(Pickled Eggplant)

8 to 10 large eggplants, unpeeled
4 1/2 quarts vinegar
8 cloves garlic, chopped
1 cup chopped parsley

2 tablespoons curry powder
2 tablespoons date syrup, or brown sugar syrup

Cut each unpeeled eggplant in slices, then into triangle sections. Place in a large enamel kettle and cover with vinegar. Boil for 2 minutes. Drain, but save the vinegar. Let the eggplant stand in the refrigerator 24 hours. Mix the garlic, parsley and curry powder and 1/4 cup of vinegar, which you saved. Add the syrup, then add to vinegar and bring all to a boil. Place eggplant in jars and pour hot vinegar over all and seal.

CHICK PEAS & GARLIC
(A very popular dish)

2 1/2 cups chick peas (Garbanzo beans)
4 cups water
4 cloves garlic crushed
salt

Olive oil to taste (1/4 cup)
1/2 lb. toasted white bread
Yogurt
Paprika

Soak Garbanzos overnight. Boil in 4 cups water until tender with the garlic salt. Mash. Add olive oil. Pour bean juice over toasted bread. Spread with mashed beans. Top with yogurt and paprika and serve hot.

Psalms 104:14
"He causes the grass to grow for the cattle, and herbs for the service of man; that he may bring forth food out of the earth."

BOLIVIA

**(DEMOCRATIC KAMPUCHEA)
CAMBODIA**

BOTSWANA

CAMEROON

BRAZIL

CANADA

BULGARIA

CAPE VERDE

BURMA

**CENTRAL AFRICAN
REPUBLIC**

BURUNDI

CHAD

**BYELORUSSIA
SOVIET SOCIALIST REPUBLIC**

CHILE

Bolivia was once part of the ancient Inca Empire. This is one of the most beautiful countries in South America. The Andes Mountains and many lakes make it especially attractive to visitors. Large deposits of tin, silver, copper, lead, petroleum, gold and natural gas are among its natural resources.

Juice of 2 limes
2 tablespoons oil
1/2 cup grated onion
1 tablespoon curry powder
1 chili, deseeded and chopped

2 teaspoons powdered ginger
2 teaspoons chopped turmeric
1 clove garlic, crushed
1 teaspoon salt
Pinch cayenne

CURRY MARINADE for SKEWERED MEATS

Marinate meat overnight after all ingredients have been well mixed together. For skewers, alternate pineapple chunks, cherry tomatoes, bell peppers, veal, lamb or chicken, after you have marinated the meat overnight. Grill to desired doneness or bake in hot oven.

Ice cubes
3/4 cup rum
1 1/2 cups cold, black coffee

6 tablespoons double cream, lightly
    whipped

RUM COFFEE ON THE ROCKS

Put all ingredients in cocktail shaker. Shake vigorously. Pour over ice and serve.
If you like, add 1/2 teaspoon vanilla
                1/4 cup chocolate syrup
                1/2 teaspoon powdered cinnamon
For Chocolate Rum Coffee!

Cook 1/4 cup each chopped onion, carrot and celery in 5 tablespoons butter. When golden, add 1/3 cup flour. Stir over low heat until brown. Add 5 cups hot beef stock, 3 sprigs of parsley, 1/2 bay leaf, 1/2 teaspoon thyme, 1 clove garlic and 1 tablespoon tomato paste. Simmer 1 1/2 hours or until thick enough to coat a spoon. Strain, degrease and season. Add raisins or black olives and serve over meat.

ESPAGNOLE SAUCE
(Brown)

17

Botswana is in Southern Africa, near Namibia and Zambia. Cattle raising and the mining of diamonds, copper, and nickle have contributed to rapid economic growth in that country.

SOUTH AFRICAN BEAN CURRY

1 lb. dried beans, black-eyed peas
  or peabeans
  washed and soaked overnight
4 quarts beef stock
2 cups chopped leeks
1 cup sliced carrots
1 cup canned tomatoes, drained and
  chopped

1 lemon sliced
1/2 teaspoon nutmeg
1 tablespoon curry powder
Salt and pepper to taste
1 cup fresh chopped parsley
2 teaspoon chopped hot peppers

Put all ingredients in a big pot and simmer about 2 hours.

TOMATO SAUCE
(Red)

Fry 1/4 lb. diced salt pork in 2 tablespoons butter until golden. Add 1/4 cup each chopped carrots, celery and onions. Sauté until soft. Stir in 2 tablespoons flour, cook until brown. Add 2 cups hot white stock, 3 cups chopped tomatoes, 1 clove garlic, 1/2 bay leaf, 1/2 teaspoon salt, pinch each sugar, pepper and thyme. Simmer 1 1/2 hours. Strain, degrease and season. Add 2 teaspoons tomato paste. Simmer 5 minutes. Serve over egg omelet.

Essential sources of nourishment of the people of the world:
Mediterranian Area — Semolina, coarsely ground wheat, couscous.
Africa — Tapioca from Cassova.
Mexico, India, South America, Caribbean, Africa — Maize or corn.
Russia — Kasha, buckwheat.
Ukraine — Wheat.
China, Japan, Orient, South India — Rice.
South Pacific — Taro root.
South America, Africa, Middle East — Yams, borghul.

Brazil is the largest country in South America, having an area of slightly more square miles than the continental United States. It is the largest coffee growing country in the world, and also contains one-third of the world reserve of iron. It is also a leader in quartz crystals and other minerals, including diamonds. It has thriving industries in textiles, steel, and automobiles, to name only a few. It has become the leading industrial power in Latin America.

FEIJOADA
(Brazil's National Dish)

2 cups dried black beans, soaked
    overnight
1/2 lb. dried beef, soaked overnight
1/2 lb. smoked tongue, soaked
    overnight
1/4 lb. hot chorizos (sausages)
1/4 lb. salt pork
2 tablespoons oil

1 large onion, chopped
1 clove garlic, minced
Pinch of cayenne pepper
3 cups hot cooked rice
1 large green cabbage, cooked
2 oranges, peeled and sliced
2 large sweet onions, thinly sliced

Drain the beans. Cover with water and simmer until done. Cook for 2 hours with the dried beef, tongue, sausage and salt pork. Add the chopped onion, garlic and pepper. Season to taste. Place beans and meat on a large platter with the cooked cabbage and the rice. Serve with the pepper sauce.

Sauce:
Put through a blender 2 large tomatoes, 4 hot peppers, and 2 cloves of garlic. Add the juice of 2 lemons, 1/2 cup wine vinegar, 2 medium onions, finely chopped, 1/4 cup minced parsley. Blend together. Serve over platter. Garnish with thinly sliced oranges, and thinly sliced onions.

CHOCOLATE CREAM ROLL

Sift together and set aside:
6 tablespoons cocoa
1/2 cup flour
1/3 teaspoon baking powder
1/4 teaspoon salt
1/4 teaspoon baking soda
2 tablespoons sugar

Beat until very light and fluffy:
4 eggs at room temperature
3/4 cup granulated sugar
1 teaspoon vanilla

Fold dry ingredients into whipped eggs and sugar; adding 3 tablespoons cold water to help blend. Turn into a 15 x 10 x 1-inch baking sheet lined with waxed paper that has been well-greased.

Bake in preheated oven of 400 degrees for 15 minutes or until firm to touch. Turn cake onto muslin cloth. Remove paper and roll up jellyroll fashion, leaving cloth on cake. Cool. Carefully unroll and remove cloth. Spread with sweetened whipped cream (1 cup whipped cream, 1/3 cup powdered sugar, vanilla). Carefully roll cake back up and ice with Chocolate Water Glaze:

1/2 cup powdered sugar
1 tablespoon cocoa
1 to 2 tablespoons hot water

Mix until smooth and dribble over cake. Decorate with maraschino cherries and pecans if desired.

CREAM WHIP FILLING FOR JELLY ROLLS AND CAKES

2 cups powdered sugar
2 cups shortening

Beat together powdered sugar and shortening for 8 minutes. In the top of a double boiler cook and stir constantly for 2 minutes a mixture of 1 cup sugar, 4 egg whites, 1 teaspoon salt and 1 teaspoon vanilla. Cool until lukewarm and beat until peaks form. Now to the whipped sugar and shortening add whipped egg mixture in 3 parts, beating well after each addition. After adding last amount of eggs, beat 8 minutes. Cover and use as needed. Will not get sugary. Delicious for coconut cakes, too.

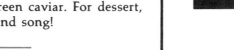

Bulgarians eat lots of cereal and fresh raw vegetables. They eat lots of yogurt. It is not unusual for these people to live to be 125 years old. a typical meal consists of a native brandy of prunes (slivovetza). A salad of egg plant and green caviar. For dessert, probably a fruit compote, wine, coffee and song!

SARMI
(Stuffed Cabbage Rolls)

3 lbs. cabbage
1 1/2 teaspoon salt
2/3 cup fat
2 large onions, chopped
3/4 cup rice, washed and dried
1 teaspoon paprika
2 tablespoon tomato juice

1 teaspoon chopped, fresh or dried mint
1 lb. lean pork, ground
1/2 lb. lean veal, ground
3 slices bacon
1 cup tomato juice

Wash cabbage, cut around the stem end with a sharp knife. Put the head, stem end down, into a kettle and cover with boiling water. Add salt. Boil 10 minutes. Remove, drain and let cool. Heat fat in frying pan and cook the onions in it until golden. Stir in rice and cook until the rice is slightly yellow. Mix in paprika, 2 tablespoons tomato juice and mint. Add the pork and veal. Mix well and remove pan from heat. Separate the cabbage leaves and cut out the heavy section of each leaf. Reserve 6 or 7 leaves for bottom of casserole. On the center of each of the remaining leaves, put a spoonful of the meat mixture. Roll around filling and fold the ends under to keep filling in. Grease a 2 quart baking dish or heavy pan and spread the reserved cabbage leaves over the bottom, to make a thick layer.

Pack the sarmi in lightly, one next to the other, with all ends carefully folded under. Lay slices of bacon on top and pour the tomato juice over all (it should reach the top of the rolls, but not cover them). Cover the dish with an inverted plate to hold the rolls down. Set the dish on very low heat and let the sarmi cook for 2 to 3 hours, longer if necessary, and at the end of 2 hours remove one roll and test for doneness. Serve hot!

The beginning of health is sleep.

The Republic of Burma is nearly the size of Texas, and is a country of rain forests and tropical monsoons. Its many rivers provide habitable valleys and means of communication, especially the Irrawaddy, which is navigable for 900 miles. Although Burma is known as a source of fine rubies, it also has oil, lead and silver in abundance, as well as sapphires and jade.

BURMESE AME NUT
(Beef Curry)

2 lbs. beef, cut into 1/2-inch cubes
8 ounces oil
3 large pieces onion, chopped
1 garlic, crushed
1 inch ginger, crushed
2 tablespoons vinegar

2 teaspoons paprika
1 tablespoon salt
3 bay leaves
3 pieces of 1-inch cinnamon
5 pieces cloves

In a saucepan, combine the meat cubes, onions, garlic, ginger, paprika and salt and mix them about 2 minutes. Add vinegar, oil and mix again. Add cinnamon, cloves and bay leaves and pour water over the mixed ingredients, just enough to cover it. Cook and let boil about 10 minutes. Cover saucepan, reduce heat and simmer until the meat is done and gravy is thickened. Turn off the heat. It is ready to serve. Serve warm. Makes about 6 servings. Serve with Rice.

FRESH FIGS IN RUM

8 fresh figs, peeled and halved
1/4 cup light rum

3 tablespoons sugar
Juice of 1 lime

Mix all together and chill. Spoon into sherbet dishes. Top with lemon sherbet and sprinkle with fresh coconut!

One man's fault is another man's lesson.

About the size of Maryland, Burundi is located in Central East Africa. Some of the inhabitants are extremely tall. Coffee is the main export. Tea and coffee plantations are numerous. Over half of the population is Christian.

For a quick, wonderful dessert:
Serve 1/2 of a ripe papaya, seeds removed, with juice from 1/2 of a lime. Sprinkle with cinnamon, sugar. Use the papaya seeds in the recipe below —

PAPAYA SEED MARINADE for PORK RIBS

1 cup white wine vinegar
1/2 cup sugar
1 teaspoon dry mustard
1 teaspoon seasoning salt

2 cups peanut oil
1 teaspoon powdered onion
2 tablespoons fresh papaya seeds

Put vinegar and dry ingredients in mixer. Gradually add the oil, then the papaya seeds. Blend until the seeds break up like coarse pepper. Brush this over pork ribs while grilling, or serve over leaf lettuce as a dressing. It also makes a perfect dressing for avocados. Papaya seeds have a hot peppery taste.

ICE CREAM PEANUT BALLS

1 quart ice cream, scooped into
   balls
1 pkg. finely chopped peanuts or
   pecans
6 squares unsweetened chocolate
   squares

2/3 cup water
1 1/3 cup sugar
1/4 cup butter

Melt chocolate with water in top of double boiler. Add sugar and boil gently over direct heat for 4 minutes. Stir constantly. Remove from heat and stir in butter. Keep warm and dip ice cream balls into chocolate and roll in chopped nuts. Freeze. Serve in orange shells or stem sherbet glasses.

Byelorussian SSR is one of the 15 union republics of the USSR. Beginning in 1939 the USSR by means of military action and negotiation included into its territory all or part of Lithuania, Latvia, Estonia, Poland, Czechoslovakia, Romania, Germany, Tannu Tuva and parts of Japan. Thecapital of Byelorussia (White Russia) is Minsk. Chief industries include machinery, tools, appliances, tractors, clocks, cameras, steel, paper and glass. The main crops are grain, flax, potatoes and beets.

KASHA

1 1/2 cups buckwheat groats, coarse	2 1/2 cups boiling water
1 egg, beaten	1 1/2 teaspoons salt

Beat the egg well. Then mix the groats with egg in a skillet. Mix and stir over heat until each grain separates. Then add salt and boiling water. Cook for 15 minutes. Serve with lots of butter. This was used by the Apostles and Christ. It was also originally a Russian food, buckwheat!

BLINIS

3/4 lb. buckwheat flour	1 ounce yeast
1 1/2 pints milk	3 eggs, separated
1/2 cup butter	Pinch of salt

Dissolve yeast in 1/2 pint warm water, and make a batter with a little of the flour. Let stand in a warm place for 2 hours. Then add rest of flour, yolks of eggs, salt and remaining milk. Mix thoroughly. Fold in stiffly beaten egg whites. Let stand 1/2 hour. Fry pancakes. Serve with sour cream and caviar!

PIROSHKI

Dough:	3/4 cup shortening
2 cups of flour	1 egg yolk
1/4 teaspoon salt	4 tablespoon ice water

Mix as for biscuits. Roll out 1/8-inch thick and cut in 3-inch circles. Place 1 tablespoon filling in circle. Fold over and press edges together. Chill and then bake for 15 minutes at 400 degrees.

Cheese filling:	1 egg yolk
1/2 lb. pot cheese	1 teaspoon salt
1/4 lb. cream cheese	1 tablespoon sugar if desired

Mix together and use as filling.

Cambodia, about the size of Missouri, is located on the Indochina Peninsula, with Thailand on the west, Laos on the northeast, and Vietnam on the east. Chief crops include rice, corn, and pepper, and the country also has rubber and kapok.

STUFFED APPLES WITH MEAT

12 tart apples (use a good eating apple)	3 tablespoons oil
	1 lb. ground beef
1/3 cup lentils, cooked until done	1/2 teaspoon cinnamon
1 onion, finely chopped	Salt and pepper to taste

Core the apples and remove some of the pulp to make holes larger.

Fry onions and meat in oil, stirring frequently until it changes color. Add the seasonings. Mix with lentils and spoon into apples. Place a little butter on each apple.

Mix 1 1/2 cups water with 1/2 cup vinegar and 2 tablespoons sugar. Pour over apples. Cover and bake in 350 degree oven for 45 minutes. If pan gets dry, add a little more water. Serve as a main course — it's different and delicious!

SHRIMP FRITTERS

use cuisinart

1 lb. shrimp 25-30 count, cut in half lengthwise	1/3 cup minced celery leaves
	2 teaspoons salt
4 spring onions with green tops (cut in 1-inch strips)	1 1/2 teaspoons ground coriander
	1/4 teaspoon ground cumin
2 cups water	1 minced clove of garlic
1 1/2 cup flour	Dash of pepper
3 whole eggs	

Beat whole eggs until fluffy. Add flour, water and spices beating until smooth. Stir in rest of ingredients and fry in hot shallow fat in a big wok or skillet using a spoon to drop each fritter into pan. Fry until golden. Serve with lemon and soy sauce.

x slotted

COCONUT JAM

1 lb. flaked coconut	2 cups sugar
1 tablespoon orange blossom or rose water	1 tablespoon lemon juice
	1/3 cup pistachio nuts or almonds, chopped
1/2 cup water	

Mix coconut with orange blossom water. Let stand overnight. Make a syrup by simmering sugar, lemon juice and water. Add the coconut and bring slowly to a boil. Remove from heat as soon as it boils. Overcooking will make coconut yellow. It should be clear and white. Mix in the nuts. Serve over cake or ice cream.

A long tongue shortens life.

Cameroon is located on the west coast of Africa. The main exports are coffee, cocoa, palm products, peanut oil, tea and bananas. The population consists of about 200 tribes. There are approximately 600,000 Moslem and 600,00 Christians.

BEAN FRITTERS

Cook dried beans until soft. Drain well and season to taste with chopped onions, chopped ginger and hot red pepper and salt. Shape into balls and roll in self-rising cornmeal. Drop into hot fat and fry until golden brown. Serve hot!

PEANUT AND PRAWN FRITTERS

These are made the same way. Ground peanuts are mixed with chopped prawns, seasoned to taste with onions, pepper and salt. All is pounded together until a smooth paste. Roll in cornmeal and fry in hot fat.

BROWN SUGAR COCONUT PUDDING

2 cups brown sugar	4 cups finely grated coconut
6 cups water	12 egg yolks
1/4 teaspoon cloves	

Beat egg yolks with brown sugar until thick. Mix coconut with 6 cups hot water and let stand 30 minutes. Combine everything and pour into a buttered baking dish. Bake in 350 degree oven for 45 minutes. Serve hot with vanilla ice cream or cold with whipping cream; sprinkled with cinnamon.
*To open a fresh coconut, draw an imaginary line around the middle of the coconut, tap with a hammer all the way around and it will split into.

PICKLED ROOTS

2 lbs. carrots, pared, cut into 1/4-inch slices	1/2 cup minced pitted green olives
	1/2 cup minced pimento
1 lb. turnips, pared, cut into 1/4-inch slices	1 clove garlic, minced
	Freshly grown pepper
2 cups olive oil	2 small onions, thinly sliced
1 cup distilled white vinegar	

Cook turnips in boiling salted water to cover in medium-size saucepan until tender, about 8 minutes. Drain; reserve. Cook carrots the same way. Heat oil, vinegar, olives, pimento, garlic and pepper in medium-size saucepan to boiling; reduce heat. Simmer uncovered 5 minutes. Combine reserved carrots, reserved turnips and the onions in large bowl; pour dressing over vegetables. Cool to room temperature. Refrigerate covered 4 hours or overnight.

Our friendly neighbor to the North, the country of Canada has a large reserve of crude oil. The canadians are also one of the top producers of wheat in the world. Canadian cities have many diverse ethnic populations, including Pakistanis, Indians, and Moslems. Thus there are many exotic food stores and restaurants catering to a wide range of special populations. Tourists can spend fascinating hours viewing the many ethnic areas of Toronto, for instance.

TOURTIERE
(French Canadian Christmas Eve Pie)

1 lb. lean, minced pork	1/4 cup chopped onion
1/2 teaspoon salt	1/4 teaspoon savory
Dash cloves	1/4 cup boiling water
Dash pepper	Pastry for 2 crust pie
1 small bay leaf	

Mix pork, onions and seasonings. Add bay leaf and water. Simmer uncovered about 20 minutes, stirring occasionally. Remove bay leaf, cool meat and skim off fat. Line 9-inch pie plate with pastry, and fill with meat mixture. Cover with pastry. Seal edges and cut small steam vents in top of pie. Brush top with an egg-milk mixture and sprinkle with coarse salt for a nice glaze. Bake at 425 degrees for about 30 to 40 minutes. Serves 6.

CRETONS du QUEBEC

2 small pork kidneys, minced	1/4 teaspoon pepper
2 lbs. leaf lard (suet from pork belly)	1 bay leaf
	2 cloves garlic, crushed
3 lbs. minced pork	1/2 teaspoon savory
2 cups boiling water	1/4 teaspoon cloves
1 cup chopped onion	1/4 teaspoon nutmeg
1 tablespoon salt	

Cut leaf lard in 1/2-inch pieces. Render over low heat until light golden, stirring occasionally. Drain and save fat. Grind cracklings in meat grinder. Simmer pork and kidney in water for 1 hour. Add cracklings and remaining ingredients. Cover, simmer 2 hours, stirring occasionally. Remove bay leaf; pour into bowls that have been rinsed in cold water, and chill until firm. Makes 7 cups. Traditionally served on bread for lunch, but now used on crackers for a snack.

One today is worth two tomorrows.

SORBET
(French Canadian)

2 cups sugar	3/4 cup lemon juice
4 cups water	1 cup grape juice
2 cups orange juice	3/4 cup claret or sherry

Boil sugar and water 15 minutes. Add rest of ingredients. Freeze until mushy. Serve as a refreshing course in the meal or after the meal.

CREPES DE BOEUF

1/2 cup minced onion	Salt to taste
2 tablespoons fat	Dash of pepper
1 cup finely chopped cooked beef	

Sauté onion in fat. Cook 1 minute. Add rest of ingredients and simmer until blended.
Now prepare crepes

1 cup flour	1 1/2 cups milk
1 teaspoon baking powder	Butter
1 egg	

Beat all together, fry quickly in butter. Spread with meat mixture. Roll up jellyroll fashion. Keep warm. Serve with chopped parsley and a dot of sour cream or Sauce Mousseline.

HOLLANDAISE SAUCE
(Yellow)

Beat 3 egg yolks in top of double boiler set over hot water. As yolks thicken, slowly beat in 2 tablespoons boiling water. Remove from heat. Slowly beat in 2 tablespoons slightly warm lemon juice and 1/2 cup melted butter. Season with salt, pepper, and cayenne and beat over water until thick. Sauce Mousseline: Fold in 1/3 cup whipped cream. For Beef Crepes add horseradish to taste.

Cape Verde is a group of Islands in the Atlantic Ocean off the western tip of Africa. The Islands are volcanic with little vegetation. It is made up of Create Mulattos, Africans, and Europeans. The official language is Portuguese. The main crops and resources are coffee, fruit, salt and fish. Most of the descendents are a mixture of Portuguese and Africans. It was uninhabited until the late 1490's when it was discovered by the Portuguese.

CRAYFISH CURRY
(South African Lobster Tails)

1 tablespoon fresh scraped ginger root
1 teaspoon chopped garlic
Salt to taste
1/2 cup oil
3 onions sliced
2 tablespoon madras style curry powder
1 teaspoon ground coriander

1 teaspoon ground aniseed
1/2 teaspoon cinnamon
4 tomatoes peeled and sliced
3 tablespoons fresh squeezed lemon juice
1/2 cup water
6 8-ounce Rock Lobsters (cold water) cut crosswise length (leave shells on)

In a heavy saucepan, sauté onion and garlic in oil with the ginger. Add rest of ingredients with lemon juice and water. Simmer for 20 minutes. Add the lobster stirring frequently around in the sauce. Cover tightly and simmer over low heat for 15 minutes. (Do not overcook) Serve over mound of rice.

BROILED SCALLOPS

2 lbs. scallops (fresh or frozen)
2 cups cold milk
Juice of 1 lemon

1/2 teaspoon ground, dried mint
Dash — pepper, paprika, nutmeg

Soak scallops in milk for at least 20 minutes. Drain well, then sprinkle with lemon juice, mint, pepper, paprika, nutmeg. Place scallops on baking tin and place under broiler 5 to 7 minutes, until lightly browned. Serves 4.

MELON WITH BLUEBERRY SAUCE

Melon
  with vanilla ice cream
Blueberry sauce
  2 cups blueberries

1/3 cup water
1/2 cup sugar
1 tablespoon cornstarch
1 tablespoon lemon juice

Cook until thick. Serve over ice cream.

In the Central African Republic, French is the official language. Diamonds are the main exports. Approximately 70 million dollars worth of diamonds are exported annually.

PEANUT BUTTER BREAD

2 1/2 teaspoons baking powder
1/2 teaspoon salt
1 1/4 cups milk
1 teaspoon grated orange rind
1/2 cup chopped dates

1/2 cup peanut butter
1 tablespoon shortening
1/3 cup sugar
1 egg
2 cups sifted flour

Cream peanut butter and shortening and sugar thoroughly. Add egg. Add alternately dry ingredients with milk and orange rind. Fold in dates. Turn into well-greased loaf pan. Bake 1 hour at 350 degrees. Slice bread and fill with this Marshmallow Creme. It's delicious with coffee!

MARSH-MALLOW CREME

2 cups sugar
1 cup water
2 1/2 cups corn syrup

Cook sugar, water and syrup to 245 degrees. Cool 15 minutes. In another bowl, place 1/2 cup warm Karo Syrup and 7/8 cup egg whites. Beat slowly until mixed. Then beat hard until light and fluffy. Beat in first mixture in a fine stream. When all is mixed, beat hard for 3 minutes. Add 1 teaspoon vanilla. Store in can or jar. Do not cover until cold.

PEANUT BUTTER

Parch 6 lbs. peanuts, shell and eliminate the husks by rubbing between fingers. Put through blender and add 2 teaspoons of salt, 1 teaspoon grated nutmeg and 2 ounces of apple jelly. Mix and blend until the consistency of stiff biscuit dough. Then add boiling hot water and mix to the consistency of cake batter. Fill 6-oz. jars and process as for canning, allowing 12 minutes in water bath.

The Republic of Chad is located in central north Africa. It is slightly smaller than Alaska in area, and grows cotton as its chief crop. Mineral sources include Uranium deposits. It has been independent since 1960.

---

2 ounces butter	Garnish with fresh, chopped
2 ounces flour	parsley
7 1/2 cups chicken stock	Pepper
12 ounces peanut butter	

PEANUT BUTTER CREAM SOUP
(Peanuts were brought to South Africa from Indonesia in 1890.)

Melt butter in saucepan. Stir in flour and cook for 2 minutes. Stir in 1/2 the chicken stock, stirring constantly; bring to a boil. Blend remaining stock with peanut butter. When smooth, stir in the soup. Season with pepper and simmer over very low heat for 10 minutes. Serve with parsley.

---

1 1/2 cups orange juice	1 clove garlic
3 tablespoons lime juice	3 tablespoons soy sauce
2 ounces butter	3 tablespoons honey
3 tablespoons chopped parsley	Salt
1 tablespoon dry mustard	

SOUTH AFRICAN CHICKEN BAR-B-Q

Mix all together. Baste chicken as you grill!

Use firm but not overripe bananas. Slit skins along one side and grill in skins until charred and soft. Open the skins and serve with lime slices, rum and sugar.

BAR-B-Q BANANAS

---

1 cup semi-sweet chocolate pieces and 1/4 cup warm water	2 teaspoons vanilla or grand marnier
6 eggs	

CHOCOLATE MOUSSE

In the top of a double boiler, melt the chocolate and water over hot, not boiling, water. Remove from heat and cool. Separate the egg yolks from whites. Beat the yolks, one at a time with the melted chocolate. In a separate bowl, beat the egg whites until they stand in peaks. Add 1/4 cup sugar. Then mix or fold the whites into the chocolate mixture. Spoon into dishes and chill. Serve with peanuts and whipped cream.

A journey of a thousand miles begins with one step.

Located on the western coast of southern South America, Chili is a mountainous country somewhat larger than the state of Texas. The Andes Mountains, containing some of the world's highest peaks, form the eastern border of the country. Although the country is chiefly agricultural, the citizens enjoy a high standard of living and education. Over 90% of the population is literate.

CEVICHE

1 lb. fresh fillet of black bass	2 tablespoons finely chopped
Juice of 3 limes	cilantro (or 2 tablespoons minced
Juice of 3 lemons	chives and parsley)
1 garlic clove, finely chopped	1 sweet potato
1 fresh jalapeno pepper, chopped	1 ear sweet corn
1/2 teaspoon salt	1/2 head romaine lettuce
1/8 teaspoon white pepper	1 medium red onion, thinly sliced

Fillet fish 1/8 to 1/4 inch thick and remove skin and bones. Slice fillets on the bias into 3/4-inch rectangles. Place in glass bowl. Mix lime and lemon juice, garlic, jalapeno pepper, salt and pepper and cilantro (or chives and parsley). Pour over fish. Cover bowl and refrigerate overnight.

Cook sweet potato in skin. Don't peel until serving time. Cook corn. Cool both to room temperature. Peel and cut sweet potato and corn into one inch slices.

To serve: Tear romaine into pieces and arrange on a serving platter.

BUNUELOS
(Pancakes with Syrup)

2 eggs, beaten	3/4 teaspoon salt
1 cup milk	1 teaspoon baking powder
4 cups flour	

Beat eggs and milk. Sift together dry ingredients and add to egg-milk mixture. Roll dough as thin as possible. Cut into rounds, about 5 inches in diameter. Fry in deep, hot fat until golden.

Serve hot with — syrup, whipping cream and berries or peaches or sapotas.

Sapota — Often called custard apple, is a delightful mellow, creamy, smooth fruit that is good served chilled.

Spanish Proverb
I wish you health, money and love and the time to enjoy them.

FLAGS OF THE UNITED NATIONS

CHINA (MAINLAND)

CZECHOSLOVAKIA

COLOMBIA

DEMOCRATIC YEMEN

COMOROS

DENMARK

CONGO

DJIBOUTI

COSTA RICA

DOMINICA

CUBA

DOMINICAN REPUBLIC

CYPRUS

ECUADOR

China (Mainland) is a fascinating highly complex country with many ethnic groups, Han Chinese, Mongols, Korean, Turks; the official language is Mandarin Chinese. Many dialects are spoken, Shanghai, Canton, Fukien, Hakka and Vigus. The main religions are Confucionism, Buddhism and Taoism. Its geographic area is slightly larger than the U.S. Its main industries and crops are textiles, chemicals, cement plastics, grain, corn, peas, soybeans, rice, sugar, hemp, jute and silk. The country has a growing stockpile of nuclear weapons and missiles and has the third largest navy in the world. It is made up of Manchuria, Guangdong, Inner Mongolia, Xinjiang and Tibet.

CHINESE ART SYMBOLS:

1. Dragons produced rain and fertility.
2. Stags bestowed old age.
3. Ducks and phoenix prompted fidelity and love.
4. Cranes lengthened life and gave happiness.
5. Tortoises endowed man with longevity.
6. Bees furthered felicity.
7. Onions heralded the advent of wise and excellent rulers.
8. Corn and pears produced wealth and pecuniary profit.
9. Rice, peas and wheat secured numerous offspring.

PEKING DUST
LI TZU KAO

2 1/2 lbs. chestnuts ground and mounded on plate. Cover with 1 cup whipped cream, sweetened with 1/2 cup brown sugar. Decorate with glazed cherries, orange slices, and nuts. Cover with spun sugar: 2 cups sugar, 1 cup water, 2/3 cup white Karo syrup. Cook to 290 degrees. Take from heat and spin. Place 2 long sticks on table, extending from table about 1 foot apart. Stand on a chair to be about 5 feet above stick. Dip and shape syrup, and dribble over stick in fine strand, shaking back and forth vigorously.

OYSTER BEEF

1 lb. beef tenderloin	1/4 cup oyster sauce (purchase at
3 tablespoons peanut oil	Chinese stores)
2 tablespoons finely chopped onion	4 tablespoons chicken broth
2 tablespoons thinly sliced fresh	1 tablespoon corn starch
mushrooms	1 tablespoon cold water } combine

Slice meat in long strips 2 inches wide. Then cut them diag-

33

onally. Sauté in oil in a very hot pan. Add onions, mushrooms, oyster sauce and broth. Steam 5 minutes. Thicken with cornstarch and water mixture.

CHINESE FORTUNE COOKIES

1 cup flour
1/4 teaspoon salt
2 tablespoons cornstarch

6 tablespoons sugar
7 tablespoons oil

Mix flour, salt, cornstarch and sugar. Add oil and 1/3 cup egg whites. Stir until smooth. Then add 3 tablespoons water and blend well. Bake by level tablespoons on foil-lined cookie tin in 3 or 4-inch rounds, at 300 degrees for 20 minutes. Remove cookies, one at a time, using a spatula and working with cotton gloves on hands. Fold cookies in half, placing fortune in center (1/2 x 3 inch strips).

CHINESE EGG ROLL

SKIN:
1 egg, beaten and divided in half
2 cups flour
1/4 cup cornstarch
Enough water to make 1/2
   thickness of pancakes

STUFFING:
2 boiled chicken breasts, minced

1/2 pound boiled shrimp, minced
1/2 head cabbage, boiled 5 minutes,
   drained and minced
1/2 teaspoon white pepper
1 teaspoon salt
2 teaspoons shortening

Make skin by beating 1/2 egg, flour, cornstarch and enough water to make a thin batter. Strain batter. Cook the skin until it pops away from small skillet. Turn the skin and cook slowly on the other side. Mix all ingredients for stuffing. Place in each egg roll skin. Roll up skin. Use other 1/2 egg to seal edges and fry to a golden brown in hot fat.

The secret to making perfect skins for egg roll is to have small pan hot and lightly greased. Pour batter into pan and then immediately pour out batter that does not adhere to the pan. This will give a thin skin for the egg rolls.

Colombia is located in the northwest corner of South America. It is a country slightly larger than Texas. Its topography is mountainous with the Andes ranging from north to south. The economy is good with main crops being coffee, rice, tobacco, cocoa, potatoes and bananas. Balsam, rubber, oil, gas, emerald, gold and silver are major industries.

COLD SPINACH SOUP

1 pkg. frozen spinach, chopped	1/4 teaspoon nutmeg
1/2 cup water	1/8 teaspoon pepper
1 chicken bouillon cube	1 can cream of mushroom soup
1 small onion, quartered	1 tablespoon soft butter
1/4 teaspoon salt	1 cup sour cream

Combine spinach, water, bouillon cube, onion, salt, and nutmeg. Cook 7 minutes. Add pepper, cream of mushroom soup, butter and sour cream. Blend well and chill.

RAW SWEET POTATO or CARROT CAKE

1 1/4 cups cooking oil	2 teaspoons baking powder
1 3/4 cups sugar	2 teaspoons cinnamon
4 eggs	1 teaspoon salt
2 cups flour	3 cups grated carrots
2 teaspoons soda	1 cup chopped pecans

*When making Sweet Potato Cake, substitute sweet potatoes for carrots!
Mix sugar and eggs together. Add oil. Blend in dry ingredients. Add carrots and nuts. Bake in sheet pan in 350 degree oven for 35 to 40 minutes, or cook in tube pan at 300 degrees for approximately 1 hour.

PINEAPPLE CREAM CHEESE ICING

4 ounces cream cheese	1/2 stick butter
1 lb. powdered sugar	1/2 cup crushed pineapple

Cream sugar, butter and cream cheese together. Add enough of the pineapple to make the frosting soft enough to spread. May use raisins that have been soaked in hot water, then drained.

The art of silence is as great as that of speech.

Comoros is a tiny island country half the size of Rhode Island located between Madagascar and Southeast Africa. The Islands are volcanic and the main industries are perfume, vanilla, copra and fruits. The Islands became independent in 1975. Arabic, French and Swahili are the main languages. Islam is the main religion.

LITTLE BIRDS IN CLAY
(Serves 4)

8 wild birds or game hens (1 lb. 4 oz.)
Salt
1/4 cup dry sherry
Heavy duty foil
1/2 cup very soft butter
1 tablespoon soy sauce
1/2 teaspoon paprika
1/4 teaspoon white pepper
1/4 teaspoon onion powder
1/4 teaspoon finely crumbled basil or oregano
Clay (red or white ceramic clay), approximately 2 lbs. for each bird

Thaw game hens, remove and save giblets for another use. Rinse in cold water, drain and pat dry. Sprinkle inside cavities with salt and tie legs together. Spoon 1 tablespoon sherry in each bird and place on large piece of foil. Combine butter with soy, paprika, pepper, onion powder and herb. Brush generously over birds. Wrap tightly in foil. Shape clay into an oval large enough to enclose each bird and about 1/4-inch thick. Wrap around foil-covered birds so they are completely enclosed. Cut slashes in top of clay. Place birds on shallow baking pan. Bake in a very hot oven (475 to 500 degrees) 1 1/4 hours. Remove from oven, knock off clay and leave in foil until ready to serve.

FRUIT SALAD

Tomato chunks peeled
Pineapple chunks
Avacado chunks
Fresh mandarin oranges

Mix and serve over lettuce with Honey Lime Dressing.

HONEY LIME DRESSING

1 egg, beaten
1/4 cup lime juice
1/2 cup honey
Dash of salt
Pinch of mace
1 cup sour cream

Cook and stir until thick. Add seasoning. Fold in cream. Serve over fruit.

Forestry is the prime resource in the Congo. Also much off-shore oil gives the government its prime revenues.

COLD BUTTERMILK SOUP

2 cups dark bread croutons, toasted in butter and ground fine
1/2 cup seedless raisins, soaked in 1 cup boiling water for 10 minutes, then drained
3 tablespoons brown sugar
3 teaspoons finely grated lemon peel
1 teaspoon fresh grated nutmeg
1/2 teaspoon fresh grated cinnamon
1 quart buttermilk, thick
2 cups applesauce

Combine all the ingredients, except buttermilk and applesauce. Blend well. While stirring, add the buttermilk and applesauce, gradually. Refrigerate for 2 hours. Serve in cups and sprinkle with sweetened cinnamon toast croutons.

SOUTH AFRICAN SAUSAGE

(Makes 4 lbs.)

3 strands natural hog casings
1 3/4 lbs. boneless pork shoulder — cut in 1-inch cubes
1 3/4 lbs. boneless beef chuck
3/4 lb. lamb suet
Salt to taste
2 teaspoons ground coriander
1 teaspoon each ground cloves, nutmeg, white pepper, cracked pepper
3 tablespoons vinegar

Grind all meat with seasonings. Adjust seasonings, stuff casings. Add vinegar.
Pan fry sausages turning once until brown and done.

GRAPEFRUIT PUDDING

3 large grapefruit
2 envelopes unflavored gelatin
3 eggs, separated
2/3 cup sugar
1/4 teaspoon salt
1/3 cup Chateau La Salle Wine
1 tablespoon lemon juice
1/4 teaspoon cream of tartar
1 cup whipped cream
Cookie crumbs

Grate rind of 1 grapefruit and squeeze the juice from all three fruits. Should have 2 cups juice. Soften gelatin in 1/2 cup of juice. Then melt over hot water. Beat egg yolks until stiff with 1/3 cup sugar and beat egg whites until stiff with remaining sugar and cream of tartar. Stir melted gelatin into grapefruit juice and then fold into egg yolks. Blend well. Fold in egg whites, whipping cream, wine, lemon juice and salt. Spoon into cookie crumb lined mold and let stand until congealed. Serve with berry juice or pomegranate juice.

This Central American country, somewhat smaller than the state of West Virginia, has both tropical and temperate regions. Its chief export is coffee, but bananas, sugar, cocoa, cotton and hemp are also important crops. Mineral resources include gold, salt, sulphur, and iron. The population enjoys a high standard of living and social services.

CREAM OF PEANUT SOUP (COLD)

1 1/2 cups of creamy peanut butter
1 quart milk
1/2 teaspoon salt
1/8 teaspoon pepper
1/2 teaspoon monosodium glutamate

In a pan over low heat, soften the peanut butter to allow easy mixing with the milk. Add the milk, salt, pepper and monosodium glutamate. Chill. Serves 8.

PUMPKIN RUM MOUSSE

1 envelope unflavored gelatin
1/4 cup rum
3/4 cup sugar, divided
5 eggs, separated
1 tablespoon grated lemon rind
1/4 teaspoon salt
1 cup cooked pumpkin
3/4 teaspoon cinnamon
1/2 teaspoon ginger
1/4 teaspoon allspice
1 cup heavy cream
Candied ginger

In top of double boiler sprinkle gelatin over rum until softened. In a small bowl, combine slightly beaten egg yolks, 1/2 cup sugar, lemon rind, and salt; mix well. Add to softened gelatin. Cook, stirring constantly over simmering water until gelatin is dissolved and mixture is slightly thickened. Remove from heat. Chill until mixture thickens. In another bowl combine pumpkin, cinnamon, ginger and allspice. Stir into thickened gelatin mixture. Beat egg whites until soft peaks form. Gradually add remaining 1/4 cup sugar, beating well, until stiff peaks form. Fold gently but thoroughly into gelatin mixture. Whip cream until thick. Gently fold in whipped cream until well blended. Spoon into lightly oiled 1 1/2-quart mold or 6 individual molds. Cover and chill at least 3 hours. Unmold on plate and garnish with more whipped cream or candied ginger.

RUM & BUTTER BREAD PUDDING

6 slices bread, several days old
1 1/2 cups powdered sugar
1/2 cup butter
3 cups milk
1/4 cup rum
3 eggs
1 cup sugar
1 teaspoon nutmeg

Cream butter and powdered sugar. Spread on bread slices. Place in 2-quart baking dish. Combine rest of ingredients and pour on pudding and bake 30 minutes at 350 degrees.

Our close neighbor off the coast of Florida, Cuba is an island republic about the size of Pennsylvania. Sugar is one of the country's most important products, but it also produces tobacco, coffee, citrus fruits and coconuts. Industries include textiles, wood products, and the famous Cuban cigars. Many Cuban dishes reflect a Spanish influence.

8 pieces beef, 1/2-inch thick	**Crushed garlic**
Lemon juice	**Salt and pepper to taste**

CUBAN BEEF STEAK

Pound meat until flat. Marinate in sauce made from lemon juice, garlic, salt and pepper for 1 hour. Fry until brown.

2 cups whipping cream	**2 egg whites**
1/2 cup powdered sugar	**1 cup bananas, sliced thin**
1 1/2 teaspoons vanilla	**Juice of 1 orange**
Pinch of salt	

BANANA CREAM
(Frozen)

Whip cream and vanilla. Fold in sliced bananas and orange juice. Beat egg whites until stiff. Add salt. Fold into cream and freeze. Serve with a spoon of rum and a cherry!

1/2 lb. butter	**1/4 teaspoon cinnamon**
1/2 teaspoon grated nutmeg	**3 1/2 ounces of rum**
1 1/2 lbs. soft dark brown sugar	**1 ounce of brandy or whiskey**

CUBAN RUM BUTTER

Just barely melt butter in frying pan. Mix in rest of ingredients well. Turn into a bowl and allow to harden.

Use as a spread for toast, or place a spoon on a slice of hot ham. Yum, yum! Or on pancakes!

Bebida — A very good Cuban Rum!

39

Cyprus is an island republic in the eastern Mediterranean, off the Turkish Coast. Two mountain ranges run east and west, separated by a wide, fertile plain. Industries include wine, clothing and shoes and the island also enjoys a flourshing tourist trade.

SPINACH TURNOVERS
(Spanakopitakia)

1/2 lb. pastry dough (Fillo)
2 pkgs. frozen leaf spinach
1 bunch chopped green onions
1/2 lb. Feta cheese
1/2 cup Parmesan or Romano cheese
1/2 cup chopped parsley

1/2 cup chopped dill
5 eggs, slightly beaten
1/2 stick melted butter, for filling
Grated rind of one lemon
Salt and pepper

Preheat oven to 375 degrees. Boil spinach according to instructions, drain very well and chop. In a bowl, mix all ingredients except Fillo. Cut each Fillo leaf 4 inches wide. Melt 1 1/2 to 2 sticks of butter. With pastry brush, brush surface of each pastry leaf. Take 1 tablespoon of filling, place on edge of pastry leaf and start folding into triangles. Place in oiled cookie sheet and bake on both sides until golden brown in 375 degree oven for 15 minutes. Lower oven to 350 degrees and bake another 10 minutes. Serve warm.
Makes about 30 pieces.
Delicious as snacks with drinks before dinner or can be served in a larger size as first course in dinner

BREAD & CHEESE "CASES"

6 thick slices of bread
6 ounces of grated cheese

Garlic seasoning salt
2 eggs, beaten

Cut off the crust and scoop out the soft part of each slice of bread to form a little case (cajicte). Mix the soft part of the bread with cheese, seasonings and eggs. Put back into cases and fry in skillet, cheese side up. To brown top run in oven.

Epicure was a famous Greek philosopher, who believed that pleasure is "God", education and virtue.

The Socialist Republic of Czechoslovakia is in East Central Europe. Terrain includes mountainous areas, with the Carpathians being the chief mountain range. Industries in the country include machinery, oil products, weapons, steel, glass, chemicals, and aircraft. Jaychmor has Europe's greatest pitchblende (for uranium and radium).

EGGPLANT SOUP

1 cup eggplant, cut in 1/2-inch cubes
2 stalks celery, cut in cubes
1 green pepper, cut in cubes
1/4 cup minced scallions
1 garlic clove, minced
1/4 cup butter

1/4 teaspoon thyme
1 cup tomatoes, peeled, seeded and chopped
Salt and pepper to taste
3 cups chicken broth
Parmesan cheese

Peel and cube eggplant. Cut up celery and green pepper. In a saucepan sauté scallions and garlic in butter until they are soft. Add the cubed vegetables and thyme and sauté mixture for 5 minutes. Add tomatoes, salt and pepper and simmer the mixture for 5 minutes. Add chicken broth and bring the liquid to a boil. Reduce the heat and simmer the soup for 15 minutes, or until the vegetables are tender. Serve the soup in heated bowls and sprinkle each serving with freshly grated Parmesan cheese.

BEAN CUTLETS

2 cups cooked dried beans
2 tablespoons fat
1/2 cup farina or semolina

1 medium sized onion, finely chopped
1 egg
Seasoned dry bread crumbs

Mix all ingredients. Roll in seasoned bread crumbs. Fry in a little melted fat until brown.

BORTSCH SALAD DRESSING

1 teaspoon salt
1 teaspoon sugar
Dash of paprika
1 cup oil
1/2 cup cider vinegar
Dash of Angostura or

Worcestershire Sauce
1/4 cup minced parsley
2 tablespoons chopped onion
2 hard-cooked eggs, chopped
1/2 cup chopped, cooked beets

Combine all ingredients and shake well. Serve on fresh greens with sliced beets!

Democratic Yemen is located on the southern coast of the Arabian Peninsula. Its population is made up of Arabs, Indians and Somalis. The official language is Arabic. Over 90% are Moslems. The country is sandy, hot and dry with a back drop of mountains. Cotton, grain and meat products as well as the fishing industry contribute to the economy. Aden, mentioned in the Bible, has been a port for trade in incense, spices and silks for over 2000 years. This port, being at the entrance to the Red Sea, is the country's most valuable resource.

SWEET MEATS

1 cup figs
1 cup pitted dates
1/4 cup seedless raisins
6 maraschino cherries

2 cups blanched almonds
1 cup English walnuts
1 cup pecans

Put all through food chopper and add 2 tablespoons fresh orange juice, 2 tablespoons lemon juice, 1/2 teaspoon of grated orange rind. Mix thoroughly. Roll into small balls and then roll in colored sugar or granulated sugar. Store in refrigerator.

HONEY PIE
(Melopitta)

2 lbs. cottage cheese or white cheese
1 lb. honey
10 ounces sugar

8 eggs
2 tablespoons powdered cinnamon
Pie crust, prepared

Mix cottage cheese with sugar and honey. Mix thoroughly adding eggs one at a time. Spread filling on pie crust and bake in 350 degree oven 35 minutes. When done sprinkle with cinnamon. Cool and cut in little diamond shaped pieces.

COTTAGE CHEESE SOUFFLÉ

In a bowl combine 3/4 cup each of creamed cottage cheese and sour cream, 1/4 cup flour, 1 tablespoon each of minced parsley and chives, 1 teaspoon salt, 1/2 teaspoon pepper, and cayenne to taste. Beat in 5 egg yolks, 1 at a time, beating well after each addition. In a bowl beat 5 egg whites until they hold stiff peaks. Fold the egg whites into the cheese mixture gently but thoroughly and pour the mixture into a buttered 1 1/2-quart souffle dish. Bake the soufflé in a preheated moderate oven (350 degrees F.) for 40 to 45 minutes, or until it is puffed and browned. Serves 4 as a luncheon entrée.

Many people think of Denmark as the home of its famous writer of fairy tales, Hans Christian Anderson. This Scandinavian country, which is the size of New Hampshire and Massachusetts combined, consists of the Jutland Peninsula and about 500 islands. The land is flat or gently rolling. Denmark is also known for its fine furniture which features pioneering designs.

DANISH BEER SOUP
(National Dish)

1 cup thin, flat egg noodles, cooked in salted water
Add 4 tablespoons butter to noodles and stir until melted
Add 1/2 teaspoon ground cinnamon, salt and pepper to taste

Place pot on stove containing noodles. Add enough beer to cover the noodles twice their depth in pan. Stir so butter will rise to top. Warm the soup until hot, but not boiling. Serve with soda crackers or rye bread and cheese. Yum!

SEAFOOD CHOWDER

6 lobster tails, cooked
6 king crab claws, cooked
6 pieces of boneless fish, cooked
2 cups small Danish shrimp, cooked
1 cup mussels or oysters
1/2 cup pimento pieces
1 teaspoon chervil
1/2 teaspoon powdered dill
1/2 teaspoon garlic salt
1/2 cup white wine
1 quart water
2 cups cream

Cook all seafood in 1 quart of water. Reserve seafood liquid and place in soup kettle with 2 cups heavy cream. Bring just to a boil and thicken with cornstarch, dissolved in water. Stir just at boiling point, while adding cornstarch. When desired thickness, add chervil, cut up seafood, dill, salt, and pepper and wine. Stir to blend and allow to sit over very low heat for 1 hour to blend flavors. Spoon into soup bowls and serve piping hot.

DANISH HONEY COOKIES

1 cup light brown sugar
1 cup Karo syrup
1/3 cup water

Mix and bring just barely to a boil. Let cool slightly. Sift 4 teaspoons baking powder, 4 cups flour, grated rind of 1 lemon; combine and add to syrup mixture. Add 1 teaspoon cinnamon and 1/2 teaspoon ground cloves. Knead dough well. Roll out on floured surface 1/2-inch thick. Cut out in desired shapes. Bake in 325 degree oven for 12 to 15 minutes. Decorate with confectioner's sugar and water icing.

*DANISH
KRINGLE*

2 cups sifted all-purpose flour
1 1/2 tablespoons sugar
1/2 teaspoon salt
1/2 cup soft shortening
   (can use part butter or oleo)

1/2 cup milk, scalded
1 egg, separated
1/4 cup warm water
1 pkg. active dry yeast

Measure flour, sugar, salt and butter into bowl; blend well. Cool milk slightly, then stir in egg yolk. Pour into bowl with first ingredients. Add yeast to warm water, and let stand a few minutes. Add to all the other ingredients, mixing thoroughly. Scrape down dough from sides of bowl. Cover tightly and chill 2 to not more than 48 hours in refrigerator.

Prepare filling before shaping kringles:

Fillings used are almond paste, prune, raisin, date pecan, apple pecan and plain pecan. Use brown sugar in all the fillings except prunes. Divide dough into two parts. Take out one part and return other half to refrigerator. Beat egg white. Grease two baking sheets.

Cover board with cloth and rub flour in well to prevent dough from sticking. Roll dough into a 6 x 18-inch rectangle. Spread a 3-inch center strip with half of beaten egg white; then with filling. Fold over one side of dough and then the other with 1 1/2-inch lap to cover filling. Pinch dough to close the fold. Arrange carefully on baking sheet in oval or horseshoe shape. Shape second kringle as first. Cover and let rise in warm place 30 to 45 minutes. Bake in 400 degree oven for 20 to 30 minutes or until golden brown. Spread with sugar icing. Serves 24.

---

*BLUE CHEESE
SMORGAS-
BORD MOLD*

1/4 lb. bleu cheese
2 tablespoons vinegar
1 tablespoon parsley
1 tablespoon onion salt
1/4 teaspoon pepper

1 tablespoon chopped pimento
1 cup well drained grated cucumber
1 cup heavy cream, whipped
1 envelope plain gelatin
1/4 cup cold water

Mash cheese thoroughly with vinegar and herbs. Add spices and seasonings. Add grated cucumber and blend well. Stir in gelatin, which has been dissolved in 1/4 cup water and melted over hot water. Fold in whipped cream. Pour into 3-cup mold and chill until firm. Unmold and serve with pears, apricots and wheat crackers.

The Republic of Djibouti is on the east coast of Africa, separated from the Arabian Peninsula by the strategically vital strait of Bab el-Mandeb. The climate is hot and dry, and much of the country is arid and sandy. Though few crops grow there, the country has a salt industry.

YOGURT SPICE CAKE

1 cup butter	1/2 teaspoon cinnamon
2 cups sugar	1/2 teaspoon cloves
6 well beaten eggs	1/2 cup brandy
1 cup yogurt	2 teaspoon soda
2 cups flour	

Beat butter and sugar for 10 minutes or until light and fluffy. Add eggs and beat thoroughly. Combine flour with spices and add yogurt. Blend well. Combine flour with soda and stir into mixture until blended. Bake 1 hour at 325 degrees in a greased 9 x 13-inch pan.

SYRUP:
1 1/2 cups sugar
2 cups water
Juice and grated rind of 1 lemon

Cook sugar, water, lemon juice and rind. Pour over hot cake.

ALMOND DROPS

1 cup ground almond (almond paste)	5 tablespoons orange blossom water
1 cup confectioner's sugar	Nuts, dates, cherries, etc.
	Candied fruits

Mix the ground almonds with confectioner's sugar and enough orange blossom water to make a stiff paste. Knead by hand until smooth. Let paste rest 20 minutes. Wash and dry hands and shape the paste into little balls the size of large marbles. Roll them in powdered sugar. Decorate with nuts and candied fruits.

This commonwealth nation is quite small, about one-fourth the size of Rhode Island. It is located in the east Caribbean, and is the most northerly Windward Island. Crops include bananas, citrus fruits, and coconuts, and because it is volcanic in origin, it also exports pumice stone. There are also numerous thermal springs.

BUTTER-SCOTCH FLAN

6 tablespoons butter	2 eggs
2 1/2 cups scalded milk	4 tablespoons granulated sugar
3 tablespoons cornstarch	1/2 teaspoon vanilla
1 1/2 cups brown sugar	

Mix all ingredients. Bake in 325 degree oven in a buttered casserole sprinkled with brown sugar. Serve cold.

FISH POACHED IN GALLIANO BUTTER

2/3 cup whole or slivered blanched almonds	Salt and freshly ground pepper to taste
2/3 cup butter	2 lbs. filet of sole or flounder
1/4 cup each: Liquore Galliano Lemon juice Fresh or dried dill or Fennel	

Make Galliano Butter as follows: In large skillet or chafing dish, sauté almonds in butter until lightly toasted. Allow butter to brown; then stir in Galliano, lemon juice and seasonings. Add sole. Cover and cook over medium heat 7 to 10 minutes, until fish flakes easily with a fork. Spoon Galliano Butter over fish frequently as it cooks. 6 servings.

MOCHA

2 cups strong fresh brewed coffee	1 cup milk
1 1/2 cups chocolate syrup	1 cup cream, whipped Grated rind of 1 orange

Combine coffee, syrup and milk. Heat to scalding. Serve in cups with a spoonful of whipped cream and a sprinkling of orange rind. Serve after dinner.

RUM AND MOLASSES FRAPPÉ

1/2 cup orange juice	1/2 cup rum
2 tablespoons molasses	Cracked ice
1/2 cup cold water	

Mix in shaker. Serve over cracked ice. Makes 4 glasses.

Dominican Republic is a small country about the size of Vermont and New Hampshire combined. It is located in the West Indies. It is bordered by Haiti on the west and it has the highest mountain peaks in the Caribbean. Its economy depends on molasses, rum, alcohol, cement, textiles, cocoa, coffee, peanuts and bananas.

Barbecuing in the Dominican Republic is done by digging a hole a suitable size. Porous rocks are placed in the bottom and on them, kindling and branches. The fire is lit and kept burning for about 2 hours, so that the stones and earth walls of the pit become very hot. Then the kindling and branches are removed. The meat is prepared for roasting and is wrapped in leaves. It is placed on top of the stones. Covered with a cloth, and with heaped earth, the pit is outlined, and a huge bonfire is made on top of the pit. It is kept burning about 8 hours. The barbecue is then unearthed, unwrapped and served.

GALLINA TOBASQUENA
(Hen Tobasco Style)

5 lb. roasting chicken, cut up
Juice of 1 lime or sour orange
1 tablespoon salt
4 tablespoons fat
4 medium size onions, chopped
6 medium tomatoes, peeled, chopped
2 tablespoons chopped olives
1 tablespoon capers
2 tablespoons seedless raisins
2 tablespoons seeded prunes, chopped

1/4 lb. ham, finely chopped
1/2 cup blanched almonds
8 cloves garlic, diced
2 tablespoons vinegar
2 tablespoons oil
1/2 teaspoon pepper
4 cloves
2-inch stick cinnamon
3 pimentos, chopped

Rub chicken with lime and sprinkle with salt. Fry until golden. Add all ingredients, except pimentos, and fry about 10 minutes. Add 1 1/2 cups water. Cover, and simmer until hen is done, about 2 hours or longer. Thicken sauce and serve over hen with pimentos.

MILK AND RUM PUNCH

3 eggs
1 tablespoon sugar
1/2 teaspoon vanilla

3/4 cup rum
1 cup cold milk
Grated nutmeg

Blend all ingredients, except milk. Divide into punch cups. Top with cold milk and grated nutmeg. Makes 6 servings!

47

Ecuador is in the northwest area of the South American continent. It is the largest exporter of bananas, but also grows rice, grains, potatoes, fruits, cocoa and kapok. The Galapagos Islands off the coast of Ecuador are the home of huge tortoises and other unusual animals.

FRIED CORN

Take frozen whole ears of corn from your freezer. Drop into deep fat and roast until golden brown. Wrap in foil or skewer and serve.

FRIED BREAD

(An Old Indian Recipe)

2 cups flour
Lard or Crisco, size of egg
2 teaspoons baking powder

Pinch of salt
Enough milk to mix

Make up like biscuit dough. Add milk. Pat out on floured surface. Cut into rounds 1/4-inch thick. Fry on greased grill until brown on both sides. Serve hot with molasses. For a different texture, use half cornmeal. Delicious!

DRIED CABBAGE

(An ancient recipe; dried in hot attic)

Quarter cabbage. Spread out to dry. Store in dry place all winter. When ready to eat, parboil and wash. Cook again with your favorite seasoning.

Green beans may be strung on a thread, hung in sun to dry and kept all winter!

TORTILLA SOUP

(Sopa Anahucacalli)

2 pints chicken stock
4 whole tomatoes peeled and chopped

1 leaf epozote (an aromatic herb)
1/2 onion, chopped
Tortillas

Fry tomatoes and onions slightly. Add broth and seasoning. Simmer 20 minutes. Cut tortillas in strips and add to soup. Serve with diced avocodo and chopped fresh onion and grated cheese.

FLAGS OF THE UNITED NATIONS

EGYPT

FRANCE

EL SALVADOR

GABON

EQUATORIAL GUINEA

GAMBIA

ETHIOPIA

GERMAN DEM. REP.

FIJI

GERMANY, FED. REP. OF

FINLAND

GHANA

Sesame, henna, sandlewood, camphor, myrrh, ambergris, and hashish greet the western visitor with an unforgettable blend of scents in the bazaars in Cairo. The food is much like that of Syria and Lebanon. For breakfast, the Egyptian might have beans, olives, cheese, eggs and tea. Milk from cows is preferred. Dried peas, chick peas and tiny small red beans are favorites. Many greens are eaten and are usually flavored with mint. Much lamb and fish are eaten. Cinnamon or Cassia, the bark of a tree, was discovered as early as 2700 BC. It was imported to Egypt in the 17th Century BC. Like several other spices, cinnamon was considered capable of inspiring love. It was used for medicinal purposes, scenting perfumes and ointments. The Arabs first carried cinnamon to the world markets. It was originally from China and Indonesia. Cinnamon has a medicinal reputation as a cure for colds. It has a strong antiseptic action. In the spice wharves, workers are free from chest troubles. Tea is brewed from cinnamon sticks in Lebanon. It is one of the most favored spices for cooking in all the world. Beer was made in Egypt.

SOYADIA
(Chilled Spiced Fish)

1/3 cup oil	1 teaspoon curry powder
1 clove garlic, minced	1/4 cup chopped parsley
Juice of 4 lemons	2 1/2 lbs. sea bass or white fish,
1 1/2 teaspoon salt	sliced and boned
1/4 teaspoon pepper	1 lemon, sliced

Heat the oil and cook the garlic in it for 5 minutes. Stir in the lemon juice, salt, pepper, curry powder, and parsley. Heat for 2 to 3 minutes. Arrange the boned fish in a 2-quart baking dish. Pour the oil mixture over all. Cover with hot water. Cover baking dish and bake in 325 degree oven for 30 minutes. Remove cover for last 10 minutes of cooking. Chill and serve with lemon, parsley and mint.

BOUHGASHA
(Stuffed Sticks)
(This is similar to the Greek pastry "Diples")

5 eggs	Juice of 1 lemon
2 1/2 cups farina	1 teaspoon baking powder
Juice of 2 oranges	1 teaspoon salt

Break eggs in bowl and add farina, 1 cup at a time. Add rest of ingredients and knead into a stiff dough. Let rest 30 minutes. Roll dough very thin and cut into strips 2 x 3 inches. Fold ends to form a triangle and fry in deep fat 2 or 3 minutes. Dip in warm honey and sprinkle with walnuts and cinnamon. To stuff the sticks, place raisins and nuts under the folds and press together after dampening edges.

49

El Salvador is in Central America, bordered by Guatamala and Honduras. The former Spanish colony became independent in 1821. Its crops include coffee and cotton, and the country also has abundant rubber forests. Its industries include cement, textiles and sugar refineries.

ESCABECHE
(Pickled Fish)

2 lbs. sliced fish (halibut or sea bass)	1 cup oil
Juice of 1 lime	5 cloves garlic
2 tablespoons salt	10 black peppercorns
1 tablespoon chili powder	1/2 teaspoon oregano
1/2 cup wine vinegar, white	1/2 teaspoon laurel
3 large onions, sliced	1 teaspoon allspice

Wash the fish and soak 10 minutes in enough water to cover with the lime juice and 1 tablespoon of the salt. Dissolve the chili powder and 1 teaspoon salt in the wine vinegar. Soak the onions in boiling water, to which 1 teaspoon salt has been added. Drain. Soak in the vinegar for 15 minutes. Remove, reserving onions and vinegar. Heat olive oil and fry 2 whole cloves garlic until brown. Discard garlic. Add fish, peppercorns, oregano, laurel, allspice and rest of garlic, chopped and wine vinegar. Simmer over low heat 15 minutes. Do not add water. Chill and serve cold on lettuce!

HERB AND WINE PUNCH

6 sprigs of fresh marjoram, crushed	2 bottles sparkling red wine
2 tablespoons sugar	2 1/2 cups soda water
1 cup rum	3 limes, thinly sliced
1 bottle still white wine	

Put marjoram, sugar and rum in punch bowl. Let stand 1 hour. Add still wine and chill. Then add chilled wines and serve over ice with lime! Serves 24

WHITE WINE FREEZE

1/2 cup sugar	Juice of 1 lemon
1 cup water	2 cups medium dry, white wine
Grated rind of 1/2 lemon	Dash of angostura

Boil sugar and water. Let cool. Mix other ingredients. Freeze in hand freezer. Let stand at room temperature for 5 minutes and serve garnished with fresh raspberries and strawberries, pineapple and bananas.

South America — Angostura is used to flavor foods and beverages.

This island country off the African coast has a volcanic terrain and a fertile valley, perfect for the growing of coffee, cocoa and other crops. Guinea is also a source of timber. The former Spanish territory became independent in 1968.

STUFFED MELON
(Slice off top to use as a cover.)

lb. prunes, soaked overnight in	4 tablespoons powdered sugar
1/4 cup Cointreau or Kirsch	2 tablespoons lemon juice
large melon	1 tablespoon orange flavoring
ripe peaches or mangoes	1 tablespoon vanilla extract
cup seedless grapes or cherries	

Scoop out melon, remove seeds and cut up. Mix with all fruits and flavoring. Place back in melon and place top on. Refrigerate for 3 hours. Serve on a buffet. Flowers may be stuck into melon for decoration. Use a knitting needle to make holes!

MOUNTAIN BEER AND RUM PUNCH
(Served in the high, cold mountains of the Andes!)

tablespoon ginger	3 eggs
teaspoon nutmeg	2 tablespoons molasses
pints beer	1/2 cup rum

Blend ginger, nutmeg and beer. Heat. Beat eggs with rest of beer and molasses. Add the warm beer to egg mixture, a little at a time, beating all the time. Add the rum and serve at once. Makes 12 glasses.

SPICED GARLIC OKRA

cups water	Dash red hot pepper
tablespoons finely chopped	Salt to taste
onions	1 lb. fresh okra, stems removed
teaspoon finely chopped garlic	

Bring water to a boil with onions, garlic, salt and pepper. Cook okra quickly for about 15 minutes. Run immediately under cold water to stop cooking and restore the green color. Sprinkle with fresh lemon and chill before serving.

Good thoughts and actions can never produce bad results; bad thoughts and actions can never produce good results!

This east African nation has an ancient culture that was influenced by the Egyptians and Greeks. Its high central plateau and mountain ranges provide a fine climate for coffee growing, which provides 50% of its export earnings. Ethiopia also has supplies of coal, iron, platinum, gold and silver. It is also said to have much potential for the production of hydro-power.

Tej — Honey wine
Wat — Hot and very spicy stew

Alechas — Less spicy and hot stew
Tolla — Wheat beer

The Ethiopians use bread to dip up foods instead of forks. They have excellent wheat, barley and millet. Injera is the best bread a pitted, pancake-like bread with a slight sour dough taste. At a small formal dinner, the hands are washed. Spiced coffee is served black with a bit of honey.

KITFO
(Raw Beef with Spices)

2 lbs. best grade beef tenderloin, ground
* 4 tablespoons Spiced Butter
1 large onion
1 large bell pepper
2 tablespoons hot chili peppers

2 pods garlic, minced
1/2 teaspoon cardamon seeds, pulverized
Juice of 1 lemon
Salt to taste

Heat butter, onions and rest of spices for about 8 minutes. Cool Stir in raw meat. Mound on plate and serve! Delicious.

SPICED BUTTER

1 lb. unsalted butter
1 onion, grated
2 cloves garlic
1 cardamon pod, crushed

1 tablespoon cinnamon, crushed
2 whole cloves
Pinch of fresh grated nutmeg

Put all ingredients in very heavy pan and place in oven at 18 degrees for 30 minutes. Pour clear butter off and store in jar to us in recipes!

INJERA
(Flat Pancake-like Bread)

2 cups millet flour
2 1/2 cups hot water
Mix and let stand overnight in warm place.

Fry in sesame oil on hot griddle by 1/4 cupfuls. Take back spatula and spread batter in big thin rounds. Do not brown. Stac while warm. This bread in used to scoop up food.

This group of 840 islands has a combined area of 7,055 square miles, approximately the size of New Jersey. Many of the islands are mountainous with tropical forests and large fertile areas. Fiji is an independent parliamentary democracy. Chief crops include sugar, coconut and ginger.

PORK ROAST

5 to 6-lb. loin of pork
Dry mustard
Thyme
Salt and pepper
Rub pork with mustard, thyme, salt
  and pepper.

1/2 cup sherry
1/2 cup soy sauce
3 cloves garlic
Cornstarch to thicken

Insert meat thermometer in pork and roast until done. Add sherry, soy sauce and cloves of garlic, chopped, to pan drippings. Thicken and serve gravy over pork.

Serve this with Horseradish Applesauce made by mixing 2 cups cold applesauce with 4 tablespoons bottled horseradish. Oh, my! How grand!

BANANA POI

3 1/2 cups mashed, very ripe
  bananas
1 1/3 tablespoon lime juice

1 1/2 cups coconut cream
  (Juice squeezed from mature,
  grated fresh coconut)

Make substitute cream by heating 1 1/2 cups packaged coconut with 1 cup coffee cream and cook for 30 minutes over very lot heat. Squeeze out juice through cheese cloth.

Mix all ingredients together and serve chilled.

HONEY-GINGER ICE CREAM

4 eggs, separated
3/4 cup honey
3 teaspoon vanilla
2 cups heavy cream, whipped

1/8 teaspoon salt
1/4 cup finely chopped, candied
  ginger

Beat egg yolks with honey and vanilla until thick and smooth. Fold in the whipped cream and egg whites beaten stiff with salt. Fold in ginger. Spoon into mold and freeze. Cut in wedges to serve.

Located in the northern Baltic region of Europe, Finland has Norway to the north, Sweden to the west, and the USSR on the east. The southern part of the country is flat, with low hills and many lakes. The northern portion of Finland is mountainous. The country's industries include machinery, metal, shipbuilding, textile, leather and chemicals. Much of the flat portion of the country is ideal for growing grain, which is one of the chief crops of Finland. Finland is oriented toward the West in trade and culture, but Soviet influence is strong politically.

FINNISH FISH PIE

2 cups flaked, cooked fish	1 cup cooked green peas
3 tablespoons minced green peppers	Salt, pepper and sage
	1 cup medium white sauce
2 medium onions, diced and fried	2 cups mashed potatoes

Mix fish, green pepper, diced fried onions, peas and seasonings. Fold into the white sauce. Place in casserole, top with mashed potatoes, and bake at 450 degrees for 20 minutes, or until brown. Serves 6.

CLOUDBERRY PARFAIT

5 egg yolks	1 cup cloudberry butter, pressed through sieve
3 cups cream	
1/2 cup cloudberry liqueur	Fresh whole cloudberries
1 cup sugar	1/2 cup cloudberry liqueur, for basting

Mix egg yolks, 1/2 cup cloudberry liqueur, cloudberry butter, and sugar in double boiler. Chill. Stir in whipped cream and pour into parfait dish and chill in freezer overnight. Unmold and moisten with cloudberry liqueur. Garnish with fresh cloudberries and whipped cream.
Cloudberries are round, soft, red or yellowish fruit somewhat like a raspberry. Raspberries or strawberries may be used also.

HEDEL-MAKEITTO
(Cold Fruit Soup)

1 lb. mixed dried fruit	1 stick cinnamon
3 tart apples, diced	2 tablespoons cornstarch
1/4 cup sugar	3 tablespoons cold water
1 1/2 quarts water	

Wash dried fruit in warm water. Soak in sugar and water overnight. Cook in same water for 5 minutes. Add cinnamon and apples. Cook slowly until fruit is soft. Strain. Combine cornstarch with water and stir into soup. Keep stirring over heat, until thick. Cool and serve!

France has a centuries-old tradition of fine cuisine, and of fine agricultural products that help make the country's many dishes so special. Flat plainland comprises almost half the country, perfect for grain crops. The eastern and southwest borders contain mountain ranges, the Alps and the Pyrenees respectively, which also gives France the perfect climate for producing wine grapes and flowers used in the art of perfumery. France is the largest food producer and exporter in Western Europe.

Poached Salmon in Court Bouillon

1 whole salmon (4-5 lbs.)	1 rib celery, minced
Make Court Bouillon with	1/4 cup minced parsley
3 quarts water	1 tablespoon coarse salt
1/2 cup white vinegar or lemon	1 teaspoon dried thyme
juice	1 bay leaf
3 minced carrots	1 lb. peppercorn, added last 15 min.
2 onions, minced	Simmer 1 hour.

Add Salmon to simmered broth and simmer covered for 20 minutes. Skin Salmon and serve with lemon butter or Aioli Sauce.

AIOLI SAUCE
(From the South of France)

2 garlic cloves	1 cup olive oil
1 egg yolk	1/2 teaspoon salt

Mix as for mayonnaise. Serve over fish or vegetables!

LEMON BUTTER
(Makes about 1 1/4 cups)

1 cup unsalted sweet butter,	1 teaspoon grated lemon peel
softened	1/2 teaspoon salt
1/4 cup lemon juice	1/4 teaspoon white pepper

Beat butter in small bowl until light and fluffy; beat in remaining ingredients gradually until smooth.

FRENCH FRIED ICE CREAM BALLS

1 1/2 quarts ice cream	6 egg whites, beaten
6 egg whites	1/4 teaspoon almond flavoring
1/4 teaspoon almond flavoring	2 lbs. graham cracker crumbs
1 lb. coconut macaroons, crumbled	

Beat the first 6 egg whites with a fork. Add the almond flavoring and coconut macaroons. Mix well. Take scoops of the ice cream and roll in this mixture. Refreeze.
Beat the next 6 egg whites until stiff. Add the almond flavoring and 2 pounds of graham cracker crumbs. Take the ice cream balls from freezer and roll again in this mixture. Fry in butter or oil at 365 degrees. Drain and serve.

COLD ORANGE OR RASPBERRY SOUFFLÉ

(Serves 6 to 8)

1 envelope unflavored gelatin
1/4 cup cold water
1 teaspoon grated orange rind
1/2 cup orange juice or raspberry juice

4 eggs, separated
1/2 teaspoon salt
1 cup granulated sugar
1 cup heavy cream
1/4 cup finely crushed macaroons

1. Fold a 20" piece of foil in half lengthwise. Wrap around a 1 1/2-quart soufflé dish as a collar.
2. Sprinkle gelatin into cold water to soften.
3. Grate orange rind, then extract juice.
4. In top of a double boiler, combine egg yolks, orange juice, salt and 1/2 cup sugar. Cook, stirring constantly until slightly thickened.
5. Stir in gelatin and orange rind.
6. Turn into a large bowl and cool.
7. Beat egg whites until they hold their shape. Beat in remaining 1/2 cup sugar gradually, until whites hold a stiff peak.
8. Whip cream until stiff.
9. Fold whites into orange mixture gently and then fold in cream until completely blended. Pour into prepared soufflé dish.
10. Refrigerate at least 3 hours. Remove foil. Press macaroon crumbs around the exposed sides of soufflé. Decorate with candy flowers.

BROWN EDGE WAFERS

1/2 cup shortening
1/2 cup sugar
1 egg

3/4 cup flour
1/2 tablespoon salt
1/2 teaspoon vanilla

Cream shortening and sugar; add rest of ingredients and beat until smooth. Place by teaspoonfuls on lightly greased cookie sheet. Bake in oven of 375 degrees. Remove from sheet immediately, before cooling. These cookies will spread; bake with a brown edge. These are wonderful!

FRENCH ONION SOUP

Serves 6-8

Ingredients:
  4 medium onions
  3 tablespoons chicken base
  3 teaspoons Maggi seasoning
  2 tablespoons melted butter
  3 tablespoons salt
  1 tablespoon black pepper
  3 quarts water

  1/4 cup sherry
  3 tablespoons flour
Bread Crumb Toppinig:
  1 cup bread crumbs
  1 teaspoon paprika
  1 teaspoon melted butter
  1 ounce old English cheese

Preparation:
Melt butter in 2 gallon pot. Sauté onions until transparent. Add Maggi seasoning, chicken base, flour, and mix well. Add water,

bring to a boil and return to simmer for 20 minutes. Remove from heat and add sherry.
Serving Suggestions:
Pour soup into bowl. Place small crouton with melted mozzarella cheese, cheese side down, in soup. Completely cover top of bowl with sliced mozzarella cheese so that all areas of the lip of the bowl are covered. Sprinkle with bread crumbs and cheese topping. Place in oven until cheese melts and bread crumb mixture is golden brown. May be served with garlic bread toast.

		STEAK
1 lb. finely ground beef tenderloin	1 small onion, minced	*TARTARE*
1 raw egg	Dash of Worcestershire sauce	
1/2 cup finely chopped parsley	2 tablespoons capers	
2 teaspoons poupon mustard	1 1/2 teaspoons salt	
1 clove garlic, minced	Coarsely cracked pepper	

Mix thoroughly until very smooth. Make into a nice round ball and serve with melba toast.

		FRENCH
1 cake yeast	2 cups boiled water	*BREAD*
1/4 cup boiled water, cooled	1 1/2 teaspoons salt	
3/4 cup flour	6 cups flour	

Knead first three ingredients into a ball. Set the ball in a bowl containing the 2 cups of boiled water that has been cooled to lukewarm. When ball floats add the salt and the rest of the flour. Knead for 15 minutes and let rise until double in bulk. Knead again, shape into long loaves. Cut furrow in each loaf and let rise until double in bulk. Bake for 10 minutes at 450 degrees then reduce heat to 300 degrees and bake for 50 minutes. Brush with beaten egg white.

Allow 6 snails per person.
Prepare snail butter as follows:
Blend 1 cup soft butter, 1/2 teaspoon garlic powder, 1 teaspoon chives, dash of Tabasco and seasoning salt to taste. Dab butter into snail shell, place in snail then seal off with more butter. Run under broiler and heat until bubbly hot. Serve with garlic bread.

The Gabonese Republic is on the Atlantic coast of Central Africa. Its major industry is oil products but the country has crops of cocoa, coffee, rice, peanuts, palm products, cassava, and bananas. Gabon became independent in 1960, and is one of the most prosperous African countries, due to its abundant natural resources and the high proportion of foreign private investment.

RED SNAPPER IN LIME OR LEMON JUICE

1 5-lb. red snapper, sliced, boned and salted. Then cover with juice of 10 lemons overnight. Next morning — fish was cooked by the addition of the lemon juice. It is served, sprinkled with pepper, fresh thyme, parsley and peanuts.

This is excellent served with a raw vegetable salad and "Coconut Dressing."

COCONUT DRESSING

To make dressing:
Grate 1 fresh coconut and add 1 cup cold milk. Squeeze all the juice from the milk and coconut. Add the juice of 2 lemons, 2 tablespoons peanut oil, salt and pepper to taste. Shake vigorously and serve over crisp greens!

PEANUT BUTTER PIE

1 cup dark Karo syrup   Dash of salt
3/4 cup white sugar   3 eggs
2/3 cup peanut butter

Blend all ingredients together quickly. Pour into unbaked pie shell. Bake in 350 degree oven for 45 minutes or until barely set. Do not over bake. Serve topped with sweetened whipped cream flavored with orange or vanilla or rum.

The secret of life is not to do what one likes,
But to try to like what one has to do.

Gambia is a tiny country on the western tip of Africa on the Atlantic Coast. Its chief industry is tourism. The main exports are peanuts and rice. It is a democratic country made up of Moslems and Christians. English is the official language.

CHICKEN LIVER AND GIZZARD CURRY

2 lbs. chicken livers and gizzards
3 tablespoons peanut oil
1 large onion
3 hot red chili peppers, minced
3 cloves garlic, minced
1 teaspoon anchovy paste
1 teaspoon curry powder
1/2 teaspoon powdered ginger
1/2 teaspoon powdered coriander
2 bay leaves
1 1/2 cups coconut cream
6 hard cooked eggs, chopped
2 tablespoon lime juice
Salt

Sauté onion in peanut oil for 3 minutes. Add spices, livers and gizzards and coconut cream. Simmer 30 minutes covered. Stir in lime juice and eggs. Simmer for a few minutes and serve hot with rice.

COCONUT CREAM

Made by combining 2 cups packaged coconut with 2 cups scalded milk. Let stand 30 minutes.

Strain and press out milk (for a very thick cream let simmer for 1 hour and strain).

CABBAGE SOUP

Boil 2 1/2 pounds green cabbage in 3 quarts of salt water for 60 minutes. Keep covered.
Herb Tea: To 1 pint of water add 2 cloves garlic, 1 teaspoon caraway seeds, 1 teaspoon whole black pepper, 2 medium bay leaves and 2 teaspoons oregano. Let simmer for 10 to 15 minutes. Let stand for another 10 minutes to cool before straining tea into cabbage mixture.
Thickening: Blend 2 cups of flour into 1/2 pound drawn butter and mix well. Add this to cabbage mixture and with wire whip stir while simmering for 10 minutes. When soup is smooth, discontinue simmering. Add 1 quart scalded milk and 4 ounces cheese grated. Add to taste: nutmeg, mace, salt, white pepper and ground oregano.

Germany is the land of beer and wurst!

Assmannhausen is one of the best known of the Red Rhine Wines. Auslese (means specially selected) is used to designate those Rhine and Moselle wines made from the best grapes of the vintage. If the process has been carried to the point of picking the best grapes from the bunches, the terms Goldbeerenauslese or Beerenauslese are used. Sometimes further qualified wines are Feine (fine).

GERMAN LIVER DUMPLINGS
(Leberknodel)

6 slices white bread	2 eggs
1 cup lukewarm milk	1 teaspoon salt
3/4 lb. liver all membrane removed	Pinch of marjoram
	Grated rind of 1 lemon
2 ounces kidney fat	1/2 to 1 cup bread crumbs
1 small onion	8 cups beef broth

Dice bread, soak in warm milk until milk cools. Squeeze out excess milk. Grind together liver, kidney fat and onions through the fine blade of a food chopper. Stir in eggs, salt, bread soaked, marjoram and lemon rind. Gradually add dry bread crumbs, 1 tablespoon at a time, until mixture can be shaped into dumplings. Can be done easier with a wet hand. Make them about 1 1/2 inches in diameter. Drop gently into boiling beef broth. Simmer uncovered fo 15 to 20 minutes or until they float. Serve in soup!

PRETZELS

1 pkg. yeast	Pinch of sugar
1/4 cup water	2 teaspoons salt
1 cup warm water	4-5 cups flour

Dissolve yeast in warm water. Mix in all ingredients except flour. Add flour; stir until stiff. Knead for 10 minutes. Place in greased bowl and let rise. Preheat oven to warm. Turn off and roll out dough to 18 inches long. Cut in strips and cross right in through left. Bring 4 cups water to a boil with 4 teaspoons baking soda. Drop 3 pretzels in at a time. Boil 1 minute or until pretzels float. Remove, drain and place on a greased pan. Sprinkle with coarse salt and bake in a 475 degree oven till brown, about 12 minutes.

Use a standard-size mixer to ensure thorough beating of the eggs.

10 egg yolks

• • •

3/4 cup butter, softened
3/4 cup granulated sugar
2 teaspoons finely shredded lemon
   peel
1 teaspoon vanilla

1 cup all-purpose flour
1/2 cup cornstarch
1/4 teaspoon salt

• • •

10 egg whites
1/4 cup granulated sugar
1 recipe Vanilla Glaze
1 recipe Chocolate Glaze

In small mixer bowl beat egg yolks at high speed on electric mixer till thick and lemon-colored, about 10 minutes; set aside. In large mixer bowl beat butter till light and fluffy; gradually beat in the 3/4 cup sugar. Add lemon peel and vanilla. Beat in egg yolk mixture. In large mixing bowl stir together flour, cornstarch, and salt; stir in butter-egg mixture. Wash beaters and the large mixer bowl thoroughly. In large mixer bowl beat egg whites to soft peaks (tips curl over); gradually add the 1/4 cup sugar, beating to stiff peaks (tips stand straight). Fold into egg yolk batter.

Grease an 8-inch springform pan. Spread 1/3 cup of the batter evenly in the bottom of the pan. Place under broiler 5 inches from heat and broil about 1 minute or till top is light brown (it may be necessary to give pan a half turn for even browning). Do not overbrown. Remove from broiler. Spread another 1/3 cup batter on top of first layer. Broil as before, turning, if necessary, for even brownness. Repeat spreading batter and broiling to make 15 to 17 layers in all. Cool in pan 10 minutes. Loosen cake and remove sides of pan; cool completely. Cut into 12 wedges. Place wedges on wire rack with waxed paper underneath. Spoon and spread Vanilla Glaze evenly over half the wedges; let dry thoroughly. Spoon and spread Chocolate Glaze over remaining wedges; let dry. Makes 12 servings. See page 177.

1/2 lb. ground beef
1/2 lb. ground pork
1 egg
1 cup onion

2 tablespoons horseradish
1 tablespoon mustard
2 tablespoons ketchup
1 cup oil
Salt, pepper and garlic to taste

Mix beef, pork, egg, onions and mustard. Shape into rounded pattie, roll in flour then into 2 beaten eggs and then back in flour. Fry in oil until golden. Serve with dab of ketchup.

PLUM CAKE
(Zwetchenkuchen)

2 cups flour
1/2 teaspoon salt
1/2 teaspoon baking powder
2 teaspoons sugar
2/3 cup butter
2 egg yolks
1/3 cup cold water
Bread crumbs
Butter

Filling:
2 lbs. fresh plums
1 cup sugar
2 egg yolks
2 tablespoons sugar
2 tablespoons cream

Sift flour, salt, baking powder and sugar. Cut in 2/3 cup butter and blend well. Make well in center and add the egg yolks and water. Mix well. Knead well. Let chill 1 hour in refrigerator. When cold, roll dough into a thin sheet. Sprinkle with bread crumbs and dot generously with butter.
Filling:
Wash plums, cut into halves, remove stones. Place plums in rows on top of crumbs. Sprinkle with 1 cup of sugar and cover with following mixture. Beat the egg yolks. Add the 2 tablespoons sugar, and the cream. Bake in 350 degree oven 45 minutes.

SAUERKRAUT SALAD

1/2 cup oil
1/2 cup white vinegar
1 1/2 cups sugar
Heat until sugar dissolves.

1 No. 2 1/2 can sauerkraut, drained

2 cups diced celery
1/2 cup diced onion
1/2 cup diced green peppers
1/2 cup diced pimento
1 teaspoon caraway seeds
1 teaspoon celery seed

Heat sugar, vinegar and oil. Chop vegetables; add to sauerkraut and mix with rest of ingredients.

Let stand 3 hours. Will keep 2 weeks.

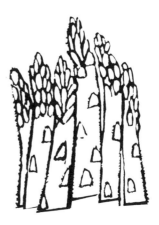

The Federal Republic of Germany was proclaimed May 23, 1949, after a constitution had been drawn up by a consultative assembly formed by representatives of 11 "states" in the Western occupied zone of the country. The country is a thriving center for steel production, shipbuilding, and production of oil products and automobiles. The country has experienced tremendous economic growth since the 1950's, and is the world's 4th greatest economic power. West Germany leads Europe in provisions for worker participation in the management of industry.

BLACK FOREST CAKE
(Schwarzwalder Kirsch Torte)

Bottom Layer: (Pastry Layer)
125 grams flour
10 grams cocoa (3 teaspoons)
1 teaspoon baking powder
50 grams sugar
1 teaspoon vanilla
1 egg white
50 grams butter

Mix all ingredients; knead well and refrigerate. Then press into a springform pan and bake 20 minutes at 300 degrees.

Biscuit Layer: (2nd and 3rd Layers, Sponge Layer)
3 eggs
1 egg yolk
2 tablespoons warm water
100 grams sugar
1 teaspoon vanilla
3 drops butter almond
1 teaspoon cinnamon
75 grams flour
10 grams cocoa
25 grams cornstarch
1 1/2 teaspoons baking powder

Beat eggs and egg yolks with sugar and water until very fluffy. Fold in dry ingredients that have been sifted together. Bake in a springform pan for 35 minutes in a 350 degree oven. Cool and split layers.

Now assemble the torte by placing over the pastry layer, pitted cherries and juice which has been heated and thickened with cornstarch.
Next layer; place sponge cake and make a — Gelatin Filling:

750 grams sour cream
75 grams sugar
40 grams cornstarch, dissolved in water
2 tablespoons kirsh
2 tablespoons gelatin
3 tablespoons cold water

Heat sour cream and sugar; stir in cornstarch and cook until thick. Dissolve gelatin in cold water and add to this mixture; add kirsh. Let cool and spread on sponge cake. Top with next layer of sponge cake.

Whip:
1 pint sweet cream
2 tablespoons kirsh
1 teaspoon vanilla
Sugar to taste

Use whip to top the torte and arrange curls of chocolate and cherries around it. Refrigerate for 2 hours, serve!

Ghana is on the southern coast of West Africa, with an area of 92,100 square miles, slightly smaller than the state of Oregon. Its low fertile plains and scrubland are used to grow cocoa, coffee, palm products, corn, rice, and casava. Industrial diamonds are also mined, and the country has a large reserve of timber, including rare woods and rubber trees. It was once ruled by Britain as the Gold Coast, but became independent in 1957.

BOBOTIE LOAF

2 onions, sliced finely
1 apple, peeled, cored and chopped
2 tablespoons butter
2 1/2 lbs. ground lamb or beef, cooked or raw
2 slices white bread, soaked in milk and squeezed dry
2 tablespoons mild curry powder
2 tablespoons apricot jam
2 eggs, beaten

2 tablespoons vinegar
4 ounces seedless raisins, soaked in boiling water
2 tablespoons ground almonds
1 cup milk
3 lemon leaves or 3 small bay leaves
1 teaspoon turmeric
1 teaspoon ginger
Salt and pepper

Fry onions and apples in butter until soft and golden. If beef or lamb is uncooked, fry it with the onion until browned. Add chopped apple and fry a little longer. Combine all ingredients and knead well until mixed and smooth. Press into a buttered pie dish and bake at 350 degrees for 45 minutes. Remove from oven and leave to stand in the pie dish for about 10 minutes and then turn out. Serve garnished with thin slices of orange and a few lemon leaves. Bobotie is good with a salad or cold rice and pineapple! Serves 6 to 8.

TRADITIONAL YELLOW RICE WITH RAISINS AND CINNAMON

1 large cup rice
1 ounce sugar
1/2 teaspoon salt
1 tablespoon butter

2 ounces seedless raisins
4 orange juice
1 teaspoon turmeric

Bring water to boil. Add all ingredients, except raisins. Boil 15 minutes. Add raisins. When cooked mix with fork. Strain off excess liquid.

To get juice from an onion, cut in half and press on lemon squeezer. Do not peel.

FLAGS OF THE UNITED NATIONS

GREECE

HONDURAS

GRENADA

HUNGARY

GUATEMALA

ICELAND

GUINEA

INDIA

GUINEA BISSAU

INDONESIA

GUYANA

ISLAMIC REPUBLIC OF IRAN

HAITI

In ancient times, Greece was a leader in learning; the traditions of their teachings in art, architecture, science, mathematics, and philosophy as well as drama and literature are still influences in the modern world. Today, the country produces textiles, chemicals, aluminum, and wines. Although large portions of the rocky countryside are unsuited for crop growing, Greece does produce corn, grain, rice, olives and citrus fruits.

DOLMADAKIA YIALANDJI
(Stuffed Grapevine Leaves)

4 medium onions, chopped
1 teaspoon salt
2/3 cup raw rice
3/4 cup olive oil
1 teaspoon mint, chopped
1 teaspoon fresh dill, chopped
1/2 cup parsley, chopped, reserve stalks
3 large bunches scallions, including green, chopped
Salt and pepper
Juice of 1 lemon
12 ounce jar grapevine leaves
Parsley stalks
1 cup boiling water
Additional lemon juice

Steam onions over very low heat with 1 teaspoon salt, stirring occasionally, for 5 to 10 minutes. Remove from heat. Add rice and 1/2 cup of the olive oil and mix. Add herbs and vegetables and mix. Add salt and pepper and half the lemon juice. Wash grapevine leaves thoroughly to remove all brine. Separate leaves carefully. Remove thick stem portions. Cut large leaves in half. Place 1 tablespoon filling on underside of leaf. Starting at base, fold over, and fold in sides, rolling tightly toward point. Interlace parsley stalks on bottom of saucepan. Arrange DOLMADAKIA in layers. Add the remaining oil and lemon juice. Weight down with a heavy plate. Cover saucepan and simmer for 20 minutes over low heat. Add boiling water and simmer for 25 minutes longer. Serve cold, sprinkled with lemon juice. Yield: 3 dozen

MOUSSAKA

2 large onions, chopped
1/2 lb. butter
4 lbs. chopped beef
Salt and pepper to taste
Oregano
Dash garlic powder
1 2-lb, 3-ounce can Italian plum tomatoes
1 cup tomato pureé or sauce
5-6 eggplants
Salt
6 eggs
4 cups milk
1/2 cup flour
1 teaspoon salt
2 tablespoons butter
Grated cheese

Brown onions in 1/4 lb. of the butter. Add ground beef and brown well. Add salt and pepper, oregano, and garlic powder. Add tomatoes and tomato pureé and cook over low heat for 1 hour, stirring frequently. Set aside.

Melt remaining 1/4 lb. butter. Peel one eggplant at a time. Cut lengthwise into 1/2-inch thick slices and arrange slices on broiler pan. Sprinkle lightly with salt and brush with melted butter. Brown 2 inches from broiler heat, turn, and brown other side. Set aside and repeat until all eggplants are broiled. Beat eggs with 1 cup of the milk, the flour, and teaspoon salt. Heat remaining milk with the two tablespoons butter. Add slowly to egg mixture, beating constantly. Stir over low heat, without letting sauce boil, until very thick.

Overlap a layer of eggplant in bottom of an ungreased 10 x 6 x 2 inch pan and sprinkle lightly again with cheese. Repeat layers until all eggplant and meat is used, ending with a layer of eggplant. Cover top with the egg sauce and sprinkle generously with grated cheese. Bake in a 375 degree oven for 1 hour or until brown. Cut into squares and serve warm. Serves 14 to 16!

GREEK EGG AND LEMON SOUP

Avgolemono

3 quarts hot chicken broth	Juice of 2 large lemons, or 6
2/3 cup rice	tablespoons lemon juice
4 egg yolks	Salt, white pepper as necessary

Add the rice to the chicken broth and cook covered until rice is tender, about 20 minutes. Beat the egg yolks until very yellow and light in texture. Stir in the lemon juice gradually. Keep stirring to prevent curdling of the egg yolk. Add, as you stir, 1/2 cup of the hot broth. Keeping the soup under the boiling point and with constant stirring, add egg-lemon mixture to soup. Heat gently and stir for 2 or 3 minutes, then season with more salt if it is needed, and a little white pepper to taste. Pepper isn't always used in this soup, and black pepper shouldn't be as it spoils the color.

MELOMAKA-RONA

(Honey Cakes)

4 cups farina or flour	2 jiggers brandy
1 cup oil	Juice and rind of 1 orange
1 cup butter	1/2 teaspoon cinnamon
1/2 cup powdered sugar	1/2 teaspoon cloves
1 cup warm honey	2 teaspoon baking powder

Work flour with oil and butter until creamy. Add sugar, honey and rest of ingredients. Work with hands to make a smooth dough about 20 minutes. Roll with hands into balls the size of an egg, flatten on 1 side. Bake on greased baking pan 20 minutes at 350 degrees. As soon as done dip in hot honey syrup made with 1 cup honey, 1 cup sugar and 1 cup water. Leave cookie in hot syrup 3 minutes. Drain and sprinkle with chopped walnuts if desired

Christopher Columbus was the first visitor to the islands of Grenada. Their main products are nutmeg, cocoa, sugar, rum, mace and bananas.

AGUACATES RELLENOS
(Stuffed Avocados)

1/2 lb. ground beef	1/8 teaspoon pepper
1/8 teaspoon salt	Pinch of cumin
1 clove garlic	20 blanched almonds, chopped fine
3/4 cup butter	10 pitted ripe olives
2 medium onions, chopped	1/4 cup seedless raisins
1 1/4 cup tomato pureé	6 avocados

Melt butter and sauté onion and meat for 15 minutes, stirring frequently. Place all ingredients in skillet and stir and simmer for 30 minutes. Cut avocados lengthwise; spoon meat mixture into halves and bake in 325 degree oven for 5 minutes, just until the avocados are hot. Garnish with grated cheese and serve hot.

COCONUT ICE CREAM

2 cups shredded packaged coconut	1/3 cup sugar
1 1/2 cups milk	1 cup whipping cream
1 tablespoon gelatin	1 cup half and half
2 tablespoons water	1 teaspoon vanilla

Combine 1 1/3 cups of coconut with the milk and allow to stand for 30 minutes. Then simmer for 10 minutes. Cool and strain through cheese cloth. Discard coconut. Soak the gelatin in water for 10 minutes. Add some of the hot coconut liquid and dissolve the gelatin in it. Chill and whip the cream. Add the half and half, vanilla, gelatin, and strained coconut milk. Stir in 2/3 cup coconut and freeze in refrigerator pan. Stir several times. May be made in ice cream crank freezer.

BANANAS À LA CRÉOLE

6 firm ripe bananas, cut lengthwise
  and remove bananas, do not
  break skin

Soak skins 2 minutes in boiling water. Drain and dip in cold water. Cut each banana half in slices and sprinkle with sugar and rum. Fill bananas skins two-thirds full of cooked rice and crushed pineapple. Arrange the banana slices in neat row on top of rice. Sprinkle with finely ground macaroons and melted butter. Broil 5 minutes and serve with apricot sauce and whipped cream.

This Central American country is south of Mexico, with Honduras and Belize to the east. Central highlands and mountain areas are ideal for the growing of coffee, which forms one-third of the country's exports. Sugar, bananas and cotton are also grown. Guatemala is the site of the Old Mayan Empire and is rich in historical artifacts. Subsequently, it was a Spanish colony, and a republic was established in 1839.

GRAPEFRUIT CONSOMMÉ

2 pints strained grapefruit juice	2-3 grapefruits
2 tablespoons strained orange juice	1 pkg. lemon jello
2 tablespoons strained lime juice	1/4 cup boiling water
Dash Angostura bitters	Mint or parsley

Blend juice and Angostura in jug. Peel grapefruit divide in segments and chop; remove all pits. Dissolve jello in water. Allow to cool slightly. Combine with fruit. Pour into glass soup cups, and chill thoroughly.

SOUTH OF THE BORDER PUMPKIN SOUP

2 lb. pumpkin	Sprig of parsley
Salt	2/3 cup chicken stock
1 large onion, finely chopped	Paprika
2 tomatoes, sliced	2/3 cup cream
2 teaspoons chopped chives	

Cut the pumpkin into 4 big pieces and cook in boiling salted water for 15 minutes. Drain and scoop the flesh from the skin. Put pumpkin and all the other vegetables with the chicken stock in a saucepan. Bring to a boil. Simmer for 35 minutes. Allow to cool slightly. Strain and sieve. Allow to cool. Then season to taste. Add half the cream and beat until smooth. Refrigerate. Top with remaining cream and serve. Sprinkle with chives!

BANANA RUM PUDDING
(No eggs)

1 sponge cake, cut in thin slices	Rum Cream:
1 dozen ripe, firm bananas	2 cups whipping cream
2 pkgs. French Vanilla Pudding	1/2 cup rum
6 cups milk	6 tablespoons powdered sugar

Whip cream and add rum and powdered sugar!

Line Pyrex dish with sponge cake and sliced bananas. Beat the instant pudding with the milk until smooth. Heat in saucepan until scalding; do not boil. Spoon hot sauce over bananas and sponge layer. Repeat, making 3 layers of sponge cake, sliced bananas and hot custard. End up with hot custard. Chill in refrigerator and serve with Rum Cream.

Guinea, which is slightly smaller than the state of Oregon, sits on the Atlantic coast of West Africa. The coastland is narrow, with steep mountains rising inland. Crops include bananas, pineapples, rice, corn, palm nuts, coffee, and honey. There are deposits of bauxite, iron and diamonds.

Pieces of Iguana are floured and browned in hot butter. Place in a casserole, sprinkle with fresh parsley, a bay leaf, thyme and sliced onions. Add a little water and cover the casserole dish. Bake at 325 degrees for 3 hours in oven.

FRICASSEE OF IGUANA
(A Large Edible Lizard)

6 tablespoons olive oil
3 tablespoons wine vinegar
2 cloves garlic, crushed
1 tablespoon prepared mustard
Salt to taste
1/4 teaspoon fresh ground pepper

1 1/2 cups thinly sliced mushrooms
6 slices cooked, crumbled bacon
1/4 cup minced, fresh parsley
2 lbs. fresh spinach leaves
*Fresh shrimp, cooked, or fried fish
    is used as a side dish.

HOT SPINACH SALAD

Break up spinach in a bowl. Heat rest of ingredients in a large skillet. Pour hot mixture over spinach and serve quickly!
To flame salad:
If you want to flame salad, add 1/4 cup cognoc or brandy to sauce. Ignite and pour over lettuce and serve immediately.

Pastry:
4 cups flour
3/4 lb. margarine
1 teaspoon baking powder

1 egg yolk
1 teaspoon salt
1/3 cup ice water
1 teaspoon vinegar

MEAT PIES

Sift together flour, salt and baking powder. Rub in margarine. Beat egg yolk, add vinegar and ice water and mix with flour. Leave overnight or at least 1 hour in refrigerator.

Filling:
Sauté 5 lbs. ground beef, 4 carrots and 3 onions. Cook until tender. Add salt, pepper and cloves to taste. Cook 3/4 cup macaroni until soft. Drain and add to meat mixture. Put through food grinder. Roll out dough and cut into squares about 2 1/2 inches square. Place 1 teaspoon of filling in each square of dough. Wet edges of dough. Take the four corners of the dough and bring up towards center. Pinch together to seal. Bake about 12 or 15 minutes in 350 degree oven.

69

Guinea Bissau is a tiny country on the central east coast of Africa. For millions of years, man has evolved from his response to his needs and environment. Racial differences arose as a result of gradual genetic diversification. The differences of pigmentation, for instance, seem to be adaptive to environment. Blond, fair-skinned people tend to go with cool cloudy habitats; burnettes, with areas of bright sun, like the Mediterranean; the darkest-skinned, with the hottest, non-forested regions like the Savannah of Africa. Those with dark, yellowish skin and crinky hair are from the rain forest area of Africa. All the same, man came from one source, and has one original home, Africa. The brotherhood of man is clearly something real. Africa was the leading continent in the world until 2000 B.C. We can say that Africa gave birth to man and is man's original home and the oldest culture on earth. The rock paintings and engravings, dating back to 4300 B.C., show that beauty and art was born on this beautiful continent.

"LEKKER POEDING"

1 cup self-rising flour	1 cup milk
1 cup apricot jam	2 eggs, beaten
2 teaspoons melted butter	

Mix milk, eggs and butter. Mix with apricot jam and flour. Add 1 teaspoon vinegar to 1 1/2 teaspoons baking soda. Add to mixture. Bake for 45 minutes in 350 degree oven. Don't panic, cake loves to sink in the middle. Let cool. Can be baked a day ahead of time.

Sauce:
2 cups cream
2 eggs
3/4 cup sugar

Beat eggs, then beat cream, adding sugar, till fairly stiff. Add eggs to cream. Pour over cake and bake 10 minutes at 350 degrees. Serve warm!

CARAMEL PEACHES

8 to 12 peaches, peeled	1 cup light cream
3 tablespoons butter	1 1/4 tablespoons cornstarch
1 cup brown sugar	

Brown butter in skillet, add peaches, brown sugar and enough water to cover half the peaches. Cook until tender.

This South American country has been independent since 1966. About the size of Idaho, Guyana is bordered by Venezuela on the west, Brazil to the south. Almost 90% of the country's population lives in the flat coastal area, which is as much as 40 miles wide in places. Inland are dense tropical forests. The rich plainlands produce abundant crops of sugar, rice, coconuts and coffee, and the country has industries which produce cigarettes, rum, clothing and furniture.

HIGADO Á LA CACEROLA
(Liver Casserole)

2.2 lbs. liver	1 tablespoon Worcestershire Sauce
4 slices bacon	1 tablespoon tomato ketchup
5 tablespoons butter	Salt, pepper and oregano to taste
5 tablespoons flour	2 cups liquid
1 medium onion	(1 cup stock and 1 cup white wine)

Brown onion in butter. Remove from pan. Fry bacon. Roll liver in seasoned flour and brown in butter. Place in casserole and cover wih bacon and onion. Stir in remaining seasoned flour into pan you browned the liver in. Add stock and wine. Cook 2 minutes and pour over liver. Cover and bake in 295 degree oven 2 1/2 to 3 hours.
*Soak liver in sweetmilk 24 hours to tenderize!

FROG LEGS

12 pairs frog legs	1/2 cup butter
2 tablespoons lemon juice	1 clove garlic, minced
1/4 cup half and half	1/4 cup Madeira
1 teaspoon salt	1 cup sour cream
1/4 cup flour	

Sprinkle frog legs with lemon juice and salt. Dip in half and half and coat with flour. Heat butter in saucepan with garlic. Brown quickly. Add Madeira and simmer for 5 minutes. Mix in sour cream. Do not boil. Serve on toast.

Haiti occupies the western third of the Island of Hispaniola in the West Indies. About two-thirds of the country is mountainous, and the rest is semi-arid. It is approximately the size of the state of Maryland, and produces coffee, sisal and sugar. The country also has a thriving rum industry.

HAITIAN RICE SALAD

Cook rice till dry and fluffy. Season with tarragon, vinegar, dry mustard, red pepper and salt. Place on plate and top with mayonnaise, sliced green olives, pineapple chunks, and tomato wedges.

HAITIAN MARINADE FOR SKEWERED GOAT

1 cup grapefruit juice
1/4 cup olive oil
1/4 cup onion
1 clove garlic
1 teaspoon chives

1 teaspoon mint
1 teaspoon sage
1/4 cup brandy
1/4 teaspoon oregano

Cut 2 pounds young goat in 1-inch cubes. Marinate for 2 days in mixture. Skewer and grill until tender.

ORANGE AND TOMATO SOUP

2 cups orange juice
2 cups tomato juice
1/2 cup white wine

Juice of 1/2 lemon
1 teaspoon sugar
Salt and cayenne pepper to taste

Mix all ingredients and serve cold!

CHILLED AVOCADO CREAM SOUP

2 large green peppers, deseeded and
  chopped
2 spring onions, chopped fine
2 large very ripe avocados
1 tablespoon strained lime juice

2 teaspoons salt
1 pint milk
1 cup cream, whipped for topping
Paprika

Mash avocados, add rest of ingredients. Place seed back into soup to prevent discoloration. Chill in refrigerator. Serve in cups with a dot of whipped cream!

Located in Central America, Honduras is bordered by Guatamala in the west, with El Salvador and Nicaragua in the south. The terrain is mountainous, but wide fertile valleys in between provide room for bananas, the country's chief export, as well as coffee and cotton. Gold and silver are also mined there. Honduras has been independent since 1838.

OSTIONES DE GUAYMAS
(Oysters with Jalapenos)

36 select oysters
2 tablespoons lemon juice
3/4 tablespoons salt
1 cup chopped spring onions
1/2 cup oil
1 cup vinegar

1 teaspoon allspice
1 teaspoon pepper
3 cloves garlic, chopped and fried
1 cup Chili Jalapeno, cut in strips

Put oysters in pot with 1 cup water, lemon juice and salt. Simmer 5 minutes. Soak onions in 1 1/2 cups boiling water with 1 teaspoon salt for 5 minutes. Drain and fry in oil about 3 minutes. Add to oysters. Add vinegar, allspice, pepper, garlic, chili and one tablespoon juice from the canned chilies. Cover bowl and let stand for 24 hours. Serve with crackers! Refrigerate as soon as prepared.

CALAS TOUT CHAUD

1 cup sugar
1 cup boiled rice
2 teaspoons baking powder

2 eggs
2 cups flour

Mix yolks with sugar, rice, flour and baking powder. Add beaten egg whites. Drop by teaspoon into hot fat. Drain. Sprinkle with powdered sugar.

LEMON PUFFS

1/2 cup milk
1/2 cup water

1 tablespoon butter
2 tablespoons sugar

Mix and bring to a boil and stir in 3/4 cup flour. Stir to a smooth paste; remove from heat and cool. Add grated rind of 1 lemon, 3 egg yolks. Fold in beaten egg whites and pinch of soda. Drop by teaspoon into hot fat. Drain. Sprinkle with powdered sugar!

This East Central European country on the Danube River (which forms the border with Czechoslovakia) is mostly comprised of a great fertile plain, the Alfold, with some hilly country in the west and north. Iron, steel, machinery, chemicals, vehicles, and communications equipment are among the industrial goods produced there, while grain and vegetables are grown on the plains.

COLD FOGAS
(Hungarian Fish from Lake Balaton)

Prepare day before serving!

2 cups water
2 tablespoons vinegar
1/2 teaspoon salt

1 medium onion, sliced
1/2 lb. fish, per person

Make marinade sauce by combining water, vinegar, salt and onion. Boil and cool to lukewarm. Clean fish and remove center bone. Tie fish in cheese cloth. Boil fish in sauce until tender. Let fish cool in sauce.

Day of serving have: cooked, diced potatoes, beets, carrots, peas; apples, cored and sliced, cut into bite size pieces; mayonnaise for salad; two tablespoons plain gelatin; 3/4 cup water.

Carefully remove skin from fish. Cut into even slices. Combine vegetable-salad ingredients. Arrange in a mound on a large serving plate. Dissolve gelatin in water and heat until melted. Then place slices of fish on top of salad, arranged like a wreath. Use gelatin glaze to brush over mound, to make shiny. Garnish with mayonnaise, using decorators tools. Decorate with curls of smoked salmon. A recipe from elegant, charming old Budapest.

DOBOS TORTE

4 eggs, separated
1 cup sugar
3/4 cup flour

Chocolate Filling:
3/4 cup sugar
6 tablespoons water
4 egg yolks, beaten

6 ounces dark, sweet chocolate
1/4 cup water
1 1/2 cups creamed butter

Beat eggs, adding sugar and beat stiff. Fold in flour. Grease cookie sheets and dust with flour. Spread batter in circles, very thin. Make 7 layers. Bake each layer 5 to 6 minutes at 350 degrees. Sandwich with —
Chocolate Filling:
Dissolve sugar in water and cook to syrup. Cool; add egg yolks and beat well. Melt chocolate with water in double boiler. Add to egg yolks and sugar. Whip in butter and spread on cake layers, top and sides.

1 1/2 sticks butter
8 ounces cream cheese
1/2 can beer
2 tablespoons paprika

1 can anchovies
1 tablespoon Worcestershire Sauce
1 tablespoon grated onion

ANCHOVY CHEESE

Mix all ingredients together. Serve with crackers!

3 tablespoons minced shallots
1 1/2 cups minced cooked ham
    3/4 lb.
3 tablespoons butter
1/4 cup Madeira
3 egg yolks
1 cup dairy sour cream

1/4 cup soft bread crumbs
1/4 cup freshly grated Jarlsberg
    cheese
2 teaspoons caraway seeds
3 egg whites
1/2 teaspoon salt
1/4 teaspoon cream of tartar

FLAUF
(Makes one 9-inch Pie)

1. Saute shallots and ham in butter in 9-inch skillet 3 minutes;
add Madeira; cook over high heat, stirring constantly, until liquid
evaporates, 3 to 5 minutes. Remove from heat; cool.
2. Heat oven to 400 degrees. Beat egg yolks in medium size bowl
until thick and lemon-colored; stir in sour cream, bread crumbs,
cheese and caraway. Stir in cooled ham mixture.
3. Beat egg whites until foamy. Add salt and cream of tartar; beat
until stiff peaks form; fold into ham mixture. Spoon into 9-inch
greased baking dish. Bake 30-35 minutes until puffy.

1/2 cup butter
1/4 pound Roquefort cheese
1 teaspoon salt
1 teaspoon chives, fresh chopped

1/2 teaspoon paprika
Juice of 1 orange (6 tablespoons)
1 tablespoon Cointreau

DESSERT CHEESE DELIGHT
WITH FRESH PEARS

Cream butter and cheese. Add remaining ingredients and blend.
Place in freezing tray and freeze. Serve with fresh pears and wheat
or rye crackers for dessert.

The Republic of Iceland is an island of volcanic origin. It is close to the Artic Circle in the North Atlantic. It is about the size of Virginia and has a moderate climate. Geysers and hot springs provide natural hot water, which is piped into the towns and used to heat the buildings. Only part of the land is productive, the rest being volcanic rock. Icelandic is spoken along with Danish and English.

KALTE FEINSCH-MECKER-PLATTE

Arrangements of cold meats, vegetables, aspic and salads are as different as the housewives and chefs who put them together.
1. In the center, 2 pounds of sliced roast beef, surrounded by aspic.
2. Boiled parslied potatoes.
3. Pickled tiny beets.
4. Radish roses.
5. Steamed asparagus and carrots with a vinaigrette sauce.
6. Steamed cauliflower marinated in vinaigrette sauce.

Garnished with raw turnip daisies with carrot centers. (These are just decorations.) If you wish you may add sliced pickles, sliced tomatoes, smoked salmon, green olives, salami slices, hard boiled eggs stuffed with pate. Serves 6.

Vinaigrette Sauce:
1 cup apple cider vinegar
1 teaspoon dry mustard
1 teaspoon Worcestershire Sauce
1/2 teaspoon salt

1 clove of garlic, crushed
1/2 teaspoon black pepper
1/2 teaspoon oregano
1 cup salad oil

In a glass jar with a tight lid, mix vinegar with mustard, Worcestershire Sauce, salt, pepper, oregano, and garlic and oil. Shake well.

LOBSTER SALAD

2 egg yolks
1 tablespoon Dijon mustard
1/2 lemon
Salt, pepper
1 tablespoon mayonnaise
1 tablespoon sour cream
*1 teaspoon mustard dill sauce

Fresh dill
2 cups lobster meat
1 teaspoon A-1 sauce
Shredded lettuce
Diced mushrooms, asparagus,
    cucumbers, celery

Mix egg yolks and Dijon mustard, add juice and pulp from lemon, salt and pepper. Add mayonnaise, mix; add sour cream mix; add mustard dill sauce, mix; add fresh dill to taste and mix add A-I Sauce, mix. Then, according to taste, add some shredded lettuce and mix; again, according to taste, add the mushrooms

asparagus, cucumbers and celery; mix. Cut lobster meat into cubes, add to mixture. Put on iced salad plate. Garnish with lobster claw, decorated with paprika and chopped parsley. Serve with hot toast. Serves 4.
*Note: For mustard dill sauce, thin prepared mustard with dill pickle juice.

6 fillets of sole or flounder	3/4 cup dairy sour cream
(about 3 pounds), cut in half	3/4 cup mayonnaise
1 quart water	1/4 cup Russian vodka
1 cup white wine	4 teaspoons Dijon-style mustard
1 small onion, cut into quarters	1 1/2 teaspoons lemon juice
1/2 rib celery	1/4 teaspoon salt
1 bay leaf	1/4 teaspoon white pepper
1/2 lemon	1 clove garlic, minced
6 peppercorns	1 shallot, minced
1 clove	1 jar (2 ounces) red caviar
1 teaspoon salt	Lemon wedges

COLD FILLET OF SOLE

Makes 6 servings

1. Roll fish; secure with wooden picks. Heat water, wine, onion, celery, bay leaf, lemon, peppercorns, clove and 1 teaspoon salt in 10-inch skillet to boiling. Reduce heat; simmer uncovered 5 minutes. Place fish rolls in skillet; cook covered until tender, 5 to 6 minutes. Drain; refrigerate covered overnight.
2. Meanwhile, combine sour cream, mayonnaise, vodka, mustard, lemon juice, 1/4 teaspoon salt, the pepper, garlic and shallot in small bowl. Refrigerate covered 6 hours.
3. Place fish rolls on serving plate. Spoon some of the sauce over fish. Sprinkle each roll with caviar; garnish with lemon wedges. Serve with remaining sauce.

Vindaloo Curries are served in the South of India and usually contain vinegar and oil. The Koorma Curries are typical of Northern India and include yogurt in their preparation. Ceylon Curries usually contain coconut milk or cream. Pickles, chopped nuts, Bombay Duck, shredded coconut, chutneys and crisp breads are side dishes.

KOORMA CURRY

1/2 stick butter
2 1/2 lbs. stewing lamb or chicken, cooked
2 1/2 lbs. shrimp
2 onions, chopped
3 cloves garlic, minced
1/4 teaspoon powdered ginger

1 teaspoon each black pepper, powdered cumin, and mustard powder
Pinch of cloves, cinnamon and coriander
3 cups yogurt
Salt to taste

Marinate meats and shrimp in spices for 1 hour. Heat butter. Sauté meats and shrimp until done with yogurt. Serve hot with rice and Bombay Duck.

POORI
(Fried Indian Bread)

1 cup all-purpose flour
1 cup whole-wheat flour
1 teaspoon salt

1 1/2 teaspoons salad oil
1/2 cup water

In a medium size bowl, mix all ingredients until well blended. Mixture will be very dry. With hands, knead dough until it holds together and is smooth. Shape dough into ball and place in greased bowl, turning over so that top of dough is greased. Cover bowl with plastic wrap; let rest 10 minutes. Meanwhile, heat 1 inch salad oil to 400 degrees in electric skillet.* With hands, shape dough into 20 balls. On lightly floured surface, with lightly floured rolling pin, roll each ball into paper-thin circle, 4 inches in diameter. Keep remaining dough and finished circles covered with plastic wrap to prevent drying out.

Drop circles, one at a time, into hot oil. With back of slotted spoon, gently hold circle under surface of oil until it puffs up about 10 seconds. Fry about 20 seconds more, turning once. With slotted spoon, remove Poori to paper towels; drain. Keep warm. Makes 20 Poori.

TO REHEAT: Preheat oven to 325 degree. Wrap Poori in foil in one layer and heat 5 minutes.

The Rijsttafel or rice table, is an Eastern type of smorgasbord of the Chinese, Indian and Malaysian dishes. Curries, spiced vegetables, pickled fruits and skewered meats accompany rice.

Cubes of beef, chicken, pork or lamb marinated in Wine Vinegar.

MARINADE PASTE:

4 tablespoons soy
2 tablespoons dark molasses
1 teaspoon crushed red pepper
1 clove of garlic, minced

1 teaspoon grated ginger root
1/2 teaspoon saffron
1/2 cup ground brazil nuts

Mix all ingredients and rub into meat. Brush meat lightly with oil and let stand 1 hour. Grill on hot coals. Serve skewered and dip into following sauce while eating.

Dipping Sauce:
1 clove of garlic, minced
1/2 cup ground peanuts
1 teaspoon crushed red pepper

3 tablespoons wine vinegar
1/2 cup soy sauce
2 tablespoons dark molasses
1/2 cup hot water

Simmer all together 15 minutes. Serve with rice.

SATE
(Grilled Meat on Skewers)

1 pint rice, washed in cold water
8 cups boiling, salted water

Bring rice and water to boil. Boil hard for 13 minutes. Then pour rice and water into a sieve. Pour cold water over it. Let drain well and toss lightly with a fork. Every grain should be fluffy!

PERFECT COOKED RICE

---

3 1/2 cups flour
1 teaspoon salt
1/4 cup melted butter

1 cup yogurt
Fat for frying

Mix all together. Knead well. Let stand 30 minutes. Divide into 1 1/2-inch balls. Roll into paper-thin pancakes. Fry in hot fat 375 degrees until puffed and golden brown. Drain. Serve immediately.

FRIED BREAD WITH YOGURT

Iran, somewhat larger than California, includes most of the area of historic Mesopotamia. Large salt deserts cover much of the land, with high mountains in the interior. There are many oases and forest areas, however. Iran is best known for its production of oil and oil products, but it also has a steel industry, and supplies cement and autos. Arable areas produce grains, rice, fruits and sugar beets. Iran is the official name for the historic empire of Persia, which has roots stretching back to 549 B.C.

KEBABS

Rules for preparing an authentic kebab: Lamb, mutton or chicken is good for Kebab.

1. Partly cook the vegetables before you put them on a skewer.
2. Always cook kebabs over coals, never over flames.
3. Slice the kebab meat thin, about 1/4 to 1/2-inch thick by 1 1/2 inches in diameter.
4. Let the meat soak or marinate 4 hours in this authentic marinade:

1/4 cup vinegar	1 teaspoon cinnamon
1/4 cup honey	3 chopped cloves of garlic
1/2 cup water	Salt and pepper to taste

5. Fry the drained, marinated meat in butter until desired doneness. Then string meat and vegetables on skewer and heat over hot coals.
6. Favorite vegetables for kebabs are mushrooms, leeks, eggplant, squash, tomatoes and peppers.

*FRESH
CARROT
RELISH*

6 red bell peppers	12 medium onions
6 green bell peppers	8 medium carrots
2 medium heads cabbage	2 or 3 hot peppers

Grind on medium size grinder. Mix well with 1/2 cup salt and let stand for 2 hours. Drain or squeeze off water. Add 2 teaspoons mustard seed, 2 teaspoons celery seeds, 6 cups sugar, and 3 pints of vinegar. Put in crock jar or bowl. Don't seal. Ready to eat.

Doogh is a refreshing drink made by whisking sparkling water into cold yogurt, adding a dash of salt.

IRAQ

JAMAICA

IRELAND

JAPAN

ISRAEL

JORDAN

ITALY

KENYA

IVORY COAST

3 tablespoons butter
2 onions, finely chopped
3 tablespoons cornstarch dissolved
   in 6 tablespoons water
1/2 cup walnuts

1 teaspoon ground fenugreek
8 cups chicken broth or meat stock
Salt and pepper to taste
3 cups yogurt

Fry the onions in butter stirring constantly until pale golden in color. Combine onions with soup stock. Stir in cornstarch and water mixture. Add seasonings. Stir in yogurt and beat well. Do not let soup boil or it will curdle. Serve immediately and sprinkle with chopped walnuts.

KUFTA
(Boiled Meat Ball)

1/2 pound lamb
1/4 teaspoon turmeric
1 cup cooked split chick peas
2 tablespoons fat
3/4 cup rice, cooked
2 eggs
1/2 teaspoon salt

1/4 teaspoon pepper
4 small onions, chopped
3 tablespoons currants
3 tablespoons chopped walnuts
2 hard cooked eggs (optional)
3/4 cup prunes
3 cups stock

Pound meat to a paste, cover with water and boil until half cooked, about 15 minutes, then drain. Mix in turmeric, sauté peas in the fat and pound with the cooked rice. Mix with meat and blend in the eggs. Season with salt and pepper. Brown 2 onions in a little fat, add the currants and walnuts. Let cool and add to the meat. Form into a large ball. Chop the hard cooked eggs and prunes and work into the center of the meat ball. Cook the remaining 2 onions and a dash of turmeric with the broth in a large kettle. Season with salt. Bring the broth to a boil. Tie the meat ball in a cheesecloth and lower into the simmering broth and cook gently for 30 minutes. Unwrap the hot cooked meat and serve with the broth with rice.

Ah, with the Grape my fading Life provide,
And wash my Body whence the life has died,
And in a winding sheet of vineleaf wrapt,
So bury me by some sweet Gardenside.
(AT OMAR KHAYYAM'S TOMB.)

One of the favorite seasonings in Iraq is tomato paste, Ma Jun Tamata. This is made by sun-drying. Cut tomatoes in quarters and spread in a large enamel flat pan. Sprinkle with coarse salt and put in hot sun for 2 hours. Strain the tomato through a sieve; add to juice, then put back in the sun. After about 3 days, in the hot sun, allow 2 hours each day, the remains will be very thick. This concentrated paste can be stored in sterilized jars. In Bagdad they have special jars called bastugas, in which to store the paste. The color is great and a spoon or two can be used to flavor sauces and soups.

TABOULI

3 bunches parsley, minced fine	1 cup peppermint leaves, minced
3 medium tomatoes, chopped	1/4 cup lemon juice
1 bunch green onions, chopped fine	1/4 cup Mazola or olive oil
	Salt and pepper to taste

Wash and soak 1 cup cracked wheat in 2 cups of water for 30 minutes. Combine all ingredients and mix with cracked wheat. Refrigerate. It's marvelous. Cucumbers and radishes may be added if you like.

LAHEM GHANIM MAFROOM

(Lamb Patties)

1 lb. lamb, ground (chuch or leg)	1 cup bread crumbs
2 medium sized onions, minced	1 pinch of allspice
1 egg, beaten	2 pinches ground cloves
4 sprigs parsley	Pepper and salt to taste
1 tablespoon mint	

Mix all ingredients and knead well. Add cold water to moisten and mix well. Add bread crumbs and onions, eggs, parsley and mint. Mix until firm. Make into patties and fry or broil.

FAR EASTERN SHRIMP KEBOBS

2 lbs. shrimp	2 teaspoons seasoning salt
1/2 cup oil	2 teaspoons chili powder
1 teaspoon turmeric	2 tablespoons vinegar
1 teaspoon garlic powder	2 teaspoons sweet basil
1/2 teaspoon cracked pepper	1 tablespoon chopped mint

Combine all ingredients and marinate the shrimp for 4 hours at room temperature. String shrimp on skewers and broil or grill until done. Baste with marinade.

This island country is a place of rolling green plains, sharp cliffs and isolated groups of hills and mountains. While many people think first of the potato in connection with Ireland, the country is also noted for the production of outstanding crystal ware and fine wool fabrics. The country's Celtic history goes back to the 4th century, B.C.

Here are two marvelous recipes using the Irish potato!

IRISH POTATO CAKES

2 cups self-rising flour
2 tablespoons butter or fat
Blend butter and flour, add a good
   pinch of salt.

1 1/2 cups mashed potatoes
1/4 cup milk

Add to butter and flour mixture; mix to a soft, but not slack, dough.
Caraway seeds, optional, to sprinkle on top. Roll out on floured board and cut into rounds about 3 inches across. Bake in 450 degree oven for 20 to 30 minutes. Makes about 10 cakes. Split and serve with lots of butter.

COLCANNON

2 onions, minced
2/3 cup milk
4 large potatoes, boiled
2 parsnips, boiled

Salt and pepper
1 cup cooked, shredded cabbage
1 tablespoon butter
1 tablespoon minced parsley

Cook the onion in milk until soft. Mash the boiled potatoes and parsnips together. Season with salt and pepper. Slowly add onions and milk, beating well. Combine with cabbage. Serve garnished with lots of butter and minced parsley.

Corinthians:
"If I give away all I have but have not love, I give nothing."

**IRISH SODA
BREAD**

2 lbs. all-purpose flour
1 teaspoon bicarbonate of soda
1 cup sour cream

1 teaspoon salt
1 teaspoon cream of tartar

Mix together the dry ingredients, and sift into a mixing bowl. Make a well in the center and stir in the cream, adding a little more if mixture is too dry. Mix well into a rather stiff dough. Divide into two rounds. Prick with fork and put in a greased, floured pan. Bake at 350 degrees for 45 minutes.

**IRISH SODA
CAKE**

1 cup flour
Pinch salt
1/2 teaspoon cream of tartar
1/4 teaspoon grated nutmeg
1/2 teaspoon bicarbonate of soda

9 tablespoons butter
9 tablespoons sugar
6 ounces currants
1/2 cup sour cream
1 egg

Grease well and flour a 6 1/2 to 7-inch cake pan. Sift the flour, salt, soda, cream of tartar, and nutmeg into a bowl. Rub in the butter, with the tips of fingers. Then add currants and sugar and mix well. Stir in beaten egg and sufficient milk to form a fairly soft mixture. Put into prepared pan and bake in hot oven of 375 degrees for 20 minutes or until brown. Then lower heat to 350 degrees and bake 30 to 40 minutes more.

**POTATO
SOUFFLE**

3 tablespoons butter
3 tablespoons all-purpose flour
1 cup light cream
1 teaspoon minced onion

1 cup mashed potatoes
3 eggs, separated
Salt and pepper

Melt butter and blend in flour. Add cream and cook, stirring, until thickened. Add onion and potatoes; heat, stirring until hot. Stir in beaten egg yolks quickly. Season, and fold in stiffly beaten egg whites. Spoon into 1 1/2-quart souffle dish, and bake in preheated moderate oven for 30 minutes, until puffed and firm. 4 to 6 servings.

A merry heart doeth good like medicine.

Israel's territory includes the oldest known evidence of human agriculture and primary town life. The Hebrews are believed to have arrived in the country in the 2nd millenium, B.C. where the traditions and culture of Judaism were established. Today, Israel is industrialized, with diamond cutting, textiles, electronics, machinery, plastics, tires, drugs, aircraft and munitions forming an important part of the country's economy. Israel, about the size of the state of Massachusetts, is on the eastern end of the Mediterranean Sea. The coastal plain is fertile and well-watered. In the center is the Judean Plateau.

EGGPLANT A LA MEDI

2 eggplants, cut in 1/2-inch slices
Salt
Oil for frying pan
1 diced onion
1 1/2 lbs. ground beef
1 sprig parsley, chopped
Sugar

Pepper
Paprika
1 fresh tomato, diced
1 small can tomato pureé

Preheat oven to 350 degrees. Salt the eggplant slices and let them sit for 1/2 hour; this gets the inner water out. Then fry the eggplant in deep oil until yellow (not brown). Drain.
In a large frying pan, brown the onion until clear. Add the ground beef, and stir continously for 5 minutes over low heat. Add parsley, salt, pepper, and paprika to taste. Place one layer of eggplant slices in a non-oiled baking dish; cover with a layer of all the meat and onion, then with a second layer of eggplant. Add some oil to the meat-and-onion frying pan and brown the diced tomato in this. Add the tomato pureé and an equal amount of water (1/2 cup). Season with a little salt, pepper, and a pinch of sugar. Bring to a boil. Pour over eggplant. Put in oven for 30 minutes. Serves 10.

SARDINE OMELET PUFFS

4 eggs, separated
1 cup cottage cheese
1 cup sour cream
1/3 cup sardines, mashed

1/8 teaspoon garlic powder
1/4 teaspoon cloves
Salt to taste
1 cup bread crumbs

Beat egg whites until stiff. Combine cottage cheese, sour cream, sardines, garlic, cloves, egg yolks, bread crumbs. Fold into egg whites. Spoon onto a hot buttered grill and cook until brown. Serve immediately!

STUFFED ARTICHOKES

8 artichokes with chokes removed. Soak in cold water with juice of 1 lemon. Fry the in oil on all sides. Grind 1/2 lb. lean lamb with 1/2 lb. chicken and 2 onions. Fry all in 1 stick of margarine or butter. Add 1/4 cup pinenuts. Salt and pepper to taste and about 1 teaspoon cinnamon. Stuff mixture in the artichoke and bake in 375 degree oven 1 hour. Serve hot as main course.

Serve with sweet and sour leeks.

SWEET & SOUR LEEKS

6 canned leeks	4 tablespoons oil
3 cloves garlic	Juice of 1 lemon
1 tablespoon sugar	

Put sugar, oil, garlic and lemon juice in pan. Put leeks in pan and coat with mixture. Simmer until hot.

MATZO BALL SOUP

1 egg	2 tablespoons parsley, finely
1/2 cup matzo meal or cracked	chopped
meal	1/2 teaspoon poultry seasoning
1/4 cup butter, melted	1/2 cup water
1/2 teaspoon salt	

Mix all together and refrigerate overnight. Form into 1/2-inch balls and drop into boiling chicken soup. Cook for about 15 minutes or until balls float.

BLINTZES

Batter:	Dash salt
2 eggs	1/2 tablespoon cornstarch
1/4 cup flour	1 tablespoon sugar
1/2 cup milk	Dash vanilla

Mix all together quickly. Let stand 30 minutes. Bake on medium sized buttered skillet, tilting pan to make a very thin pancake. When pancake sets up, remove from pan and continue to bake the rest.

For Filling:	Dash salt
1 cup dry cottage cheese	1 teaspoon vanilla
1/2 cup currants (if desired)	1/2 teaspoon cinnamon
1 tablespoon cornstarch	3 tablespoons sugar

Combine all ingredients. Place 1 tablespoon in center of each pancake. Fold sides over and roll up like jelly roll. When ready to serve brown in butter and sprinkle with sugar.

6 lbs. filleted white fish, pike and carp or any freshwater fish of your choice. Reserve skin, heads and bones and combine with 4 sliced onions, 2 teaspoons salt, 3/4 teaspoon pepper and 1 quart of water. Cook over high heat while preparing the fish.

Grind fish with 1 large onion. Place in bowl with 3 eggs, 3/4 cup ice water, 1/2 teaspoon sugar, 4 tablespoons matzo or cracker meal, salt and pepper to taste. Chop all the ingredients and mix until very fine. (I like to beat this all together in my mixing bowl until it's fluffy.) Moisten hands and shape fish into balls. Drain the fish heads and skins from the stock and carefully drop the balls into the fish stock. Add 4 sliced carrots, cover pot and simmer for 1 1/2 hours on very low heat. Taste to correct seasoning. Cool slightly, remove to earthenware bowl. Strain stock and pour over fish. Arrange carrots around gefilte fish. Chill and serve with horseradish.

| 4-5 lbs. Tongue fresh | 2 cloves garlic |
| 1 onion | 2 bay leaves |

Wash tongue. Combine with garlic and bay leaves. Cover with water and bring to a boil. Reduce heat and simmer 4 hours until tender. Let cool in water. Then skin and slice. Sprinkle with Tarragan vinegar and fresh herbs.

The Italian artichoke has a delicate, nutty flavor, but it is a curious fact that tea and most wines lose their flavor entirely when taken with the artichoke.

Barolo is one of the best red table wines of Italy. Asti Spumante is the best known sparkling wine of Italy.

As you know, "pasta" is one of the Italian's favorite dishes. Here is a recipe for a summer easy pasta dish:

PASTA ALLA CECCO

Take some fresh tomatoes, peel them and take out the seeds, cut them in pieces and put them in a bowl. Add fresh mozzarella, also cut in small pieces, and fresh basil leaves. Add some oil and butter. Salt and pepper to taste. Mix everything and let stand for an hour. In a separate saucepan, boil water, add salt and paprika. When the water is boiling, put in spaghetti or penne, and let boil for not more than ten minutes. When ready, drain and place in bowl. Mix them immediately with the tomatoes and the rest and serve them very hot.

TORTELLONI
(Spinach Ravioli)

3 1/2 cups flour	5 ounces ricotta cheese
3 eggs	6 1/2 oz. spinach

Place flour on board; mix in the eggs, working them together into a soft dough. Add cooked, drained and finely chopped spinach. Knead dough until smooth and elastic. Roll dough paper-thin. Let rest 5 minutes. Cut with round ravioli cutter and put teaspoon ricotta cheese in each pasta. Press firmly together and boil 4 minutes. Drain and serve with tomato sauce.

CHICKEN CACCIATORE
(From Naples)

1 cup olive oil	1 1/2 teaspoons black pepper
8 cloves garlic, sliced thin	Salt to taste
4 fryers, cut up	3 teaspoons chopped parsley
4 No. 2 cans of tomatoes, sieved	3 bell peppers, chopped
3 teaspoons oregano	

Sauté garlic in olive oil until lightly browned. Place well floured chicken in oil. Turn heat to medium and brown on all sides. Add salt and pepper to each piece. While chicken is browning, combine: tomatoes, oregano, pepper and salt, parsley, bell peppers. Add tomato mixture to chicken. Turn into casserole. Bake 1 hour at 325 degrees. I put 1 lb. fresh, sliced mushrooms in the sauce, too.

1 medium head cabbage, shredded
1 medium onion, sliced thinly
7/8 cup sugar
1 cup vinegar
3/4 cup salad oil

2 teaspoons sugar
2 teaspoons salt
1 teaspoon dry mustard
1 teaspoon celery seed

Mix vinegar, salad oil, 2 teaspoons sugar, salt, mustard and celery seed and bring to a boil. Alternate layers of cabbage and onion rings in a large bowl. Top with 7/8 cup sugar. Pour hot mixture over cabbage and onion. Cover and let stand 4 to 6 hours. Mix well and serve. Will keep 2 to 3 weeks in refrigerator.

---

1 1/2 cups butter
2 cups sugar
6 egg yolks, beaten
3 cups sifted cake flour
1 teaspoon salt
1 teaspoon cinnamon
1 teaspoon cloves
1 teaspoon allspice

1/4 cup buttermilk
1 scant cup of wine
1 teaspoon soda
1 1/2 cup blackberry jam
1 teaspoon vanilla
6 egg whites, well beaten
3/4 cup shortening may be used
    instead of using all butter.

Cream butter and sugar. Mix in dry ingredients, alternately with buttermilk and wine. Mix well. Add jam and vanilla. Beat in egg whites until creamy. Bake at 350 degrees until done in the center when tested with toothpick.

Sift together:
    3 cups all-purpose flour
    1/2 teaspoon salt
    1/4 cup sugar
Rub into dry ingredients until like
    fine meal:
    3 tablespoons shortening

Beat with mixer on high speed:
    4 eggs
    1/2 teaspoon orange flavoring
    2 tablespoons water

Add this to meal-like ingredients and mix together. It will seem to be not enough liquid, but do not add more liquid. Turn onto a floured board and knead until smooth ball is formed. Let rest about half an hour and then roll into a thin sheet of dough — about 1/8th of an inch thick. Cut strips to the size shell you desire. Wrap around metal or wood forms and seal together with water. Fry in deep hot (360 degrees) fat until brown. Cool. Fill with whipped ricotta cream sweetened to taste and flavored with cinnamon and vanilla. Roll in powdered sugar.

The national dish is Fou Fou, which consists of yams, boiled in water, peeled and pounded in a mortar. It is highly seasoned with salt, pepper, red peppers and grated nutmeg. This is eaten with chicken or meat fricassee.

Palm oil is used extensively in cooking.

YAM PUDDING

2 eggs, separated
3/4 cup brown sugar
2 tablespoons melted butter
1 teaspoon cinnamon

1 1/2 cups boiled, mashed sweet potatoes
1 cup milk

Beat all together, except egg whites. Beat egg whites in separate bowl. Fold into potato mixture and bake in 350 degree oven about 40 minutes. Serve!

BANANA SOUP
(Cold)

1 quart orange juice
5 ripe bananas
2 cups whole milk

2 ounces kirsch
Nutmeg to taste (1/2 teaspoon)

Blend all ingredients. Chill thoroughly and serve with a dab of whipped cream and finely chopped roasted peanuts.

POACHED FRUIT

4 peaches
4 nectarines
4 apricots
8 plums

2 dozen bing cherries
1 cup water
1 cup sugar

Heat water in deep kettle. Add 1 cup sugar. Stir until dissolved. Drop in first 3 washed unpeeled fruits. Let come to boil and cover. Simmer for 6 minutes, dip out apricots. Place in deep bowl. At the end of 8 minutes dip out nectarines, at the end of 12 minutes dip out peaches. Now add plums and cherries to the kettle of boiling syrup. Cook 4 minutes only, do NOT let skins pop open. Remove to bowl. Now add 1 cup more of sugar and a drop or 2 of red food coloring. Boil syrup 5 minutes. Pour over fruits, add 2 teaspoons lemon juice. Cool in refrigerator. To serve give each person some fruit, cherries and plums. Elegant for breakfast or dessert.

The island of Jamaica in the West Indies is mostly mountainous, perfect for the growing of coffee, sugar cane, bananas, coconuts, and some spices. Its beautiful beaches and warm climate make it a popular tourist haven as well. The country was once held by Spain, and then by Britain, but became independent in 1962.

JAMAICA
PEPPER POT
(Hot and Spicy)

1 lb. kale, ground
1 lb. cabbage, ground
1/2 lb. beef, cubed
1/2 lb. cooked chicken
1/2 lb. corned beef
1 cup coconut
12 okra, stems removed
2 onions, ground

1 quart water and chicken stock
1/2 teaspoon salt
1/8 teaspoon cayenne pepper
1/2 teaspoon thyme
2 green onions, sliced
1 pod garlic
2 tablespoons Worcestershire Sauce

Mix kale, cabbage, beef, chicken, corned beef, coconut, okra, onions and water and chicken stock and cook over low heat for 1 hour. Add remaining ingredients; cook 15 minutes longer. Serve hot!

RUM BUNS

2 lbs. flour
7 ounces sugar
6 1/3 ounces shortening
4 ounces whole eggs
1 1/3 ounces yeast
1 ounce whole milk

1/2 tablespoons salt
2 teaspoons lemon rind
1 1/3 ounces brown sugar
2 ounces raisins

Place in mixing bowl, sugar, whole eggs, finely grated lemon rind, salt, and yeast, which is dissolved in 2 2/3 ounces of warm water. Melt shortening on low temperature, to texture of oil. Add to the above, and blend well, slowly adding first milk, then flour. Continue on slow blend until well mixed. Allow enough time for proper rising, or until batter has risen to top of bowl level. Roll this to 1 inch thickness, being sure enough flour is used on table, or dough board, to prevent sticking.
Then dissolve brown sugar in warm water, to syrup consistency and spread evenly over dough. Sprinkle same with seedless raisins, then roll and cut into 3-ounce portions, place in well-greased muffin tins. Again allow to rise to top of pan level before baking. Bake in preheated oven at 375 degrees for 15 to 18 minutes. This will make 2 dozen Rum Buns.

See Rum Topping on next page.

RUM TOPPING

1 lb. 10X Confectioner's sugar	2 2/3 ounces milk
2 2/3 ounces cream	1 1/3 teaspoons Arrac Rum

Place sugar in mixing bowl, slowly add cream and milk. When texture becomes smooth, add rum and blend at high speed for 3 minutes. Use pastry brush to apply to Rum Buns while hot.

MILK AND RUM PUNCH

3 eggs	3/4 cup rum
1 tablespoon sugar	1 cup cold milk
1/2 teaspoon vanilla	grated nutmeg

Blend all ingredients, except milk. Divide into punch cups. Top with cold milk and grated nutmeg. Makes 6 servings!

BANANA DAIQUIRE FRAPPE

4 bananas, peeled and chopped
4 tablespoons orange juice
3/4 cup rum

Blend all together and freeze. Whip up with spoon and serve. Makes 4 cups.

RUM SWIZZLE

1/2 cup sugar	1 1/2 cups rum
1 cup lime juice	Cracked ice
8 sprigs mint	

Put everything except ice in jug. Swirl and swizzle until frothy. Pour over cracked ice and serve. Makes 8 glasses!

We enter life alone. We depart alone. But life is meant to shar with others.

Japan is comprised of four main islands: Honshu (designated as the "Mainland"), Hokkaido, Kyushu, and Shikoku. Today it is a flourishing industrial country, producing cars, camara equipment, electronics, micro-circuits, steel, and some wood products. There are small mineral deposits, but most minerals and metals are imported. A large portion of the Japanese diet is made up of various types of seafood and a rich variety of vegetables, all quickly cooked to maintain crispness and fresh flavor.

JAPANESE OYSTER PANCAKES

1 pint small oysters and liquor	1/2 teaspoon baking powder
1/4 cup minced scallions or shallots	2 tablespoons corn oil
2 tablespoons chopped parsley	1 teaspoon soy sauce
4 eggs, beaten	1/2 cup cider vinegar
1/2 teaspoon salt	1 teaspoon Japanese hot pepper
Pinch of pepper	sauce
1/2 cup flour	

Strain oysters and chop coarsley. Mix oysters, scallions, parsley, beaten eggs, salt, pepper, flour and baking powder. Add oyster liquor or milk to thin out. Drop by teaspontuls onto hot grill. Brown quickly on both sides. Keep warm until ready to serve, in slow oven. Serve hot with Pepper Sauce Dip.

TEMPURA BATTER

2/3 cup flour	2/3 cup water
1/4 teaspoon salt	1 egg white, beaten stiff
2 tablespoons salad oil	Fat for frying

Mix flour, salt, oil and water. Fold in stiffly beaten egg whites. Dry fish or vegetable dip in batter and fry. Serve with favorite dipping sauce.

Favorite foods for Tempura:
Mushrooms, eggplant, leek, shrimp and fish.

Some of the staple Japanese foods are:
Miso — Cooked yellow soybeans, mixed with fermented rice and salt.
Tofu — Soybean curd (white, cheese-like), pressed into 3-inch cubes and used in soups.
Wakome or Kombu — Dried seaweed used to flavor soups, custards, etc.

Miro Shiru — Hot breakfast soup made with fish and vegetables and seaweed.

Sashime — Raw fish sliced very thin and served with Shoyu sauce, grated horseradish or fresh ginger.

ONION DIPPING SAUCE HOT

1/2 cup soy sauce
1/2 cup lemon juice
2 tablespoons green onion tops

1 tablespoon freshly grated ginger
1/4 teaspoon cayenne pepper
Mix and let stand 1 hour.

DIPPING SAUCE WITH SESAME

1/4 cup toasted ground sesame
1/4 cup soy sauce
1/4 cup chicken broth

2 tablespoons vinegar
Mix and serve cold!

SWEET AND PUNGENT SAUCE

1 cup vinegar
2 cups brown sugar
1/2 cup of chicken broth

1/2 cup of tomato ketchup
Cornstarch to thicken

Boil vinegar and sugar then add broth, tomato ketchup and thicken with cornstarch.

To Serve: use toothpick for fried shrimps and dip them in sauce.

HOT BEEF ON STICK TERIYAKI

1 1/2 lbs. beef tenderloin cubed
1/4 cup soy sauce
3 tablespoons sliced fresh ginger
4 cloves of garlic or 3 teaspoons sliced

1 1/2 teaspoons sugar
Tops of 3 green onions, sliced
4 hot chilies, crushed

Marinate beef cubes in above marinade for 30 minutes. Then heat 2 tablespoons salad oil in an electric frying pan. Cook meat quickly 2 minutes. Turn on warm tray, sprinkle with black sesame seeds toasted. Serve with heated marinade with wooden picks.

The Arab country of Jordan is located in West Asia, with Israel to the west, Saudi Arabia to the south, Iraq to the east, and Syria to the north. Chief industires include textiles and plastics. Although about 88% of Jordan is arid, crops of grains, olives, vegetables and fruits are grown in fertile areas in the western part of the country. In area, Jordan is slightly larger than the state of Indiana.

ROAST LEG OF LAMB

1 young 5 lb. leg of lamb	1 can mushrooms
4 pods garlic	1 can tomatoes
Handful of parsley	1/2 cup olive oil
1 green pepper	Pinch of basil
1 onion	1 bay leaf
1 pint red wine	Salt and pepper

Stab holes in lamb and stuff with parsley and garlic. Put in 500 degree oven. Brush top well with olive oil and roast until tender, allowing 25 minutes to the pound. Pour red wine over roast the last 30 minutes of cooking time. In the meantime, make sauce as follows: Sauté chopped pepper and onion in olive oil until tender. Add tomatoes, mushrooms, basil, bay leaf, salt and pepper and simmer until reduced to 1/2 amount. Add drippings from lamb and thickening if desired. Serve with lamb.

HOT SPINACH SOUP

2 quarts chicken stock	1/2 cup minced celery
1/2 lb. chopped spinach	1/2 cup julienne carrots

Cook together until tender.

3 tablespoons cornstarch	1/4 cup lemon juice
6 tablespoons water	1/4 cup minced parsley
3 egg yolks	

Combine cornstarch with water. Beat in egg yolk, lemon juice and parsley. Add 1 cup of the hot broth to mixture, stirring quickly, then add to the soup pot (do not boil).

CURRIED EGG SALAD

2 pkgs. plain gelatin, dissolved in 1/2 cup water	1/2 cup chutney or chili sauce
	1 cup yogurt
1 cup chicken broth	1 teaspoon salt — pepper to taste
10 hard cooked eggs, chopped	1 teaspoon curry powder

Melt gelatin over hot water. Stir into rest of ingredients. Congeal in refrigerator. Slice and serve on lettuce leaf.

Coconut is almost as important a food in Africa as yams, peanuts and palm nuts.

Fish barbecues are popular in all of Africa. Much of the beef and mutton is very tough and used in stews. Chicken, generally, is less tender than we are accustomed to.

Rice is often boiled in coconut milk, which imparts a marvelous flavor. On rare occasion, one has elephant, which is a rather stringy and coarse meat, I am told.

MARINATED WEST AFRICAN CHICKEN

8 pieces chicken
4 tablespoons oil, peanut
1 cup water
1 cup lemon juice, fresh
2 cups finely chopped onion

2 tablespoons finely chopped garlic
Dash of fresh hot chilies
1 teaspoon ground ginger
Salt and white pepper to taste

Combine all ingredients and mix well. Place chicken in a large Pyrex or crock and pour ingredients over chicken. Marinate overnight in the refrigerator. Remove chicken from marinade and pat dry. Heat about 4 tablespoons oil in heavy skillet. Brown the chicken a few pieces at a time. Then strain the marinade and cook the strained vegetables in oil until done, about 8 minutes, stirring often. Now combine vegetables, browned chicken and marinade in a baking dish. Bake 45 minutes at 350 degrees, or simmer on top of stove over low heat until done. Serve with boiled rice!

BLACK BEANS WITH GARLIC

1 lb. dried black beans (or other dried beans)
1 or 2 heads of garlic, separated into cloves and peeled
1 dried hot pepper (optional)

4 tablespoons olive oil
1 teaspoon whole cumin seeds
2 cloves garlic, sliced thin
1 taplespoon salt

Soak beans overnight in water to cover; or boil for two minutes and let sit for an hour or longer. Drain the beans and cover with fresh water. Add whole garlic cloves and hot pepper and simmer until beans are tender, about 1 hour.

In a heavy flame-proof casserole heat olive oil and saute the cumin seeds and garlic slices until lightly browned. Transfer the cooked beans and garlic to the casserole with some of the cooking water. Stir in salt and bake, covered, at 350 degrees for about an hour. If the beans seem dry, add a little more of the cooking liquid. These beans are very good served with a dollop of sour cream. Serves 6.

FLAGS OF THE UNITED NATIONS

KUWAIT

MADAGASCAR

LAOS

MALAWI

LEBANON

MALAYSIA

LESOTHO

MALDIVES

LIBERIA

MALI

LIBYA

MALTA

LUXEMBOURG

Kuwait is a small Arab state. Oil is its mainstay. Crude oil production is around 7 billion barrels and annual payments to the Kuwait government in royalties and taxes, exceeds 8 billion dollars. Per capita income is in excess of $10,000.00.

SPICED HARD COOKED EGGS

8 hard cooked eggs	1/2 teaspoon paprika
1/4 cup butter	1/4 teaspoon pepper
1/4 teaspoon salt	1 teaspoon cinnamon

Shell the eggs. With a sharp fork, prick them all over. Heat the butter in a frying pan over low heat and sauté the eggs, turning them with a spoon so the butter penetrates all sides. Let them get very hot. Mix the spices and salt. Roll the eggs in the mixture. Serve hot with curry.

EXOTIC FRUIT DESSERTS

Exotic Fruits for excellent light desserts!

Fresh Lychee Nuts — With White Creme de Menthe.
Loquats — Serve chilled with pineapple and a dash of orange liqueur.
Kiwi Fruit — Slice and serve with sliced bananas and strawberries with lime juice and rum.
Figs — Serve peeled with fresh sweet cream and grated orange rind.
Mangoes — Serve fully ripe with slices of fresh oranges.
Papayas — Peel, slice and serve with a wedge of lemon.
Oriental Persimmons — Try freezing them whole and serve on dessert plate with spoon. Eat frozen with a squeeze of orange.
Pomegranates — Use as a garnish; eat the seeds and red flesh, discarding the pulp. Try sprinkling them on any dessert when you serve whipped cream.

97

Laos is on the Indochina Peninsula, with Burma and China to the north, Vietnam on the east. It is a landlocked country with mostly jungle terrain, but there are high mountains on the eastern border. The country's chief industry is the production of wood products. Grain, olives, vegetables and fruit are grown as well as cotton and opium.

MANDOO
(Meat filled Dumpling Soup)
Similar to Won Ton

Cook one chicken for 3 hours, until very tender, in 2 quarts of water. Cut up into tiny cubes. Season with soy, toasted sesame seeds, garlic, pepper, and onions. This mixture is served as a side dish to Mandoo.

Dumpling (Won Ton):
3 cups flour
1 egg
1 cup water
Pinch of salt

Put flour on board. Make well; add egg, salt and water. Stir in a spiral motion until all water is used up. Divide into 100 pieces. Roll, paper-thin.

Filling:
1/2 cup bean sprouts
1 cup cabbage, finely chopped
1 egg or 1 fresh soybean cake
1 tablespoon oil
1/4 lb. meat, chopped (beef, chicken or pork)
1/4 cup finely minced green onions and tops
1 1/2 tablespoons soy sauce
1 1/2 teaspoons toasted sesame seeds
2 quarts soup stock

Sauté all in oil, except soup stock, until almost done, stirring constantly. Divide mixture into dumpling squares. Fold in half diagonally. Dampen edges and seal. Refrigerate for 2 hours. Drop into simmering hot broth, seasoned with soy. Cook only 20 at a time. After they rise to top, simmer 4 minutes. Remove and repeat process until all dumplings are cooked. Serve in bowls with dumplings and broth. Top with green onions, chopped.

FRIED DUCKLING

Take the breast of the duck; skin and slice into 1/4-inch thick slices. Tenderize by pounding as you would a beef steak. Fry in butter, sprinkle with powdered ginger and a dash of almond flavoring.

Lebanon lies on the eastern end of the Mediterranean sea, with an area of 4,015 sq. miles, smaller than Conecticut. There is a narrow coastal strip and two mountain ranges running north and south which enclose the fertile Beqaa Valley. Fruits, olives, tobacco, grapes, vegetables and grains are grown in the fertile area, and the country also produces textiles, cement, oil products, and food products. Lebanon was originally formed from 5 former Turkish Empire districts. The country's economy is run under the free enterprise system.

This is the national dish of Lebanon!

KIBBE
(Baked Lamb and Wheat Dish)

1 cup cooked, cracked wheat pilaf	1 lb. lean and fat lamb, ground fine
1 lb. lean, lamb, ground fine	1 1/2 teaspoon salt
2 onions, chopped	1/2 teaspoon pepper
1/2 cup butter	
1/4 cup pinenuts	

Prepare the cooked wheat as described in pilaf. Drain; chill in refrigerator 1 hour or longer. To the ground lean lamb, add 1/2 the onion and grind again. Sauté the rest of the onion in 2 tablespoons butter till golden. Add the nuts and mix. Stir in meat mixture and set aside to cool.

To the other pound of ground meat, add the chilled wheat. Knead this in quickly, adding the salt and pepper. When well blended, divide into two parts. Spread 1/2 in a greased 12-inch square pan. Spread the onion and meat mixture on this. Cover with the rest of wheat and meat mixture. Pat down firmly; then with a thin, sharp knife, cut the cake in diamond-shaped pieces. Run knife around the edge of pan. Dot the top with remaining butter. Bake in 375 degree oven for 1 hour.

BUTTERBALLS
(For Soup)

3 tablespoons butter	1/4 cup flour
2 beaten egg yolks	Salt and nutmeg

Cream butter, add alternately with small amounts of egg yolk and flour. Season to taste with salt and nutmeg. Drop into hot soup by teaspoon-size lumps. Cook 5 minutes.

Ecclesiastes 3-13
"It is God's gift to man that everyone should eat and drink and take pleasure in all his toil."

The kingdom of Lesotho, the southern Africa, represents an interesting geographical phenomenon — it is completely surrounded by another country, the Republic of South Africa. Lesotho, about the size of Maryland, is a center for diamond polishing, but up to 70% of themale population work outside the country, in South Africa. The chief exports of Lesotho are its fine wool and mohair.

LARDED SPICED MEAT

2 tablespoons curry powder	1 clove garlic, minced
1 teaspoon powdered clove	1 small piece suet
1 tablespoon cinnamon	2 lbs. rump steak
1/2 teaspoon pepper	3 small onions, peeled
3 tablespoons salt	1 bay leaf
1/8 teaspoon cayenne pepper	

Mix the spices, seasonings and garlic and pound in a mortar. Cut a gash through the steak and beat the meat with some of the spice mixture. Roll the suet in the spice and insert in the gash. Rub the remaining spices over the outside of the meat. Roll the steak and tie with a string. Put in a 2-quart saucepan and cover with hot water. Add onion and bay leaf to remaining spices. Bring to a boil and skim off. Cover the pan tightly. Cook over very low heat for 2 hours. Uncover and cook for 1/2 hour longer. Let cool and slice very thin.

SARDINE CRACKERS

Mix 1 cup thick white sauce with 1/2 cup chopped sardines, 1 teaspoon lemon juice, 1/4 teaspoon nutmeg, and salt to taste. Mix well and spread on warm toast or crackers. Wonderful as a hot dip!

EGG PLANT CHUTNEY

1 medium eggplant	1 cup sugar
4 cups (8 lbs.) chopped tomatoes	1 cup vinegar
1 1/2 cups chopped onion	3/4 cup water
1 1/2 cups chopped green pepper	1 teaspoon Tabasco
1-3 cups raisins	

Do not peel eggplant; chop into cubes (about 4 cups chopped). Place all ingredients in medium size pot. Bring to boil, stirring occasionally, do not boil. Simmer 10 minutes. Seal in hot sterilized jars. Makes about 3 pints.

The Republic of Liberia on the southwest coast of Africa is slightly smaller than Pennsylvania. A marshy Atlantic coastline rises to low mountains and plateaus. Although Liberia engages in some light industry and food processing, it is mainly agricultural. Crops include fibers, palm kernels, rice, cassava, and coffee. Liberia was founded in 1822 by black freedmen from the United States who settled at Monrovia, now the nations's capital.

BRAISED SPICED DUCKLING
With Orange Sauce

2 cups water	2 whole oranges
1 duckling, cut in 8 pieces	1/4 teaspoon cloves
1/2 onion	1/4 teaspoon chili pepper
1/2 cup celery	1/4 teaspoon salt
1 bell pepper	1 cup orange juice
1/2 cup chopped carrots	1/4 cup lime juice

Place duck and all ingredients in a baking pan, with tight cover and bake at 300 degrees for 4 hours. Serve after skinning off excess fat. I like to thicken the gravy with a bit of cornstarch, dissolved in cold water.

PEANUT PIE SHELL

1 cup sifted flour	1/3 cup crushed salted peanuts
1/2 teaspoon baking powder	1/3 cup liquid shortening
1/2 teaspoon salt	3 to 4 tablespoons cold water

Sift flour, baking powder and salt into mixing bowl. Cut in shortening with knives, or blend with pastry blender until mixture resembles coarse cornmeal. Add peanuts.
Sprinkle cold water over mixture, a little at a time, stirring with fork until dough is just moist enough to hold together and form a ball.
Roll out on lightly floured surface to a circle. Fit loosely into 9-inch pie pan and flute edges. Prick over entire surface with a 4-tined fork. Bake in hot oven (425 degrees) 12 to 15 minutes. Cool.

Put banana ice cream in pie shell and top with whipped cream and chocolate sauce.

GREEN TOMATO PIE

6 cups thin sliced tomatoes
1 cup sugar
3 tablespoons flour
1/4 teaspoon salt
1/4 teaspoon ground cinnamon

1/4 teaspoon nutmeg
1/8 teaspoon ground cloves
1 tablespoon grated lemon peel
1/4 cup fresh lemon juice
2 tablespoons butter

Cover tomatoes with boiling water and let stand for 3 minutes and drain. Mix all ingredients and put in an unbaked pie shell. Bake in 350 degree oven for 35 to 40 minutes.

APPLE CAKE

Beat 1 1/4 cups Wesson oil
2 cups sugar
2 eggs
1 teaspoon vanilla
Sift and add to the above
1 teaspoon soda

2 teaspoon baking powder
2 1/2 cups flour
Add 1 cup chopped pecans
3 cups chopped apples, raw

Bake 1 hour or until done at 350 degrees. Use tube pan, ungreased. Ice with Vanilla Glaze: 1 cup powdered sugar
1 teaspoon vanilla
3 teaspoons milk

PEANUT SALAD

1 cup nuts, peanuts
2 cups chopped celery
1 dozen finely chopped ripe olives

Enough mayonnaise to bind
ingredients
Lettuce
Grapefruit sections

Mix peanuts, celery, olives with mayonnaise. Serve on crisp lettuce. Garnish with grapefruit sections.

Libya is on the Mediterranean coast of North Africa, with Tunesia and Algeria on the west, and Niger and Chad on the south. Although it is an important supplier of crude oil to the west, it also produces textiles, carpeting (Oriental) and shoes. In ancient times Libya was ruled by Carthage, Rome and then the Vandals and the Ottoman Empire. It became an independent constitutional monarchy in 1952, but in 1969 a junta seized power and instituted socialist policies.

BUTTERMILK SOUP

1 lb. potatoes	3 strips bacon
1 tablespoon flour	1 onion, peeled and chopped
1 quart buttermilk	Salt and pepper

Scrub potatoes, rinse, drain, pare and chop. Cover with salted water and cook until tender. Drain; mix flour smoothly with a little buttermilk. Stir into rest of buttermilk. Bring to a boil. Chop bacon and cook with onion until brown. Combine potatoes, hot buttermilk-flour mixture, bacon and onion. Season with salt and pepper.

FRIED CHEESE SQUARES

5 cups grated white cheese (Swiss type)	Combine with batter
	1 1/3 cup milk, canned
4 1/2 cups milk	4 eggs
4 cups flour	1/2 cup water
1 teaspoon salt	3 cups seasoned bread crumbs

Bring milk and salt to a scald. Add the flour and stir with a heavy spoon until blended. While hot add cheese. Stir well. When cool enough to handle; knead smooth. Press the dough into an oiled pan and spread out to 1/2-inch thick. Chill. Cut in inch squares, dip in beaten egg-milk mixture. Roll in crumbs. Fry in deep fat until golden. Serve with soup.

Cloves
There is a saying in Zanzibar that the clove tree will not grow except within sight of the mountain and within the smell of the sea. It is very fragile and has to be hand picked. Cloves are the dried unopened bud of an evergreen tree. It grows in East Africa, the Caribbean, South America, Pacific Islands, Burma, etc. In the third century B.C., the State Officers of the court in China were compelled to hold cloves in their mouth, while addressing the Sovereign. The custom of chewing gum, flavored with cloves to sweeten the breath, is in wide practice throughout the world. Cloves were first found in the Moluccas Islands. Wars were fought over the Island. Clove oil stimulates the flow of gastric juices to the stomach.

103

The Grand Duchy of Luxembourg is only 999 sq. miles in area, smaller than the state of Rhode Island. The southern part of the country is a low, open plateau, with heavy forests to the north. Steel represents 90% of its export products, and one of its chief crops is roses for the perfume industry. Luxembourg has a history reaching back many hundreds of years to 963.

STUFFED CABBAGE

Green, white, or red cabbage can be used for this recipe. The red is especially good with game or pork. As a change, add meat — about 3/4 cup of chopped ham or sausage, or ground beef to the stuffing. Little new potatoes boiled in the water with the cabbage are delicious!

1 medium size cabbage, 1 1/2 to 2 lbs.	1/2 teaspoon freshly cracked white pepper
3/4 cup butter	1/4 teaspoon freshly grated nutmeg
1/2 cup finely chopped onion	3 tablespoons chopped parsley
1/4 cup fine bread crumbs	2 lightly beaten eggs
4 teaspoons salt	2 tablespoons lemon juice

Remove and discard damaged leaves from cabbage, then peel off five or six leaves, keeping them as perfect as possible. If the cabbage head is firm, run it under warm water to loosen the leaves.

Line a 2-quart bowl with a cloth at least 12 inches square and place the six leaves, stem ends up, in it, overlapping them to form a cup or nest. Remove the core from the remaining cabbage and chop the cabbage very fine. Melt 1/4 cup butter in a large skillet and sauté cabbage with chopped onion over high heat for about 15 mintues, or until cabbage is limp. Do not let it brown. Put the sautéed cabbage and onion into a bowl and add bread crumbs, one teaspoon salt, other dry ingredients and the beaten eggs. The cabbage will be hot, so stir the eggs in quickly to avoid curdling. Stuff the mixture into cloth lined with cabbage leaves and twist the cloth very tight. Tie with string long enough to pull cabbage out of water. Drop tied cloth into kettle of boiling, salted water, reduce heat and simmer uncovered for 1 hour. Turn once during cooking. Serve with Sauce Mirepoix.

SAUCE MIREPOIX

1/2 lb. bacon, cut up and fried	1/2 lb. ground round of beef
3 small onions, cut up fine	1 cup beef broth
3 teaspoons parsley	

Brown onions in bacon drippings; add parsley. Cook beef in grease with onions and parsley. Keep stirring beef so it remains in small pieces. Add 1 cup beef broth and thicken with cornstarch.

Add:
4 ounces mushrooms
1/16 teaspoon ground cloves

1/4 teaspoon thyme
1 cup diced carrots, cooked
1 cup white port wine

Fry pieces of venison in bacon drippings and serve with sauce above.

APRICOT SOUP

3/4 lb. dried apricots
3 ripe fresh peaches
1/4 lb. fresh cherries

5 cups water
1/2 cup sugar
1/4 cup tapioca

Wash apricots in warm water. Combine with rest of fruit. Add water and sugar. Let stand overnight. Next day, cook fruit in water it was soaked in. Strain through a sieve. Heat to boiling point. Add the tapioca, gradually, and cook until soup is thick and clear. Remove from heat and stir in the juice of 1 lemon. Serve warm or cold.

BLUEBERRY SOUP

1 1/2 cups blueberries, washed
1 quart water
1/4 cup sugar

2 tablespoons cornstarch
3 tablespoons water

Place in saucepan 1 quart of water with the blueberries. Bring to boil and simmer until very soft. Strain berries through fine sieve, and return to the saucepan. Mix cornstarch and water, add to soup and cook until thickens. Stir adding 1/4 cup sugar. Simmer 3 minutes. Chill and serve.

PEAR PICKLE

Select small, sound pears. Remove blossom end. Stick them with a fork. Allow to each quart of pears — one pint of apple cider vinegar and 1 cup of sugar. Put in a teaspoon of allspice, cinnamon, and cloves to boil with the vinegar. Add the pears and boil until tender. Seal in jars.

Madagascar is in the Indian Ocean off the southeast coast of Africa. The island, slightly smaller than Texas, has a humid coastal strip in the east, and fertile valleys in the mountainous center plateau. Madagascar supplies 80% of the world's vanilla.

GLAZED SHRIMP

1/2 cup vinegar
1/2 tablespoon paprika
1 1/2 teaspoons salt
Dash red pepper
1 clove garlic

1 tablespoon sugar
1 egg
Dash red food coloring
1 cup salad oil

Mix all ingredients, except oil. Mix well. Slowly add oil, beating until thick. Combine 1 1/4 teaspoons plain gelatin with 2 tablespoons cold water. Let stand until thick. Remelt over boiling water. While hot, add slowly to french dressing mix until smooth. Place in refrigerator until thick. Stir occasionally. Dip shrimp into mixture. Let drain 30 minutes in refrigerator. Top with pale-pink cream cheese!

COLD ANCHOVY SAUCE FOR RICE OR MEATS

2 cups fresh parsley, finely chopped
3 cloves garlic
1/4 cup fresh basil or 1 teaspoon dry
2 tablespoons wine vinegar

1/4 cup chopped anchovies
Black pepper to taste
3 tablespoons oil
1/4 cup pimentos
3 tablespoons capers

Blend oil, vinegar and anchovies. Add rest of ingredients. Mix well. Serve over Hearts of Palm and Rice.

GARLIC SOUP

1 head of garlic (12 to 16 cloves)
1 tablespoon olive oil
4 cups chicken stock
Several sprigs of parsley

Salt and pepper to taste
A pinch of tarragon or rosemary
2 egg yolks

Separate garlic into cloves and remove loose outer husks but don't bother to peel. Heat olive oil and sauté garlic cloves until they just start to brown. Add chicken stock, the parsley stems (reserve the leaves for garnish) and other seasonings. Bring to a boil then lower the heat and simmer for about 30 minutes. Run the soup through a food mill, to remove the skins, and return soup to the pot. Beat the egg yolks with a little of the soup, then pour egg yolk mixture slowly into the remaining soup, stirring constantly. Reheat the soup if necessary, but do not let it boil. If you like, place a thick slice of French bread in the bottom of each bowl and pour the soup over it. Sprinkle with chopped parsley. Serves 3 to 4.

Malawi is one of the most scenic countries in Africa. Its high mountains and dense forests and broad plains make it very beautiful. Eighty-five percent of its work force is agriculture. Tea, tobacco, peanuts and cotton are its main exports.

6 sweet red or green peppers, sliced thin
6 onions, sliced
6 green tomatoes or firm, ripe ones
1/4 clove garlic, minced
1 teaspoon salt
1/8 teaspoon cayenne pepper
1/4 cup olive oil

Make layers of vegetables in a greased 2-quart baking dish. Season each layer with garlic, salt and cayenne pepper. Pour the oil over the casserole and bake, covered, in 350 degree oven for 45 minutes.

1 cup chopped Spanish onion
1/4 cup butter, softened
2 tablespoons lemon juice
12 juniper berries, crushed
1 teaspoon dried thyme leaves
1/4 teaspoon salt
1/8 teaspoon pepper
3 guinea hens (about 2 lbs. each)
1/2 cup strained red currant or apricot preserves

1. Combine onion, 1/4 cup softened butter, the lemon juice, juniper berries, thyme, salt and pepper. Rub inside and outside of each hen with onion-butter mixture. Refrigerate covered overnight.
2. Heat oven to 425 degrees. Place hens in roasting pan. Bake, basting occasionally with pan juices, 25 to 30 minutes. Brush with preserves during last 5 minutes of roasting. Remove hens to serving platter; garnish with leaf lettuce and artichokes.

1 cup dark brown sugar
1/2 cup butter
1 cup chopped peanuts
1 cup hot water
3 tablespoons cornstarch, dissolved in cold water
Pinch of nutmeg
2 tablespoons rum

Combine all ingredients except rum; bring to a boil. Cook until thick. Stir in rum. Serve over ice cream and bananas.

This tropical country, slightly larger than New Mexico, is located on the southeast tip of Asia and the northeast half of the Island of Borneo. Industries include rubber, pottery, and fertilizers, but it is also blessed with other abundant natural resources, including 35% of the worlds tin.

KEEM-CHEE

(Oriental Pickle)

(Spring)

3 cups celery or cucumbers
3 cups cabbage (Chinese)
3 tablespoons salt (uniodized)
3 green onions
3 clove garlic

1/2 teaspoon chopped red chili pepper
1 teaspoon chopped candied ginger
1 1/2 cups water

Wash vegetables. Do not peel cucumber, if used. Cut in 1-inch pieces. Sprinkle with 2 tablespoons salt. Let stand 15 minutes. Cut onion in 1 1/2-inch lengths and shred lengthwise. Chop the garlic, red pepper and ginger in fine pieces. After cabbage has stood 15 minutes, wash twice in cold water. Mix the prepared vegetables with the cabbage. Add remaining 1 tablespoon salt and put into a stone jar or glass jar. Add enough water to cover the cabbage and let stand several days. In very hot weather, 1 day is needed. In cold weather, up to 5 days is needed. Can be kept several weeks in the refrigerator.

KEEM-CHEE

(Soy with dates & nuts)

3 heads celery cabbage
1 cup thinly sliced turnips
1 cucumber
1 1/4 cups soy sauce
1 teaspoon candied ginger
1 tablespoon chopped red pepper, hot
1 tablespoon salt

4 green onions
1/4 cup shredded celery
1 firm pear
6 sliced water chestnuts
6 dates, chopped
1/4 cup pine nuts
1/3 cup sugar

Let stand 2 or 3 weeks.

Wash cabbage.
* Cut into 1 1/2-inch pieces. Add 1/2 cup soy sauce. Let stand 3 hrs. Slice rest of vegetables thin and let marinate in rest of soy. Drain vegetables and layer them in stone crock with pine nuts and seasonings. Put sugar on top and cover with mixture of soy and water, using 2 cups water to each 1/2 cup soy sauce.

4 envelopes Knox gelatin (or 2
   swifts or swallow nests)
1/2 cup cold tangerine juice
1 quart hot water
1/2 cup of olgae or cooked

   pumpkin
1/2 cup grated radishes
1/2 cup Chinese celery leaves or
   regular celery leaves
Salt and pepper to taste

BIRDS NEST
SOUP

Mix gelatin, tangerine juice and hot water. Let stand for 1 hour.
Add rest of the ingredients. Serve cold or hot.

Six to eight people are seated around a table, at the center of which
is a hot broth-filled vessel. Arranged around the vessel are various platters of raw ingredients cut into bite-size pieces. Fish,
seafood, beef, pork and vegetables are dipped into the boiling hot
broth and cooked to the desired doneness. The morsel is dipped
into various sauces and eaten. I have found that thinner slices of
meat can be had if you freeze the meat before slicing. Only the
white meat of chicken should be used. Noodles are added to the
simmering broth at the end of the meal and this is served to
finalize the meal. Chinese cabbage and spinach are favorite vegetables. Sherry and soy combined make an ideal dipping sauce, as
do mustard and plum sauces.

ORIENTAL
FIREPOT

1 cup chicken broth
1 cup rice wine
1 cup seedless raisins
1 cup pistachio nuts or pine nuts
2 tablespoons curry powder

1 tablespoon cornstarch, dissolved
   in 1/2 cup water
Hot boiled rice
Sliced bananas, mangoes, peaches,
   apricots, litchis and longan

FRUIT & RICE
WITH CURRY
SAUCE

Combine broth, wine, raisins, nuts, curry and cornstarch. Bring
to a boil and stir until thick. Arrange fresh fruit around a mound
of hot rice. Pour over sauce and serve.

Maldives is a group of about 1087 small islands in the Indian Ocean. The terrain is flat. The chief crops are coconuts, fruits and millet. Fish processing and tourism are the main industries. The ethnic groups are Singalese and Arabs. Most people are Sunni Moslems.

CHICKEN AND PEANUT STEW

good

1 fat frying chicken, cut in pieces
1 tablespoon salt
1 tablespoon ginger, ground
1 tablespoon curry powder
1/2 cup peanut oil *(or sesame)*
1 cup finely chopped green onions
1 cup pureed fresh tomatoes

1/2 cup tomato paste
1 teaspoon finely chopped fresh garlic
1/2 teaspoon hot red pepper
1 cup peanut butter mixed with 1 cup cold water

Pat chicken dry and coat with mixture of salt, ginger and curry powder. Then heat oil and brown pieces of chicken until a rich brown. Put chicken on plate and reserve 1/4 cup of oil and cook the onions until transparent and done. Add the tomatoes and paste, garlic, peanut butter and water. Simmer 15 minutes, being careful not to let it stick. Now return the chicken to stew pot and reduce heat and simmer for 1 hour. Be sure to spoon off any fat that rises to top of stew during cooking. This is a very thick delicious dish.

ALMOND STRIPS

A very sweet cookie with a meringue-like top.

4 ounces ground almonds
4 ounces sugar

1 egg yolk
1 teaspoon vanilla

Mix in order listed and work to dough. Form into fingers or press into 1/4 x 7 x 7-inch sheet, and cut into sticks with diagonal ends. Frost down center and bake in very slow oven, 280 degrees for 25 minutes. They should dry, rather than bake, and must not brown. FROSTING: Beat 1 egg white until stiff, and gradually beat in 4 ounces sugar. Frost center of each cookie, as it will crack if cut.

The Republic of Mali has an area of 464,873 square miles — about the size of Texas and California combined. It is located in the interior of West Africa. It is a landlocked country, mostly grassy plain, and is largely agricultural. Crops include millet, rice, peanuts and cotton, and it also has rubber trees.

DRIED FIG CONSERVE

2 lbs. dried figs	2 tablespoons lemon juice
5 cups water	1 cup blanched almonds
2 cups sugar	1 cup chopped pine nuts
3/4 teaspoon anise seed, pounded	

Chop figs into quarters and soak in cold water 4 hours. Heat water and sugar in a large saucepan. Bring to boil and add the anise seed and the figs. Cook slowly, be sure and keep heat low, until figs are transparent and tender and the syrup has cooked down. Takes about 1 1/2 to 2 hours. Stir in lemon juice and nuts. Serve as a sweet!

DATE NUT BREAD

3/4 cup pecans	3/4 cup boiling water
1 cup dates	2 eggs
1 1/2 teaspoons soda	1/2 teaspoon vanilla
1/2 teaspoon salt	1 cup sugar
1/4 cup shortening, melted	1 1/2 cups sifted flour

Beat eggs and add to dry mixed ingredients.

Grease 4 soup cans with oil. Fill two-thirds full. Cover and bake at 350 degrees for 10-25 minutes.

NASTURTIUM VINEGAR DRESSING

1/2 cup chopped nasturtium stems	Pepper to taste, coarse fresh cracked
1/2 cup finely minced celery	1/2 teaspoon thyme
1/2 cup finely chopped onion	1/2 teaspoon basil
1/3 cup red wine vinegar	1 cup salad oil
Salt to taste	

Shake all ingredients together and serve over fresh leaf spinach or lettuce. Garnish with hard cooked eggs. It's peppery and good. Let dressing stand for 4 hours to blend flavors.
Tiny green chrysanthemum buds may be used instead of nasturtiums.

A Long Tongue Shortens Life.

The island of Malta is in the center of the Mediterranean Sea, with Italy its closest neighbor, to the north. Malta is 95 sq. miles in area. Other islands in the group are Gozo, 26 sq. mi., Comino, 1 sq. mi. The country is a center for ship repair. The country became independent in 1964, but retained a British naval base until 1979. Maltese is a Semitic language, with Italian influences, and is written in the Latin alphabet.

This is the most popular dish on the Maltese Menu.

TIMPANA

1 1/2 lbs. macaroni	1/2 eggplant
3 eggs	1/2 lb. ricotta cheese
2 hard boiled eggs	1/4 lb. liver or bacon
1/4 lb. lard	1 or 2 small onions
1/2 lb. minced meat, pork or beef	1/4 lb. cheese
1 small can tomato purée	Puff pastry

Place macaroni in boiling salted water. Peel the eggplant and cut up into small pieces. Soak in water diluted with a little vinegar. Fry the chopped onions in a saucepan, together with eggplant. When these are cooked, add the minced meat and liver. Let simmer. Dissolve the tomato purée in hot water and add to the contents of saucepan. Beat the eggs separately and grate the cheese for use when required. Prepare a deep casserole by greasing it. Line the bottom and sides with puff pastry. Next, mix meat sauce with the ricotta. Strain the macaroni. Place first a layer of macaroni, followed by a layer of meat sauce. Sprinkle with grated cheese. Slice hard boiled eggs and place on grated cheese. Repeat the process, finishing with a layer of meat and ricotta filling. Add the well-beaten eggs, spread over top. Sprinkle grated cheese on top and cover with layer of puffed pastry. Bake till golden color!

RIS DE VEAU ARCHIDUC

1 1/2 lbs. veal sweetbreads	1 cup heavy cream
Salt	1 ounce Madeira wine (Malmsey)
6 small fresh mushrooms	Pepper
Butter	

Parboil sweetbreads for 30 minutes in salted water. Cool, then cut in 1-inch pieces, removing excess membranes. Sauté mushrooms in butter. Add cream, wine and sweetbreads. Simmer until sauce is cooked down about half and thickened. Season to taste with salt and pepper. Makes 2 servings. Notice sauce is thickened by reducing and is not thickened by addition of any starch or flour.

FLAGS OF THE UNITED NATIONS

MAURITANIA

NETHERLANDS

MAURITIUS

NEW ZEALAND

MEXICO

NICARAGUA

MONGOLIA

NIGER

MOROCCO

NIGERIA

MOZAMBIQUE

NORWAY

NEPAL

Mauritania is a West African territory, about one-fifth the size of Alaska. There are large herds of cattle, camels, sheep and goats. The land is rich with mineral deposits.

FISH IMOJO
(Cold Salad)

2 lbs. halibut or haddock simmered
   until done; flake fish and chill.
Mix with:
1 cup finely chopped tomato
1/2 cup finely chopped onion

1/4 cup bell pepper
2 tablespoons fresh parsley
1 tablespoon hot chili
1 tablespoon chopped garlic

Make dressing by mixing 1/3 cup lemon juice with 1/4 cup olive oil and 2 tablespoons tomato paste. Pour over fish and sprinkle with ground pepper. Serve with Tomato Chutney and beans.

CORN MEAL DESSERT

1/2 cup butter
1/2 cup blanched almonds, chopped
2 cups fine cornmeal

3/4 cup milk
1 tablespoon cinnamon
4 tablespoons sugar

Melt the butter in a deep skillet. Add the nuts. Stir in the cornmeal, slowly. When the nuts are brown, slowly add enough milk to make a thick mush. Stir well. Cover with cheesecloth and put on pan cover. Cook very slow for 30 minutes. Stir and fluff up mixture with a fork. Serve with sweet cream, cinnamon, sugar or honey or foam sauce!

FOAM SAUCE WITH RUM

2 eggs, separated
1 cup sugar

1/2 cup butter
2 tablespoons rum

Cream egg yolks and sugar; add soft butter and continue to beat 5 minutes. Add rum. Fold in stiffly beaten egg whites and serve over hot puddings!

TOMATO CHUTNEY

5 lbs. tomatoes, red or yellow
2 lbs. sugar
1/2 teaspoon salt
1 orange, thinly sliced
1 lemon, thinly sliced

1 stick (3-inch) cinnamon
1 piece whole ginger
2 cups seedless raisins
1/2 cup lemon juice
1/4 teaspoon Tabasco

Peel tomatoes and chop. Combine with sugar, salt, sliced orange and sliced lemon. Stir over heat until sugar dissolves. Add cinnamon and ginger, bring to a boil; cook over low heat until thick, about 1 hour, stirring occasionally. Remove cinnamon and ginger. Add raisins and lemon juice and bring again to a boil. Stir in Tabasco, pour into hot pint or half-pint jars, and seal at once. Makes 3 1/2 pints.

Mauritius is an island in the Indian Ocean, 550 miles east of Madagascar, and has a very complex population of Hindus, Europeans, Africans, Moslems, Americans, and Chinese. Indian language, French and many dialects of various languages are spoken. Sugar is the main industry. The people live to be very old here. Tea and sugar are the main crops.

CHEESE LAYER CAKE

1/3 cup sifted cake flour	2 tablespoons vinegar
1/8 teaspoon salt	1 tablespoon olive oil
1 egg, beaten	3/4 cup oil
1 cup water	Butter

Sift the flour with the salt. Mix the egg with water and vinegar. Gradually add to the flour mixture. Mixing well, add the oil a little at a time, and mix to a good dough. Divide into 8 pieces and roll each piece as thin as possible.

Filling:

2 cups cottage cheese	
3 eggs, beaten	1/4 teaspoon salt
3 tablespoons sugar	1 cup melted butter

Mix all filling ingredients together. Place 1 layer of dough in a lightly greased round cake pan. Spread with the filling and repeat using each dough layer and filling until all is used. Dough should end up on top. Brush each layer of dough with butter before adding filling. Bake in 375 degree oven for 35 minutes or until brown on top and crisp. Very rich!

CHAPATI
(Indian Bread)

3 cups whole wheat flour
2/3 cup water
1 teaspoon salt

Put flour into a bowl and make a little indentation in the center. Add just enough water to make a very dry dough. Add salt to taste. Knead well with the fingers and divide the dough into a lump the size of an egg. Roll out very thin. Brown on both sides on an ungreased griddle. Press with a cloth before removing from griddle.

Mexico, in southern North America, is officially called the United Mexican States, with a governmental organization comprised of states with governors with legislatures. About 45% of Mexican land is arid, but some crops, including cotton, coffee, sugar cane, tomatoes, and 50% of the world's supply of sisal are gorwn there. Mexico was once the site of advanced Indian civilizations, including the Mayas, the Toltecs, and the Aztecs. The economy of the country has improved with the discovery of vast oil and natural gas reserves.

LA PALOMA TEQUILA
(Dove in Tequila)

12 doves, or 4 game hens, picked
    clean
1/2 cup fat
2 small onions, minced
2 whole cloves
1 teaspoon peppercorns
2 cloves garlic, minced
1/2 bay leaf
1 cup tequila

1 cup warm water
1/2 teaspoon salt
1/4 teaspoon pepper
Few grains cayenne
1 teaspoon minced chives
2 cups heavy cream

In large skillet, melt fat. Add onions, cloves, peppercorns, garlic and bay leaf. Cook several minutes then add birds and brown on all sides. Add tequila, warm water, salt, pepper, cayenne, and chives and simmer till tender, about four minutes. Remove doves to warm serving dish. Strain sauce, add cream and heat to boiling. Pour over birds. Serves 4 to 6.

MOLE DE QUAJOLOTE

The turkey symbolizes Mexican hospitality. Mole is the Aztec word for sauce, a very unusual combination of chocolate and chili peppers, which comprises one of Mexico's national dishes.

Cut cooked turkey meat into serving pieces. Brown in fat. Place in casserole. Keep warm. Add 2 onions, chopped, and 4 cloves of minced garlic to oil in pan and sauté until soft, not brown. Place onions, garlic in blender with 2 bell peppers, 2 teaspoons cumin, 1/2 teaspoon powdered aniseed, 4 tablespoon toasted sesame seed, 3/4 cup roasted peanuts, 6 tomatoes, 1/4 cup chili powder, 1 teaspoon salt, 1/4 teaspoon cinnamon, pinch of black pepper, 3 ounces bitter chocolate. After blending heat with 3 cups turkey stock. Pour over turkey and heat until sauce is thick. Serve with rice.

This is a very popular Mexican dish!

115

VEAL IN NOGADA OR IN WALNUT SAUCE

3 lbs. fillet of veal
1 1/2 quarts of water
2 medium onions
2 cloves garlic
1/4 teaspoon thyme
Salt and pepper to taste
3 tablespoons butter

1 cup ground walnuts
1 can evaporated milk
5 cups veal broth
1/4 cup blanched almonds, toasted, slivered
Avocado tips
Green or red pepper tips

Cook the veal with water, thyme and 1 onion. When half done, add salt and pepper. Cook well until tender. Cool to cut in thin slices. Chop very thinly the second onion and cook in butter until transparent. Add the ground walnut and evaporated milk and broth. Bring to a boil, moving it constantly until it thickens. Add the slices of veal. Before serving, sprinkle with almonds and if desired garnish with tips of avocado and pepper tips.

ICED ZUCCHINI SOUP

2 tablespoons butter or margarine
1 onion, chopped
2 cloves garlic, sliced
2 to 3 teaspoons curry powder
Handful of parsley stalks

1 1/2 lbs. zucchini, coarsely chopped
3 cups chicken broth
Salt and pepper to taste

Sauté onion and garlic in butter until limp. Stir in curry powder and cook a few minutes longer. Chop parsley leaves and place them in a plastic bag. Add parsley stems, zucchini and chicken broth to the pot and simmer, uncovered, until the vegetables are tender — about 15 minutes. Run soup through a food mill and season to taste. Chill, then pour soup into a cold thermos bottle. Bring along the chopped parsley to sprinkle on top. Shake thermos well before pouring soup into mugs. Serves 6

TEQUILA PUNCH

8 tender lemon leaves
1 peeling of whole grapefruit
1 stick cinnamon

8 cups water
2 cups sugar
1/2 pint tequila

Mix all ingredients, except tequila, and boil for eight minutes. Let stand 1 hour. Strain. Add tequila. Place in jar for two weeks before serving. WOW!

Mongolia is one of the world's oldest countries. It reached the zenith of its power in the 13th century, when Genghis Khan and his successors conquered all of China and extended their influence as far west as Hungary and Poland. Later, the empire dissolved and came under the rule of China, but became independent in 1911. Industries include food processing, textiles, chemicals, and cement. The country's chief crop is grain.

PUMPKIN CHIP PICKLES

2 lbs. pumpkin, sliced or in chips (should be thin like potato chips)	1 teaspoon whole cloves
1 pint vinegar	1 teaspoon whole allspice
2 lbs. sugar	1/2 cup crystalized ginger
1 teaspoon salt	4 lemon slices
	Pieces of stick cinnamon

Place all ingredients in a saucepan, bring slowly to boil and cook until pumpkin is transparent. Lift out the pumpkin and pack in jars with a slice of onion and a little of the ginger. Continue boiling syrup until thick. Spoon over the chips and fill jars with syrup while hot. Seal. Place in refrigerator before serving. For a sweeter chip, instead of vinegar, use 1 cup water and 1 cup lemon juice. Makes 2 1/2 pints.

FRIED SPINACH BALLS

1 1/2 cups finely chopped, cooked spinach	1 egg
1 tablespoon onion, grated	Dash of allspice
1 tablespoon grated parmesan cheese	1/2 cup cracker crumbs

Mix ingredients and let stand 15 minutes so crumbs can soak up moisture. Make in balls. Dip in 1 egg beaten with 4 tablespoons water. Roll in cracker crumbs or meal and fry 3 minutes in oil.

CONGEE

Congee is rice simmered with water using the proportion of 15 parts liquid to 1 part of rice. Any ingredients can be added to this bland concoction. Any liquid may be used. This is a very popular dish in Asia.

Philippians 2-14:
"Do all things without grumbling or questioning."

MOROCCON TAGINE

(Stew) with Couscous

The main crops of Morocco are citrus fruits and olives. The main occupation is sardine fishing, and cork is also found in Morocco.

A typical meat and fruit stew made with honey!

2 lbs. cubed leg of lamb (water to cover)
2 tablespoons oil
1/4 teaspoon ground ginger
Salt and black pepper
1/2 teaspoon ground coriander
1/2 teaspoon ground cinnamon

1/2 cup chopped onion
1/2 lb. prunes, soaked overnight, pitted
2 tablespoons honey
1 teaspoon orange blossom water or
1/4 teaspoon orange flavoring

Put meat in large saucepan. Cover with water. Add all ingredients, except prunes, honey and orange blossom water. Simmer gently for 2 1/2 hours. Add the prunes, orange blossom water and honey. Simmer 20 minutes longer. Serve, sprinkled with roasted sesame seeds.

Serve with Couscous prepared in a couscousiere. The stew is placed in the bottom of the steamer. After it is done the couscous is steamed in the top of the strainer until light and fluffy. Best results are had by first moistening the semolina and then placing into the cloth-lined steamer above the stew and then it is steamed for about 10 minutes until each grain stands out.

Diners are seated cross-legged and in a circle around a low table and eat from a communal bowl. Etiquette describes that they hold their wooden spoons in the right hand and eat from the outer edges, leaving the center for the blessing of Heaven to descend upon it. The meal concludes by passing a communal bowl of water or milk, followed by coffee.

Mozambique is a country on the southeast coast of Africa. Cement, alcohol, textiles are the chief industries. Cashews, copra, sisal, tea and sugar are the main crops. Literacy is 7%. Portuguese is the official language.

EGGS AND YAMS

Boil, skin and mash the yam (large enough for 6 servings). Mix with it a dash of onion, red pepper, curry and salt. Spread the hot yam over a greased baking dish, about 1/2-inch thick. Make 6 holes in sweet potato and break 6 eggs into the holes. Place in 325 degree oven and cook until eggs are desired doneness. Delicious for breakfast.

CARDAMON COOKIES

1 cup butter	1/2 teaspoon soda
2 egg yolks	1/2 teaspoon ground cardamon
3/4 cup sugar	3 1/3 cups flour
Juice of 2 oranges and grated rind	

Cream butter. Add egg yolks and sugar. Beat until fluffy. Add rest of ingredients with flour. Roll thin. Cut in rounds. Bake until crispy but not brown. Roll in powdered sugar.

3/4 cup cake flour	3/4 cup sugar
3/4 teaspoon baking powder	1 teaspoon vanilla extract
1/4 teaspoon salt	1 cup jelly
4 eggs	

Start oven at 400°. Grease a 15 x 10 x 1 1/2—inch jellyroll pan. Fit with layer of greased wax paper. Sift flour. Beat eggs, baking powder and salt until fluffy. Add sugar gradually and beat until mixture is smooth. Fold in flour and vanilla. Bake for 13 minutes. Roll up cake — let cool — spread with jelly, creme filling, whipped cream, etc.

The Kingdom of Nepal is in the Himalaya Mountains, with China on the north and India to the south. Virtually colosed to the outside world for centuries, Nepal is now linked to India and Pakistan by roads and air service and to Tibet by road. The country's industries include animal hides and drugs, and it has a supply of quartz.

BATEN GEN MIHSHEE
(Stuffed Eggplants)

1 dozen small 3 to 5-inch eggplants	1/8 teaspoon cloves
1/2 cup tomato catsup	Pinch of allspice
3 cups rice or wheat pilaf, cooked	2 tablespoons butter
1 teaspoon salt	1 onion, minced and sautéed in
1/8 teaspoon cinnamon	butter

Place eggplants, unpeeled, in baking dish with two cups water. Cover and steam. Bake until tender, for about 30 minutes. Slice off top and scoop out eggplant; mix with remaining ingredients. Pile back into eggplant skin and dot with butter. Bake about 10 minutes. Add a little water to pan to prevent sticking. Serve with Tomato Dressing!

BANDOORA MAHLOOBEE
(Tomato Dressing)

2 tablespoons butter	1/8 teaspoon cinnamon
1 medium can diced tomatoes	1 teaspoon salt
1 onion, minced	Pepper to taste
1 stalk celery, minced, use leaves too	1 teaspoon chopped mint

Slightly sauté onion and celery in butter. Add tomatoes and seasoning. Simmer 12 minutes. Serve over Stuffed Eggplant.

CURRY PASTE

1 teaspoon saffron and enough water to make paste	1 teaspoon black pepper
6 tablespoons coriander	1 teaspoon mustard seed
1 heaping teaspoon anise seed	
1 heaping teaspoon clove	3 garlic pods
1 teaspoon jera	1 large onion
1 teaspoon mehti	Red pepper to taste

Mix and mash all ingredients in a mortar. Use as a seasoning.

The Netherlands is a flat country in northwest Europe on the North Sea. The average height is 37 ft. above sea level, with much land reclaimed from the sea and protected by a system of dykes. The Netherlands is the site of the world's busiest seaport, Rotterdam, which handles the most cargo of any ocean port in the world. The country is also a center for diamond cutting, and its other industries include metals, machinery, food products, chemical and textile production.

ROTTERDAM
(Liver Paste)

1 lb. calves or veal liver	1/4 teaspoon dry mustard
1 lb. bacon	3 eggs, separated
2 medium onions, chopped	1 cup thick cream sauce, made
1 teaspoon pepper	with:
1 tablespoon salt	3 tablespoons flour, 3 tablespoons
1/2 teaspoon allspice	butter, 1 cup milk
1/4 teaspoon powdered cloves	

Remove membrane from liver and grind 3 or 4 times with the 1 pound bacon. Combine pepper, salt, spices, the cream sauce. Cool. Then add liver, blend in the well-beaten egg yolks. Last fold in 3 egg whites, beaten stiff. Pour into buttered 2-quart Pyrex dish. Bake over water in preheated oven of 350 degrees for 1 1/2 hours. Cool in pan. Serve on crackers or toast.

*STUFFED
TROUT*

6-8 ounce whole boneless trout, buttered inside and out (Filet of Sole may be used)

Stuffing:

1/4 cup butter	1 cup raw, chopped shrimp
1/4 cup chopped onion	1 egg
1/4 cup chopped celery	1/2 teaspoon thyme
4 cups bread cubes	1/2 teaspoon sage
1/2 cup dry white wine	1/4 teaspoon marjoram
1/4 cup parsley	Salt and pepper to taste

Sauté butter, onion and celery. Combine with rest of ingredients. Stir until blended. Stuff the trout and place on baking sheet. Bake at 450 degrees for 15 to 20 minutes.

*APPLE
FRITTERS*

Make batter using	1/2 can beer
1 3/4 cups flour	Pinch of salt

Dip slices of tart apples (which have been sprinkled with cinnamon sugar and allowed to stand 30 minutes) in batter. Fry in hot oil until light brown. Sprinkle with powdered sugar and serve hot.

121

Two main islands comprise New Zealand. Both are hilly and mountainous, but the coastal areas have fertile plains. The islands were located by the Dutch, who were not permitted to land by the native Maori Indians. The islands were later settled by the British, who continued to rule the country until it became a dominion in 1907. It is now an independent member of the Commonwealth. The country produces fine wool and timber, and industries include food processing, paper manufacture, and production of steel and aluminum.

ENGLISH BREAD SAUCE

1 cup milk	2 ounces fresh, soft bread crumbs
1 small onion	1/2 ounce butter
1 small clove	1 tablespoon cream
1 blade mace	Salt and pepper

Crumble bread. Slowly heat the milk with mace and the onion, in which the cloves have been stuck. Bring to the scalding point in double boiler. Remove the mace. Stir in the crumbs, beating constantly. Add salt and pepper to taste and 1 tablespoon butter. Cook for 20 minutes, stirring often. Add cream and 1 more tablespoon butter. Remove the onion and clove. Serve at once over Grouse, Partridge or game.

ENGLISH MUSTARD SAUCE

1 cup mustard (4 ounces)	Add:
1 cup vinegar, white	1 cup sugar
	2 beaten eggs
Mix and let set overnight.	Pinch salt

Cook until it coats the spoon. Put in jars and refrigerate.

PAVLOVA
(National Dessert of New Zealand)

6 egg whites	1 1/2 teaspoon vanilla
1/8 teaspoon salt	1 tablespoon vinegar
3/4 cup fine sugar	

Line an 8-10 inch springform pan with waxed paper. Beat egg whites to a foam with rotary beater or electric. Add salt and beat to a stiff foam. Beat in sugar, 1 tablespoon at a time, beating well after each addition. Add vanilla and vinegar. Beat thoroughly. Turn meringue mixture into prepared pan. Bake in 250 degree oven for 1 1/2 hours. Remove from pan while still warm. Cool on cake rack. Place on serving dish. Top with swirls of whipped cream sweetened to taste. Decorate with sliced Kiwis or fresh berries.

2 8-ounce cans shad roe, drained
1 tablespoon lemon juice
1 envelope plain gelatin dissolved
    in 1/2 cup juice from shad roe,
    then heated over hot water until
    melted.

2 onions, finely minced
1 teaspoon paprika
5-10 dashes of Tabasco
2 anchovies, minced
1/2 cup mayonnaise
1 cup yogurt

Mash shad roe with lemon juice, add onions, paprika, Tabasco, anchovies, mayonnaise and yogurt. Blend well. Add hot melted gelatin. Stir well. Turn into mold and congeal. Serve with sesame crackers.

3/4 cup butter
1/2 cup sugar
3 eggs
1 cake yeast (dissolved in 1/4 cup
    lukewarm water)

1 1/2 cups warm milk or water
Flour to stiffen dough
Almonds
Sugar

Cream margarine and sugar. Add eggs, beating thoroughly after each addition. Add yeast cake dissolved in water, and the warm milk. Add enough flour to make a semi-stiff dough. Let rise overnight. Then add enough flour to make a stiff dough. Knead until smooth. Roll out 1/2-inch thick in 3 long strands and braid. Let it rise again. Brush top with melted butter. Sprinkle with sugar and decorate with almonds. When the braid has doubled size bake in 350 degree oven until done.

Anise (served as iced drink during summer)
        1 teaspoon anise in 1 glass warm milk and 1 teaspoon honey induces sleep.

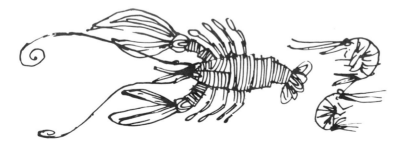

The Republic of Nicaragua in Central America is slightly larger than the State of Wisconsin. It is bordered by Honduras on the north, Costa Rica on the south. A mountain range bisects the country. Oil refining, chemicals, and textiles are among the industries. There are deposits of gold, silver, copper and tungsten, and chief crops include bananas, cotton, fruit, yucca, coffee, sugar, cocoa, and rice.

PEANUT WAFERS

1/2 cup butter	1 1/2 cups flour
1 cup sugar	Chopped, unsalted peanuts
1 cup milk	Vanilla

Mix all ingredients, except peanuts. Spread very thin on a cookie sheet in strips; only spread 3 at a time. Sprinkle with chopped peanuts; bake in 350 degree oven until slightly brown; take from oven and roll up so that the peanuts are on the outside.

LACE COOKIES

1 cup quick-cooking oats	1/4 teaspoon salt
1 cup sugar	1/2 teaspoon vanilla
1/4 lb. melted, butter	1/4 tablespoon baking powder
1 egg, beaten	3 tablespoons flour, scant

Mix all ingredients together well. Using a pastry tube, drop 1/2 teaspoonful of the batter onto a 4-inch waxed paper round. Place very thin slivers of almonds on top of each and bake in 350 degree oven until slightly brown, approximately 7 minutes. Cool completely; and peel off paper and serve. Thin and crispy.

I prefer to bake these on well greased, floured pan. As soon as they come out of oven, lift them off of pan before cooling.

BUNUELITOS deJAMON
(Breakfast Ham Fritters)

2 eggs, separated	2 cups ground ham
2 tablespoons flour	Salt and pepper
2 tablespoons milk	

Beat egg whites until stiff. In another bowl, beat yolks, flour and milk. Stir in ham and season to taste with salt and pepper. Fold in egg whites. Drop by teaspoons into hot deep fat and fry until golden. Serve immediately with mustard sauce and scrambled eggs.
Potato fritters are made the same way. Use 2 cups mashed potatoes instead of ham. Add juice of 1/2 onion, 1 finely grated bell pepper and 2 tablespoons parsley.

In Niger the main crop is peanuts. Camels and donkeys are seen a lot in Niger. Ostriches, once very plentiful throughout the Middle East, are almost extinct everywhere except Africa. For special occasions, one ostrich egg will make an omlette for 12 people. The eggs weigh around 3 pounds.

BEID HAMINE
(North African hard cooked eggs)

12 hen eggs
12 skins from brown onions

Plenty of cold water to cover eggs. Add a thin layer of oil to keep water from evaporating. Bring egg in water to a simmer and simmer 6 hours over very, very low heat. The lengthy cooking produces a delicious creamy egg. The whites are à soft beige from the onion skin and the yolks a very creamy pale yellow. Serves over brown beans.

FUL MEDAME

1 lb. brown beans soaked overnight
4 cloves garlic, crushed
1/4 cup finely chopped parsley

Quartered lemon
Salt and black pepper
6 hard cooked eggs

Let beans simmer in unsalted water until tender, about 5-7 hours. When beans are soft add crushed garlic and serve in soup bowls with hard cooked egg in center and sprinkle with fresh parsley. Pass quartered lemons to be squeezed over top.

ICE CROWN WITH FRUIT AND FLOWERS

To make a clear ice block, one merely uses distilled water.

All that is needed is a well-shaped mold that holds 1 1/2 quarts or more. (The tower mold is perfect for this.) Also needed are a nosegay of flowers and a few berries (strawberries are nice), toothpicks and a freezing compartment.

Make an old-fashioned bouquet of edible flowers (roses, fruit blossoms, nasturtiums or carnations). Tie stems tightly. Stick berries with toothpicks and insert in other end of bouquet. Pour water about an inch deep into bottom of mold, place bouquet upside down (stem out) and cut off stems level with edge of mold. Then fill with water. Place plate over mold to hold bouquet down near, not touching, the bottom of mold. Freeze 8 to 10 hours or several days. To unmold, dip momentarily in warm water.

The Federal Republic of Nigeria on the south coast of Africa is more than twice the size of California. Topographically, the country is divided into four east-west regions: a coastal mangrove swamp, a rain forest, a plateau of savanna and woodland, and an area of semi desert. Cocoa is the main export crop, and the Nigerians also grow tobacco, palm products and peanuts.

AKARA BALLS
(Black-eyed Pea Fritters)

2 cups dried, black-eyed peas
1 1/2 teaspoon garlic salt
1/2 cup green onions, minced

1/2 cup green peppers, minced, or 1
  tablespoon hot peppers

Cover peas with water and soak overnight. Drain. Barely cover with water and simmer until soft. Do not overcook. Blend with other ingredients. Drop by teaspoons into hot oil. Brown. Serve hot!

HONEY BREAD
(Makes 1 8 1/2 inch round loaf)

1 pkg. dry yeast
1/4 cup lukewarm water

1 egg
1/2 cup honey
1 tablespoon ground coriander

1/2 teaspoon ground cinnamon
1/4 teaspoon ground clove
1 1/2 teaspoons salt
1 cup lukewarm milk
6 tablespoons melted butter
4 1/2 cups flour

Dissolve yeast in warm water and set aside.

Beat egg, honey and spice together until fluffy. Add the yeast mixture, warm milk and melted butter. Stir in flour. Knead the dough until smooth. Add a little oil to your hand to keep dough from sticking, don't add more flour. Let rise until double in size, about 1 hour. Punch down and knead for a couple more minutes. Shape into round loaf or place in a greased loaf pan. Let rise again until double, about 1 1/2 hours. Bake in 300 degree oven 1 hour. Warm. Serve with butter and honey.

MOLASSES VINEGAR

4 pints molasses
6 gallons soft water
1 pkg. yeast

Mix ingredients and let stand 3 weeks in a warm place. Strain and bottle.

VANILLA ESSENCE

Soak 3 vanilla beans in 1/2 pint rum (nip). Use as flavoring.

Norway occupies the western part of the Scandanavian peninsula in northwest Europe, and extends further north than any European country. Originally part of Denmark and then of Sweden, Norway became an independent country in 1905, with Prince Charles of Denmark as king. Norway's industries include paper manufacture, ship building, and engineering. Abundant hydroelectric power has helped in the industrialization of the country. Norway's merchant marine is the world's fourth largest.

NORWEGIAN FISH PUDDING

2 lbs. boneless haddock or trout	2 tablespoons flour
2 teaspoons salt	2 eggs
1/8 teaspoon pepper	1/3 cup butter
Dash nutmeg or mace	1/2 cup heavy cream

Grind fish until fine. Stir in seasonings and flour. Beat in thoroughly one egg at a time, then the softened butter. Add cream and beat until fluffy and light. Turn into greased fancy mold. Set in a pan of hot water and bake in a 350 degree oven for 1 hour or until firm in center. Serve with Caper Sauce!

CAPER SAUCE

1 cup chicken stock	1 teaspoon capers
2 tablespoons butter	1/4 teaspoon paprika
1/4 teaspoon salt	2 tablespoons parsley
Dash white pepper	1 tablespoon cornstarch

Put all ingredients in saucepan. Dissolve cornstarch in 2 tablespoons cold water, add to sauce and bring to boil. Serve over fish.

NORWEGIAN OMELETTE
(Dessert)

Cover a wooden bread board with heavy aluminum foil. Take white cake or sponge cake, cut in 2 1/2-inch squares. Sprinkle cake with apricot brandy. Place a slice of orange sherbet on cake. Cover with orange marmalade.

Whip 4 egg whites until stiff. Fold in 3/4 cup sugar. Cover the cake and orange marmalade. Brown quickly in a hot oven. The so-called "Baked Alaska" is a poor imitation of this delightful treat.

LEFSE
(A Norwegian Food)

7 potatoes, medium size
3 tablespoons cream
3 tablespoons butter
3 tablespoons honey or brown
　sugar

Pinch of salt
3 cups flour

Steam potatoes until tender, mash. Add other ingredients, mix until this is not too sticky. Roll out 1/8-inch thick, like a big pancake. Brown 1 minute on each side in oil. Good hot, cold or wrapped around food!

SILDESALAT
(Herring Salad)

Soak 10 salt herring in cold water 6-8 hours. Remove from water and dry the fish. Weigh. Take same weight of cooked veal, cooked potatoes, cooked beets and raw apple, chopped fine. Add 2 dill pickles, diced. Mix 2 tablespoons of vinegar, 2 tablespoons oil, 1 tablespoon sugar, 1/2 cup claret and beet juice. Mix all with chopped herring and potatoes, etc. Let stand overnight.
To serve combine 2 tablespoons more of oil with 2 tablespoons more of vinegar. Stir over hot water until it is thickened. Pour over salad and garnish with hard boiled eggs.

OLLEBROD

1/2 lb. whole wheat bread
1/2 lb. pumpernickel
4 1/2 cups water
4 1/2 cups dark beer or ale
6 tablespoons sugar

1/4 teaspoon salt
1-inch stick cinnamon
1/2 teaspoon grated lemon peel
1/2 cup heavy cream, whipped

Combine bread in 3-quart enamel kettle. Pour water in kettle, let stand overnight. Next morning, place kettle over low heat. Cook until it forms thick paste. Stir in beer, sugar, salt, cinnamon and lemon peel and bring to a boil. Serve hot with whipped cream on top.

FLAGS OF THE UNITED NATIONS

OMAN

POLAND

PAKISTAN

PORTUGAL

PANAMA

QATAR

PAPUA NEW GUINEA

ROMANIA

PARAGUAY

RWANDA

PERU

SAINT LUCIA

PHILIPPINES

The Sultanate of Oman has a long history of rule by other lands, including Portugal in the 16th century. By the early 19th century, however, Muscat (the capital) and Oman was one of the most important countries in the region, controlling much of the Persian and Pakistan coasts. The discovery of oil in 1964 has been the major source of income for the sultanate. The country, roughly the size of Kansas, is on the southeast coast of the Arabian Peninsula. There is a narrow coastal plain up to 10 miles wide, a range of barren mountains, and a mostly waterless plateau. Some crops, including dates, fruits, vegetables, wheat and frankincense are grown.

YOGURT

1. Heat 1 quart fresh milk to 180 degrees, simmering for 1 minute.
2. Cool the milk immediately by placing in bowl of ice water. Cool to 115 degrees.
3. Innoculate the milk with 2 tablespoons dry yogurt culture or 2 tablespoons yogurt.
4. Pour in pre-rinsed jars or glasses. Let set at room temperature for 3 to 4 hours. Place in refrigerator and eat as desired.

HONEY COMB CANDY

1 cup sugar
1 cup dark corn syrup
1 tablespoon vinegar
1 tablespoon baking soda

Combine sugar, syrup and vinegar in heavy saucepan. Cook over medium heat until sugar dissolves. Continue cooking without stirring, until candy thermometer reaches 300 degrees. Remove from heat; quickly stir in soda and mix well. Pour into lightly buttered 9 x 9 x 2 inch pan. Candy will spread itself. Cool, break in pieces. Yields 1 pound. Keep in airtight tin.

GRANOLA STICKS

4 cups rolled oats
1 1/2 cups rolled rye
1 cup rolled wheat
2/3 cup wheat germ
10-ounce pkg. shredded coconut
1/2 cup brown sugar
1 teaspoon salt
1/2 cup corn oil
1 teaspoon vanilla
2/3 cup chopped almonds
1/2 cup chopped dates
1/2 cup sesame seeds
1/2 cup dried chopped apricots or bananas
3/4 cup water

Mix all ingredients and press together to form 1 x 4-inch sticks. Bake in 300 degree oven until brown, about 45 minutes. Let cool. Wrap and store to use as food snacks.

Pakistan, somewhat larger than Texas, is in the western part of South Asia. The country is mountainous, including the Hindu Kush and Himalaya Mountains in the north, and it is watered by the Indus River, which rises in the mountains and flows over 1,000 miles through a fertile valley into the Arabian Sea. Pakistan shares the 5,000 year history of the India-Pakistan sub-continent. Beginning with the Persians in the 6th century B.C., then with Alexander the Great, successive nations ruled and influenced Pakistan, ultimately separating the nation from Indian influence. Industries in modern-day Pakistan include textiles, cement and paper.

A traditional chicken and rice dish, flavored with herbs and spices!

MURGHI BIRYANI

1 3 1/2-lb. chicken, fryer	1 teaspoon powdered ginger
Salt to taste, about 1 teaspoon	1/2 teaspoon powdered cinnamon
2 cups yogurt	1/2 teaspoon powdered cumin
1/3 cup butter	4 or 5 sprigs fresh mint leaves
1 large onion, finely chopped	2 cups long grain rice
4 cloves garlic, minced	2 cups water
5 green chili peppers or	1/2 teaspoon saffron
Cayenne pepper to taste	1 tablespoon rose water
4 or 5 whole cloves	

Disjoint the chicken. Sprinkle with salt and cover with yogurt. Leave for 30 minutes. In a large, deep skillet, melt the butter and sauté the onion. Add the garlic, chili peppers, cloves, ginger, cinnamon, cumin and mint. Place chicken in pan and simmer 30 minutes. Add the rice and 2 cups water. Season to taste. Swirl in the saffron, so as to streak the rice. Cover and steam for 25 minutes. Add rose water.

PICKLED LIMES OR LEMONS

Scrub limes well and slice them thin. Sprinkle generously with salt and let stand 24 hours in a colander. They will become very limp and lose their bitterness. Arrange in layers in a glass jar, sprinkle paprika between each layer. Cover with corn or nut oil. Cover jar and let stand 3 weeks until they are a beautiful orange color.

The Republic of Panama occupies the isthmus between Central and South America. Two mountain ranges run the length of the isthmus, and tropical rain forests cover the Caribbean coast and eastern Panama. Industries include oil refining, shipping, and international banking. Christopher Columbus visited the isthmus in 1502, and Vasco Nunez de Balboa crossed the country and "discovered" the Pacific Ocean in 1513. Panama was under Spanish influence until 1821, when it joined Columbia. It declared its independence from Columbia in 1903.

Fish is the national emblem of Panama.

ARROZ CON SENORITAS
(Rice and Little Scallops)

2 cups raw rice	1 teaspoon chili powder
4 cups water	1 clove garlic
Salt and pepper	2 tablespoons butter

Combine all in a large saucepan. Cook over low heat until rice is tender and fluffy. Add 2 cups scallops and juice of 1 lemon. Put in casserole and bake 8 minutes, at 325 degrees. Do not overcook scallops.

CHOCOLATE FRUIT

1 6-ounce package semi-sweet chocolate chips	1/4 cup half and half
	1 teaspoon vanilla extract

Melt chocolate chips in double boiler, add half and half. Stir until hot, add vanilla. Cut up slices of bananas, fresh pears, apples, pineapple, seedless grapes and chop some nuts. Serve each person sliced fruit, a small cup of hot chocolate and nuts. Let each dip his fruit into chocolate and then into nuts. If chocolate is too thick, thin with hot milk or cream. A marvelous dessert!

FABULOUS SOUR CREAM DIP
For Fresh Strawberries

4 cups sour cream (extra thick commercial)	1/3 cup dark brown sugar
	1/4 cup grand marnier or Curacao

Mix all together very quickly. Serve with fresh strawberries. *Do not over mix.

GOLD BRICK ICE CREAM BARS

Cut ice cream in sticks. Insert wooden skewer in end. Dip in melted mixture of 6 ounces semi-sweet chocolate pieces, 1 cup chopped peanuts and 1/4 cup butter. Allow to harden in freezer.

131

PEARS IN CHOCOLATE

12 firm ripe pears with stems, peeled. Core each pear from the bottom leaving the stem. If necessary, slice off bottom so they will stand up right.

Mix:

2 cups sugar	1/2 cup lemon juice
8 cups water	4 3-inch pieces of cinnamon

Bring to a boil and simmer about 15 minutes. Then add peeled pears and poach gently 15 minutes turning the pears several times. Cool pears overnight in syrup.

Next day remove pears from syrup and pat dry with paper toweling.

Melt 8 squares semi-sweet chocolate in top of double boiler. Add 1 stick of butter. Use a spoon and dip pears into chocolate to coat evenly. Place on waxed paper to drain. Place on serving dish. Keep cold. Serve with a dab of whipping cream.

RUM PUDDING
(Congealed)

2 egg yolks	1/2 cup sweet milk
2 tablespoons rum	1/2 pint whipped cream
Scant 1/2 cup sugar	2 beaten egg whites
1 tablespoon Knox gelatine	

Beat egg yolks until thick, add gradually 1/2 cup sugar. Dissolve gelatin in 1 tablespoon cold water. Heat milk and add softened gelatin mixture to hot milk. Add this to the eggs and sugar. Let cool until syrupy, then fold in whipped cream and stiffly beaten egg whites. Add rum last. Pour into sherbet cups and place in refrigerator to congeal. Serve with a small amount of whipped cream, sweetened, and sprinkle with nutmeg.

Papua New Quinea is the eastern part of the Island of New Guinea. Its population is made up of Papuano, Chinese, Austrialians and Polynesians. The country is slightly larger than California. Its terrain is mountainous with lowlands on the coast. The chief crops are coffee, coconuts and cocoa. The fishing industry is important to the economy as well as its mineral resources. Human remains have been found in New Guinea dating back 10,000 years. Many tribes of people live on the Islands with practically no communication, since so many languages are spoken.

1 lb. raw fish (tuna, red snapper or sea bass). Remove skin and dark meat and cut in strips 1 1/2 inches long, 3/4 inches wide and 1/8-inch thick. Chill. Serve with sauce made using 3/4 cup shoyu, and 1 1/2 teaspoons grated fresh ginger root, 1/2 teaspoon mustard and 1/2 teaspoon chili pepper.

RAW FISH WITH GINGER SHOYU SAUCE
(Sashime)

2 1/2 lbs. fresh spinach   3 cups shredded packaged coconut
1 teaspoon salt   2 cups coffee cream

Wash spinach and remove tough stems. Combine coconut and cream, let stand 30 minutes and simmer for 10 minutes over low heat. Cool and strain using a cheesecloth. Add salt to coconut cream and pour over spinach in a Pyrex dish or earthenware. Bake in a 300 degree oven until spinach is tender. Sprinkle with nutmeg if desired.

BAKED SPINACH WITH COCONUT CREAM

133

Paraguay is one of two landlocked countries in South America. The country is bisected by the Paraguay River. On the east are fertile plains and wooded slopes. To the west is the Chaco plain with marshes and scrub trees. Paraguay produces corn, wheat, cotton, beans, and peanuts, and has a growing food processing industry as well as wood products.

SOPA PARAGUAYA
(A National Dish)

1 large tomato, chopped	2 cups cornmeal
2 onions, chopped	1/2 lb. cheese, grated
Butter	1 tablespoon shortening
1/2 cup meat or chicken stock	1 cup milk
Salt	1 teaspoon baking powder

Fry the tomatoes and onions until brown. Add the stock and a dash of salt. Allow to boil. Mix the cornmeal with the cheese, shortening and milk in which the baking powder has been dissolved. When thoroughly blended, add the cooked tomatoes and onions. Pour into greased pan and bake in 350 degree oven until brown. Serve hot, cutting in thick slices. It's great served with Cevici!

CEVICI

1 lb. cod or white fish	1 bell pepper, chopped fine
1 cup lemon juice	1 red pepper, chopped fine
Salt	Boiling water
3 onions, sliced	

Cut fish in strips. Cover with lemon juice and salt. Place in refrigerator overnight. The lemon juice "cooks" the fish. Drain fish and serve covered with the onions and peppers, prepared by covering them with lemon juice. Then pour boiling water over the onions and peppers. Let stand 5 minutes. Then rinse with clear water. Serve over fish. Delicious!

CHOCOLATE LEAVES

Wash and dry thoroughly 10 to 12 small leaves with stems. Melt 1/2 cup semi-sweet chocolate chips in top of double boiler over hot, not boiling, water. Stir; remove from heat. Cool slightly. Carefully brush a thin layer (about 1/8-inch thick) of melted chocolate on underside of each leaf. Chocolate and leaf will separate more easily if edges are not covered. Place leaves on baking sheet. Chill until firm. Carefully peel leaf from chocolate. Store in refrigerator or freezer.

Peru, on the Pacific coast of South America, has been the world's top fishing nation in recent years, taking 1/6 of the world's tonnage. The temporary disappearance in 1972 of anchovies seriously affected the fishing industry until their return in 1974 with a shift of the ocean current. The land has an arid coastal strip which is irrigated to provide crop growing land. The Andes cover 27% of the land area. The uplands are well watered however, producing crops of cotton, sugar, coffee, rice and potatoes. Industries include fish meal and steel.

A wonderful salad that is very popular in Lima, Peru!

ENSALADA PARA PAELLA

Shred lettuce. Place sliced tomatoes, anchovies and pitted olives (black and green), sliced sweet onions, and grapefruit sections over top of lettuce. Serve with garlic dressing:

1/2 cup sugar	1 clove garlic
1/4 cup tomato catsup	1/3 cup vinegar
2 tablespoons Worcestershire Sauce	1 cup salad oil

Mix all ingredients together. Serve over salad! This dish is great served with Paella.

---

1 lb. rice	1 teaspoon garlic, minced
1/2 lb. pork spareribs	1 bell pepper
1 chicken, cut in pieces	2 onions
1 cup shrimp	1 cup olive oil
1 cup peas, cooked	1 quart water
1 can mussels	Salt to taste
1 can or 1/2 cup pimentos	Dash of saffron
4 cups tomatoes	

PAELLA

Fry chicken, spareribs and saffron lightly in oil. Add seasonings, tomatoes, garlic, pepper and onions. You can pureé these. I like them in pieces. Let cook until meat is tender about 45 minutes to 1 hour. Add rice, water and salt. When rice is almost cooked, add sweet pimentos, peas, shrimp and mussels. Cook very slowly until rice is done. Mixture should be dry with each grain of rice fluffy. You may need to add a little more water. Do not stir! Cook in earthenware if possible.

GAZPACHO
(Quick)

12 cups tomato soup
2 cups minced cucumbers
1/2 cup minced green onions
1 cup finely cut celery

2 bell peppers, finely cut
Dash salt
4 cloves garlic, run through press

Mix all ingredients. Thin down with tomato juice. Chill overnight. Serve ice cold!

CHICKEN WITH CURACAO

3 tablespoons all-purpose flour
1 teaspoon salt
4 chicken breast, skinned, boned, and halved
4 chicken thighs, skinned and boned
1 tablespoon butter
1 tablespoon cooking oil

2 tablespoons curacao
2 cups chicken boullion
1 cup sliced fresh mushrooms
1 tablespoon butter, melted
1/2 cup whipping cream
Orange wedges
Seedless grapes

Combine flour and salt, coat chicken pieces in flour mixture. Heat 1 tablespoon butter and oil in a large skillet. Add chicken and cook for 5 minutes on each side. Place chicken in a 9 x 9 x 2-inch baking pan and bake in a 350 degree oven uncovered for 20 minutes. Pour fat from skillet and add curacao and boullion. Bring just to a simmer. Add chicken and simmer uncovered for 20 minutes or until tender. Cook mushrooms in 1 tablespoon butter, add to chicken along with cream. Spoon into a chafing dish and garnish with orange wedges and grapes, or serve fruits in compotes. Serve with black beans and rice. Makes 4 servings.

The Philippino's cooking has an international flavor. The Chinese brought bamboo shoots, bean sprouts, cabbage, egg noodles and soy to this country. The Spaniards introduced tomatoes, garlic, cocoa, sweet potatoes, squash, eggplant, peppers, and garbonzas.

---

1 6-lb. sea bass or other choice fish	1/4 teaspoon bay leaf, powdered
1/4 cup lime juice	1/4 teaspoon cayenne
Salt to taste	1 cup dry bread crumbs
3 cups chopped, salted nuts	1 cup milk
1 cup cheddar cheese, grated	1/3 cup butter
1/4 cup scraped onion	1/4 cup sherry

PESCADO
TAGALOG
(Fish Bake)

Rub clean scraped fish inside and out with lime juice. Sprinkle with salt. Chill 2 hours in refrigerator. Drain the lime juice off the fish. Place on well-greased baking sheet. Mix 2 1/2 cups nuts, cheese, onion, bay leaf, cayenne, and 1/2 cup of the bread crumbs. Pour in milk and stir to a thick paste.
Cover fish with the nut mixture. Sprinkle the remaining bread crumbs over and bake 45 minutes in 375 degree oven. As the fish bakes, baste several times with melted butter and sherry. When ready to serve, transfer to platter and sprinkle with remaining nuts.

3/4 cup sugar, caramelized	1/4 cup butter
1/2 cup plain sugar	Pinch salt
1 cup canned milk	3 eggs

CARAMEL
BUTTER
CUSTARD

Caramelize sugar until amber colored. Heat milk, butter and remaining sugar and salt to scalding. Have pan large so when you pour the hot caramelized sugar into the hot milk it has room to bubble up. Take 1 cup of the hot milk-caramel mixture and combine with beaten eggs. Then add egg mixture back with rest of custard, beating quickly. Pour into individual buttered custard cups. Bake until set 15-20 minutes. Chill and serve with whipping cream and chopped ginger.

Poland has a national cookery that dates back hundreds of years. An old Polish custom is to have the larder filled and well stocked always for unexpected guests. Quite often in olden days, an extra plate and chair was provided for the wayfarer, who might be the Christ, come in disguise. The Polish people are fine gourmets and enjoy good food!

BIGOS
(Sauerkraut with Meat and Game)

2 1/2 lbs. sauerkraut
1/2 lb. cooked poultry or game
1/4 lb. Polish sausage, sliced thin
2 apples, diced
4 tablespoons shortening
2 tablespoons flour

2 tablespoons meat glaze or
   seasoning
2 tablespoons tomato purée
1 onion, chopped
1 cup vodka
1/2 cup white wine

Wash sauerkraut in water. Scald in hot water. Drain. Melt shortening in skillet and fry onion until brown. Add the flour. Then add the meat glaze, tomato purée, vodka and wine. Mix well. In a Pyrex dish, layer the sauerkraut, meat, sausage and diced apples. Repeat. Moisten each layer with vodka and wine mixture. Cover and bake 2 hours at 300 degrees.

SNIEZKI
(Snowballs)

2 egg whites, beaten stiff
2 1/2 tablespoons powdered sugar

1/2 teaspoon vanilla
1 1/4 cups milk

Beat egg whites. Add powdered sugar and vanilla. Bring milk to a boil in saucepan. Drop egg whites in by spoonfuls. Cover pan. Set off heat and let stand 10 minutes. Remove snowballs and serve with Custard Sauce!

POLISH PIEROGI

1 cup sifted flour
1 teaspoon salt
1 egg
1 tablespoon dairy sour cream
1/4 cup water

1 8-ounce small curd, cottage
   cheese, drained
1/2 cup butter
1/2 cup fine dry bread or vanilla
   cookie crumbs

Combine flour, salt, egg, sour cream and water and mix until dough is easy to handle. Turn dough out onto lightly floured board and knead until smooth, using as little flour as possible. Roll dough out very thin, thinner than pie crust. Sprinkle a small amount of flour on rolling pin if it sticks to pin. Cut dough into circles with a 3-inch glass. Place 1 teaspoon cottage cheese in center of circle. Fold circle in half and press edges of dough together with fingers.

Fill a large kettle with water, cover and bring to a boil over high heat. Drop in a few Pierogi at a time. Cook 3 minutes, drain in colander. Melt butter, add crumbs and cook until crumbs are browned. Sprinkle crumbs over Pierogi just before serving. Makes about 30.

500 grams pork		1 onion
800 grams sauerkraut		2 cloves garlic
400 grams potatoes, diced		50 grams salt pork or bacon
1 carrot		2 tablespoons flour
1 parsley root (parsnip)		

SAUERKRAUT SOUP

Stew the pork until done. Cut into cubes. Strain the stock, add the strained sauerkraut and stew until it is done. Sauté the onion, parsnip and carrot in butter. Blend in flour and lightly brown. Add diced raw patotoes. Season to taste with salt and pepper and simmer for 30 more minutes or until potatoes are done. Serve with a dab of sour cream and minced parsley.

Pare and dice vegetables. Cook in chicken stock until tender, about 20 minutes. Add 1 tablespoon of sugar, 2 tablespoons butter. Salt to taste. Thicken juice with a little flour if desired. Serve immediately.

A Guest in my home is God in my home.

Slightly smaller than the state of Indiana, Portugal sits at the southwest extreme of the European continent. The northern part of Portugal is mountainous, cool and rainy, while the south has drier, rolling plains. Portugal has been an independent state since the 12th Century, and was a monarchy until 1910. Current industries include textiles, pottery and shipbuilding. The Portuguese grow grain, corn, rice, grapes and olives.

From Portugal comes a great white wine, Amarante. Use when new, not aged.

Great with roast pork!

FRIED SWEET POTATOES

Use large sweet potatoes, boiled in jackets until tender. Cool overnight. Peel and slice 1/4-inch thick. Dip in batter and fry until brown. Serve with powdered sugar and grated orange rind.

Batter:	2 tablespoons oil
2/3 cup flour	2/3 cup milk
1/4 teaspoon salt	1 egg white, beaten stiff
1 teaspoon baking powder	1 teaspoon cinnamon

Combine all these ingredients and mix into a thick batter. Use to dip yams into. Fry in butter.

TARRIJAS de NATA
(Fried Cream)

3 egg yolks, beaten lightly	Cinnamon
1 cup whipping cream	Powdered sugar
1 egg, beaten	

Whip the beaten egg yolks into the cream. Grease a pan well and spread the whipped cream mixture in it, about 1/2-inch thick. Place over a very slow flame, until set. Allow to cool. Cut into slices, lift out with spatula. Brush with beaten egg and fry in hot butter. Serve hot with sprinkled cinnamon and powdered sugar.

LOIN OF PORK
(LOMBO DE PORCO)

3 lbs. loin of pork	1/3 cup parsley
3 onions, sliced	3 tablespoons oil
3 tomatoes, sliced	3/4 cup wine (Maderia)
3 carrots, sliced	

Rub pork with salt. Place in pan with oil and cook until brown on all sides. Add vegetables and wine. Cover and bake for 3 hours until tender in 300 degree oven. Thicken sauce and pour over pork.

The State of Oatar is 4000 square miles, smaller than Connecticut, on a peninsula on the west coast of the Persian gulf. The land itself is mostly flat desert, but crude oil reserves have made the country prosperous. The state was under the control of Bahrain until the Ottoman Turks took power in 1872. Oatar became independent in 1971.

AUBERGINE SALAD
(Eggplant Salad)

1 large eggplant	Salt and pepper to taste
3 to 4 tomatoes, peeled and seeded	2 to 3 tablespoons olive oil
1 large Spanish or Bermuda onion	1 tablespoon lemon juice
3 tablespoons olive oil	1 to 2 heads lettuce, Boston or Bibb
1 clove garlic, put through garlic press	Yogurt dressing
	3 hard cooked eggs
2 large green peppers, shredded	1 small can black olives, pitted

Cut eggplant in half lengthwise, sprinkle with salt and place on paper towels for 30 minutes. Wipe dry and remove as much salt as possible. Peel and slice the eggplant into 1/2-inch slices. Blanch tomatoes by dipping them in boiling water for 20 seconds. Then peel and seed. Peel and thinly slice onion. Heat 3 tablespoons olive oil in frying pan; add garlic and sliced onions. Sauté for 5 minutes, then put eggplant on top of onions and continue cooking, covered, until eggplant and onions are soft. Add green pepper, salt to taste, and pepper. Cook for half a minute, stir, add tomatoes, stir again, take pan off heat. Do not cook tomatoes. Put into dish and cool. Moisten cooled salad with 2 or 3 tablespoons olive oil and 1 tablespoon lemon juice. Refrigerate for 1 hour. To serve, arrange lettuce leaves on platter. Spoon salad onto leaves and put a dab of yogurt dressing on top.

YOGURT DRESSING

1 clove garlic, put through garlic press	Freshly ground pepper
1/4 teaspoon salt	1 cup yogurt
1 teaspoon paprika	Squeeze of lemon juice

Mix garlic, salt, paprika and pepper into yogurt with a fork. Add a squeeze of lemon juice, if desired. Taste for seasoning.

Try 3 tablespoons honey, 3 tablespoons boiling water over green Gatorade for a refreshing drink. Serve over crushed ice.

Romania is in southeast Europe on the Black Sea. The Carpathian Mountains encase the North Central Transylvania Plateau. There are wide plains south and east of the mountains. Romania produces steel and other metals, machinery, and oil products. Romania became a separate country in 1861, and in 1877 declared its independence from Turkey.

GARLIC SOUP
(With Dill)

6 garlic buds, chopped
2 large onions, chopped
Salt and pepper
2 tablespoons fat
1 tablespoon scallions

1 tablespoon parsley, chopped
1 tablespoon flour
1 tablespoon dill, chopped
2 quarts water

Boil garlic and onions in 2 quarts water until tender. Fry scallions in 2 tablespoons fat until tender. Stir in parsley and flour. Add 1 cup boiling water and stir until smooth. Add to garlic and onions in broth. Simmer 10 minutes longer. Strain soup if desired and serve sprinkled with chopped dill.

CABBAGE STUFFED WITH MEAT
(Sarmale)

1 head of cabbage
Scald with boiling water; let stand 30 minutes

Brown together for stuffing:
1 onion chopped with 2 tablespoons oil

1/4 teaspoon thyme, 4 tablespoons rice
1 tablespoon chopped leek
1 lb. ground beef
Salt and pepper to taste

Put a teaspoon of filling in each cabbage leaf; roll right and left sides toward center, then roll up each cabbage leaf into a loose roll.

Make layers of bacon drippings, drained bacon, sauerkraut, and sliced pork loin and cabbage rolls until the pot is full. Cover with sauerkraut juice or tomato juice and simmer for 2 hours over very low heat. Then place in 300 degree oven for 1 hour. Serve with sour cream and hot cornmeal dish (Mamaliga).

Rwanda, in East Central Africa, is approximately the size of Maryland. Grassy uplands and hills cover most of the country, with a chain of volcanos in the northwest. Crops include coffee, cotton, tea, pyrethrum, and tobacco. Tin and gold are mined as well. Rwanda, which had been part of the Belgian UN trusteeship, became independent July 1, 1962.

CREAM OF PUMPKIN SOUP

1/4 cup chopped onion	1 cup canned pumpkin
1/4 cup butter	1 teaspoon salt
4 cups chicken broth	1/2 teaspoon black pepper
1 can evaporated milk	

Sauté onion and butter in large saucepan. Add 4 cups chicken broth and canned milk and pumpkin. Simmer for 20 minutes. Do not boil. Season with salt and pepper. Serve hot!

CUCUMBER BUTTERMILK SOUP

(Cold) 6 Servings

2 10-oz. cans mushroom soup	1/2 cup minced celery
2 cups buttermilk	2 tablespoons minced green onions
1 cup minced seeded cucumbers	

Mix all together and chill. Serve with a dab of sour cream and paprika.

GIN SOUP

2 cups clam juice	2 tablespoons minced parsley
2 cups chicken broth	Onion salt
1 pint heavy cream	Celery salt
1 tablespoon chopped dill or dill seed	2 to 3 tablespoons cornstarch
2 tablespoons chopped chives	2/3 cup gin

Dissolve cornstarch in a little water. Mix other ingredients, except gin and cornstarch, and bring to a boil. Thicken soup with cornstarch mixture. Add gin, bring to a boil and let simmer a few minutes. Season to taste. Serve hot or cold.

Saint Lucia is second largest of the Windward Islands located in the eastern Caribbean, with Martinque to the north and St. Vincent to the southwest. The island is volcanic in nature and mountainous. The island is visited by tourists, but also has a construction industry. Chief crops include bananas, coconuts, cocoa, citrus fruits and spices.

GLAZED HAM

5 lb. ham	1/4 teaspoon ground cloves
1 orange, large, sliced	1 orange (juice and peel)
1 teaspoon whole cloves	1 tablespoon Dijon mustard
3/4 cup brown sugar	2 cups Port wine jelly

Score ham. Garnish with orange slices and stud with whole cloves. Bake in preheated 350 degree oven 1 hour and 40 minutes (20 minutes per pound). Meanwhile, prepare glaze by mixing together all remaining ingredients. Half an hour before ham is done, remove from oven and spoon on glaze; baste with additional glaze occasionally during last half hour. Serve with additional Port wine jelly.

PORT-SPICES JELLY

3 cups sugar	2 whole allspice
2 cups ruby Port	1/2 bottle liquid pectin (Full bottle
2 sticks cinnamon	is 6 ounces)
1 teaspoon whole cloves	

Warm Port and spices slowly in saucepan. Simmer 5 minutes. Strain mixture into top of double boiler. Add sugar and stir over boiling water until it completely dissolves. Remove from heat. Stir in pectin, and skim off any foam. Pour or ladle into containers. Seal with melted paraffin.

SANGRIA-ORANGE JELLY

3 1/2 cups sugar	2 tablespoons grated orange rind
2 cups sangria, bottled, pre-mixed	1/2 bottle liquid pectin (Full bottle
type	is 6 ounces)
1/2 cup orange juice	

Combine all ingredients except pectin in top of double boiler. Stir over boiling water until sugar dissolves completely — about 10 minutes. Remove from heat. Stir in pectin and skim off any foam. Pour into containers and seal with melted paraffin.
Note: Flavor improves if jelly sets at least two weeks.
Serve with roast beef, boiled steak or baked ham. Or mix one jar (about 8 ounces) jelly with 1/2 cup brown sugar and use as baked ham glaze.

FLAGS OF THE UNITED NATIONS

SAMOA

SOLOMON ISLANDS

SWAZILAND

SAO TOME e PRINCIPE

SOMALIA

SWEDEN

SAUDI ARABIA

SOUTH AFRICA

SENEGAL

SPAIN

SEYCHELLES

SRI LANKA

SIERRA LEONE

SUDAN

SINGAPORE

SURINAM

Samoa is a group of islands with a total area about the size of Rhode Island. The chief islands are Savai'i and Upolu. The Samoans grow cocoa, coconuts and bananas. They also export hardwoods. The Samoans are a warm and friendly people with a special reputation for hospitality.

5-6 lb. loin or pork roast	3 cloves garlic, finely chopped
dry mustard	2 tablespoons grated fresh ginger,
thyme	or 6 pieces of candied ginger cut
1/2 cup and 2 tablespoons sherry	in slivers
1/2 cup and 1 tablespoon soy sauce	8-ounce jar apple or currant jelly

COLD BARBECUED LOIN OF PORK

Have the roast boned and tied. Rub with dry mustard and thyme. Make a marinade of the 1/2 cup soy sauce, garlic and ginger and pour over the pork. Marinate for about 2 hours, turning several times as it soaks. You may let it stand all night in the refrigerator and roast it the next morning.

To cook, remove from the marinade and arrange a meat thermometer in the thickest part of the roast. Cook at 325 degrees, allowing about 25 minutes per pound. Baste with the marinade. When the thermometer reads 175 degrees, the pork is done.

Melt the jelly in a heavy pan over a medium flame and when it is bubbly, add the 1 tablespoon soy and 2 tablespoons Sherry. Let it cook down for a minute or two, stirring constantly. Spoon over the pork and cool. Do not refrigerate unless the day is exceptionally hot (and you lack air-conditioning!).

Garnish with sliced tomatoes, thinly sliced onions and sliced cucumbers. Serve with a bowl of horseradish applesauce, made by blending 2 cups applesauce and 6 tablespoons fresh grated horseradish or 4 tablespoons bottled horseradish, drained. Chill before using.

Sao Tome e Principe is located in the Gulf of Guinea about 125 miles from West Central Africa. These volcanic islands have lush forests and productive croplands. They were discovered in 1471 by the Portuguese who brought the first settlers. Their principal crops are coffee, cocoa, coconut and cinchona (the dried bark is used for quinine).

JOLLOF

| 1 whole frying chicken rubbed with lemon, salt and garlic | Marinate one night. |
| | 4 tomatoes and onions sliced |

Stew chicken in 4 cups of water until tender. Strain off broth and remove chicken from bones and brown in deep fat. To the chicken broth add 1/4 teaspoon thyme, 2 bay leaves, juice and grated rind of 2 lemons and 1 cup of browned rice (sautéed in oil until brown). Mix browned pieces of chicken with rice and steam covered until rice is fluffy, about 20 minutes. Serve with fresh coconut grated over top. Serve with green salad.

HOT HONEY PUNCH

| 2 tablespoons lemon crystals | 2 cups hot boiling water |
| 6 tablespoons strained honey | 1 cup brandy |

Add lemon crystals and honey to boiling water. Stir until blended. Add 1 cup brandy and serve in punch cups with a sprinkling of ground nutmeg.

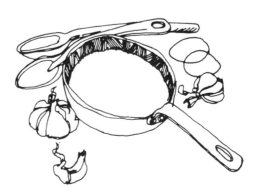

The kingdom of Saudi Arabia occupies most of the Arabian Peninsula in the middle east. Arabia was united by Mohammed early in the 7th Century. Arabia was not really united again until the founder of the Saudi dynasty, Saud, overthrew Turkish rule in 1913. The country is governed by a monarchy, the king exercising authority with a Council of Ministers. The Islamic religious code is the law of the land. The discovery of oil in the 1930's transformed the country.

---

2 lbs. ground lamb	1/2 cup milk
1/4 teaspoon allspice	1 teaspoon baking powder
1/4 teaspoon cloves	3 sprigs mint, chopped
Juice of 1/2 lemon	1/2 cup bread crumbs
1 onion, minced	1 teaspoon salt
1 egg, beaten	Pepper to taste

KAFTA KABOBS
(Lamburgers on skewers with Vegetables)

Mix all ingredients and knead well. Shape around skewer in balls. Alternate with bell pepper pieces, tomatoes and onions. Broil over charcoal or in oven until done.

1/2 lb. butter	1 teaspoon orange flower water
1/2 lb. flour	Almonds, walnuts and pistachios
1/2 lb. powdered sugar	

GHOORABEE
(Cookies)

Cream butter and sugar. Add flour. Add a little milk, if necessary, to make a light dough. Form round cookies, press nuts on top and bake in 350 degree oven until light brown.

1 cup rice
1/8 teaspoon allspice
1 cup orange juice

RIZ BOOR-DOO-KAU
(Rice in Orange Juice)

Cook rice until done. Add orange juice and allspice. Simmer 3 minutes. Serve with Kabobs. If used for dessert, add honey to sweeten and serve with whipped cream.

1 teaspoon Arabian coffee to each cup of water. Bring water to a boil, then add coffee. A creamy topping will form. Add 1 tablespoon rosewater to each 8 cups of coffee. Allow to perk for 3 minutes. When serving, add 1 cardamon seed to each cup. Sweeten with honey.

ARABIAN COFFEE

147

The Republic of Senegal is on the western extreme of Africa. The country's industry includes food processing, chemicals, and cement. Peanuts are its chief export. The country was settled first by Portuguese in the 15th century. Senegal became independent in 1960.

LACY-EDGED CORNMEAL PANCAKES

1 cup cornmeal
1/2 teaspoon salt
1/2 teaspoon soda

1 whole egg
1 1/4 cups buttermilk

Blend all ingredients together. Drop by tablespoons from 7 inches high, onto hot skillet; this spreads batter to make lace. Serve with Brown Sugar Syrup:

1 cup dark brown sugar
1/4 cup water
1 tablespoon butter

Mix all ingredients, and cook until thick like syrup.

YAM BALLS FUFU

1 lb. yams
Salt to taste
1 cup cold water

Peel yams, slice and put in cold salted water. Set on stove and simmer for 1 hour. Drain well. Mash yams, and shape into round balls and serve around or in stew.

Time is that great straightener of crooked ways,
That great curer of angry and unpoised minds,
That great evener of all inequalities.

The Seychelles are a group of 86 islands located in the Indian Ocean about 700 miles from Madagascar. The chief industry there is food processing, and the islanders grow coconuts, cinnamon, vanilla, and patchouli.* Originally under the dominion of France and then of England, the Seychelles became independent in 1976.

CINNAMON CRISPIES

1 pkg. active dry or compressed yeast	2 well-beaten eggs
1/4 cup water	1 teaspoons vanilla
1 cup milk	5 cups sifted flour
1/2 cup sugar	3/4 cup sugar
1/3 cup shortening	1 tablespoon cinnamon
1 1/2 teaspoons salt	1/2 cup soft butter

Soften yeast in water. Scald milk, add sugar, shortening, salt and cool to lukewarm. Stir in eggs, vanilla and 2 cups flour. Add softened yeast and beat well. Add remaining flour to make a soft dough. Place in greased bowl, cover and let rise in warm place until double in bulk (about 1 1/2 hours). Punch down, roll out on lightly floured board in a rectangle 12 x 16 and 1/4-inch thick. Mix 3/4 cup sugar and cinnamon. Spread dough with 1/3 of butter and sprinkle with 1/4 of sugar and cinnamon mixture. Fold in thirds and roll to a 12 x 16-inch rectangle. Again spread with 1/3 of butter and sprinkle with 1/4 of sugar mixture; fold and roll to 12 x 24-inch rectangle. Spread with remaining butter and sprinkle with 1/4 the sugar mixture. Roll as for jelly roll. Cut into 24 one-inch slices. Sprinkle remaining sugar-cinnamon mixture on a sheet of waxed paper. Dip cut side down in sugar mixture and roll thin with rolling pin. Place on greased cookie sheets, cover and let rise 15 minutes. Bake in 350 degrees oven about 10 to 12 minutes or until lightly browned and crisp. This is a delicious breakfast roll. (You may find, as I did, that you will need to make more sugar-cinnamon mixture to roll out the crispies in.)

* Patchouli is a well-known perfume with a dry musty odor. It is very popular in Asia. The perfume is made from the oil in the leaves of the Patchouli plant belonging to the mint family.

Sierra Leone means mountain of the lion. The ocean roars so loud that its early settlers named it for a roaring lion. Here the smell of the sea, the gorgeous sunsets over the Atlantic, and the smell of the jungle leave one with a lasting memory of unforgettable Africa.

BAKED PUMPKIN

Cut pumpkin into large servings, leaving skin on. Sprinkle with powdered cinnamon and dark brown sugar. Dot with butter or palm oil, if you can find it. Bake in covered pan with just a little water for 1 hour at 350 degrees. When ready to serve, squeeze a fresh lime over it and eat while hot.

8 slices pineapple, drained on paper towels

PINEAPPLE PEANUT FRITTERS

1 cup sifted flour	1 egg, slightly beaten
1 teaspoon baking powder	1/4 cup peanuts, finely chopped
1/2 teaspoon salt	3/4 cup milk
2 tablespoons sugar	1 tablespoon oil

Mix all ingredients. Dip pineapple in batter and fry in hot deep fat until golden, brown. Serve hot with a dot of whipped cream flavored with rum.

SOUR CREAM LEMON SHERBET

1 1/3 cups sugar	Pinch of salt
2/3 cups lemon juice	1 pkg. gelatin dissolved in 1/4 cup
3 cups milk	water and then melted over hot
1 cup sour cream	water

Dissolve sugar in lemon juice. Add rest of ingredients and freeze in freezer.

150

The island country of Singapore is 226 square miles in area, smaller than New York City. It is off the tip of the Malayan Peninsula in southeast Asia. The flat, formerly swampy nation includes nearly 40 isles. Chief industries are shipbuilding and oil refining. Singapore was founded in 1819 by Sir Thomas Stanford Raffles, and was a British Colony until 1959.

BEEF WITH MUSHROOMS

1 lb. beef, cut in strips
1 cup mushrooms
2 teaspoons thick soy sauce
4 teaspoons onions, finely sliced
2 teaspoons fresh ginger, shredded

2 teaspoons cornflour, mixed with
   1 cup mushroom juice
Salt and pepper to taste
8 teaspoons oil

Heat 1/2 the oil in a pan, brown the onions. Remove fried onions. Use rest of oil to fry beef till brown. Add onions, mushrooms, ginger, salt, pepper and soy sauce. Mix together, then add the cornflour and mushroom juice. Cook a few seconds to thicken. Serve.

SWEET SOUR PORK RIBS

2 lbs. pork ribs, 3-inch pieces
3 tablespoons sugar
2 teaspoons salt
1/2 cup soy sauce

4 cloves garlic, crushed
2 tablespoons dry sherry
2 tablespoons honey
1/2 teaspoon fine spice powder

Rub the ribs with 2 teaspoons sugar and salt. Let stand 1 hour. Mix all ingredients, except honey. Pour over ribs and marinate overnight. Place on rack over hot water and bake 2 hours in 350 degree oven, basting with marinade. When done brush with honey and bake 20 minutes longer. Serve with Chinese Mustard and Plum Sauce!

SPICE POWDER

2 teaspoons ground coriander
2 teaspoons dried tarragon leaves
2 teaspoons ground allspice
1 teaspoon freshly grated nutmeg

1 teaspoon ground cinnamon
1/2 teaspoon ground cardamon
1/2 teaspoon dried marjoram leaves
1/8 teaspoon ground cloves

Blend all ingredients in blender container; store in tightly sealed jar.

Located in the Melanesian archipelago in the western pacific, this group of 14 islands is nearest to Papua New Guinea. The Islands' chief industry is fish canning, but crops of coconuts, cocoa, rice, and oil palm are grown, also. Independence was formally obtained in 1978.

FISH BAKED IN TI LEAVES

1 1/2 lbs. fish slices (butterfish, halibut or mahimahi)	1 1/2 tablespoons ice cream salt Ti leaves or corn husks

Clean and scale fish. Reek with salt, wrap in ti leaves tying ends together. Bake the fish in a 350 degrees oven for 1 hour. I like to add 1 slice of bacon, 1 bay leaf, and slice of onion and 1 slice green pepper to package before tying up. Add just enough water to baking pan to cover bottom. Serve with baked sweet potatoes or taro root or bread fruit.

TORO ROOT

Wash and scrub root. Bake 1 1/2 hours at 350 degrees. Peel and serve hot with butter, salt and pepper.

BREAD FRUIT

Bread fruit can be washed, scraped and baked until the outside is charred. The inside is then mashed with various seasonings or coconut cream.

PLANTAIN

Boil Plantain in skin for 30 minutes. Peel. Mash and serve with salt and pepper and butter.

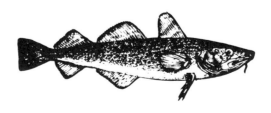

Somalia, which is slightly smaller than Texas is on the eastern horn of Africa. Crops include incense, sugar, bananas, and sorghum. There is not a large amount of industry, but there are deposits of iron, tin, gypsum and sandstone.

BANANA JAM

2 cups sugar
1/2 cup strained lemon juice
1 tablespoon finely, grated lemon
   peel

6 medium sized ripe bananas,
   peeled and sliced in 1/4 inch pieces

Combine sugar, lemon juice and lemon peel in a Pyrex bowl. Stir until sugar is dissolved. Drop in bananas and stir until they are evenly coated. Handle gently. Let bananas marinate for 2 hours. With a stainless steel spoon, transfer the banana mixture to a 2-quart stainless steel pan. Bring to a boil, then reduce heat and simmer uncovered for 30 minutes until jam is thick. Stir frequently. Ladle into hot sterilized jars and seal.

PEAR CHIPS

4 lbs. sugar
4 cups water
2 lemons, sliced paper-thin
1/4 cup chopped crystalized ginger

6 whole allspice
4 lbs. firm ripe pears,
   peeled and sliced very thin

Combine sugar and water in a large saucepan. Place over medium heat and bring to a boil. Get all the other ingredients and boil until the pears are transparent and tender and the syrup thickens. Pour into sterilized jelly glasses and seal.

LEMON GARLIC PICKLE

12 large lemons
1/2 cup salt
8 garlic cloves, peeled
1 tablespoon each mace,
   nutmeg
   allspice

1 teaspoon red pepper
4 tablespoons dry mustard
1/2 gallon vinegar

Wash and dry lemons and cut lengthwise into 8 pieces. Put cuts in enamel pan with the salt, garlic, mace, nutmeg and allspice, red pepper and mustard. Add vinegar. Bring slowly to a boil. Simmer 30 minutes. Pour into a large stone jar. Stir daily for 1 month. Then seal in sterilized jars.

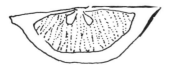

The Republic of South Africa, at the southern extreme of the continent, is 4/5ths the size of Alaska. The large interior plateau reaches close to the country's 2,700 mile coast line. Industries include steel, tires, motors, textiles, and plastics. The most important resource is the country's large deposits of gold and gem diamonds; they are the largest producers of these resources as well as antimony, platinum and chrome in the world. South Africa became a republic in 1861.

MARINATED SOUTH AFRICAN LOBSTER TAILS

12 4 to 6-ounce lobster tails, cooked
1 large bottle Italian Dressing
1 cup olive oil
3 tablespoons wine vinegar
1 teaspoon oregano
Juice of 1 lemon
3 cloves garlic, minced

1/2 cup parsley flakes
1/2 teaspoon salt
1 teaspoon cracked pepper
1/2 cup Parmesan cheese
2 tablespoons red or white wine
2 tablespoons Worcestershire Sauce

Mix all ingredients together and refrigerate overnight.

SOUTH AFRICAN PICKLED SPICED PEACHES

1/4 cup oil
1 1/2 cups onions, cut in strips
6 pods garlic, finely chopped
1 tablespoon curry powder
1 teaspoon coriander, ground
1 cup vinegar

1 cup sugar
2 teaspoons hot peppers, crumbled
1 tablespoon whole cloves
1 teaspoon salt
12 large peaches

Heat the oil in a large, heavy saucepan and cook the onions and garlic for about 4 or 5 minutes, until soft, but not brown. Then add all the rest of the spices. Bring to a boil and let simmer for 10 minutes. Skin the peaches by dropping them into boiling water for about 1 minute. Take a knife and slip off skin. Cut the peaches in 1/2-inch wide wedges. Put in hot syrup, stirring to coat each piece. Cover and let simmer until tender, 20 to 25 minutes. Put in hot sterilized jars.

GREEN SEASONING

2 medium carrots
10 green onions
1 cup parsley
1 1/2 tablespoons thyme

1/4 cup hot chillies, minced
4 cloves garlic
1 teaspoon salt
3/4 cup vinegar

Grind all ingredients as fine as possible; mix with vinegar. Bring to a boil and simmer for 20 minutes. Put in hot sterilized jars. Use to season foods.

The interior of Spain is a high plateau broken by mountain ranges and river valleys. The northwest is heavily watered; the south has lowlands and a Mediterranean climate. Spain grows grains, olives, grapes, citrus fruits, onions, and almonds. Industrial production includes machinery, textiles, shoes, paper, ships, cement. Spain has been transformed from an agricultural nation to one of the world's most important industrial powers.

Alella is a good white, Spanish table wine that is sold in a long, fluted bottle.

GAZPACHO ANDALUZ

2 tomatoes, peeled
1 cucumber, peeled and sliced
2 green peppers, seeded and sliced
1 small onion, peeled
1 clove garlic
3 tablespoons wine vinegar

6 slices white bread, trimmed and cubed
4 cups water
1 1/2 teaspoons salt
3 tablespoons olive oil

Combine all ingredients. Put in electric blender, purée until very smooth. Chill. Just before serving, check consistency. The soup should be thick, but not solid. Add a little ice water if necessary. Serve in cups, with the following garnish in individual bowls. Serves 8.

Garnish:
1 cup croutons

1/2 cup chopped green onions
1 cup diced cucumbers

PAELLA VALENCIANA

2 dozen clams
2 1 to 1 1/2-lb. live lobsters
1 3-lb. chicken, disjointed
1/2 cup lard or olive oil
2 sweet red peppers, cut julienne
4 cups long grain rice

1/2 teaspoon powdered saffron
8 cups boiling chicken broth or water
1 clove garlic, minced
2 1/2 teaspoons salt
1 cup canned green peas

Wash and scrub the clams. Cut the live lobsters into small pieces and put in the shells. Wash and dry the chicken. Heat the lard in a skillet. Brown the chicken pieces in it. A "paellera", a shallow, large two-handled metal pan, is customarily used for making paella. Any large shallow pan can be used. Arrange the chicken in the pan, then over it the clams, lobster and peppers. Spread the rice over all. Mix together saffron, broth, garlic and salt. Pour the mixture into the pan. Cover, bring to a boil and cook over high heat 10 minutes. Arrange the peas on top of the rice. Re-cover and cook over low heat 10 minutes longer, or until the rice is tender. Serve directly from the pan. Serves 8.

155

Sri Lanka, formerly Ceylon, is an island republic in the Indian Ocean with a flat coasted area, and inland the mountains rise to over 8,000 feet. The climate is hot and humid, with swift mountain streams. The islands produce many precious stones including sapphire, ruby and cat's eye. The principal agricultural products are tea, rubber, coconuts, rice, cocoa, cinnamon, citronella and tobacco.

HUMMUS bi TAHINA GARBANZO SPREAD
(About 2 1/2 cups)

1 can drained Garbanzo beans (chick peas)	2 tablespoons lemon juice
1/2 cup water *from beans*	1/2 cup Sesame Sauce (see recipe below)
1 clove garlic	Parsley or mint for garnish
1 teaspoon salt	

Place all but last two ingredients in blender container and blend smooth, gradually adding the Sesame Sauce. Serve in a bowl with parsley or mint garnish. This is to be eaten with Arab bread.

SESAME SAUCE
(Taratoor)

(Use 1/2 cup in the Hummus, remainder as a sauce for the fried cauliflower)	3/4 to 1 cup cold water
2 cloves garlic	1/2 cup fresh lemon juice
1 cup tahina paste (ground hulled sesame seeds)	1 teaspoon salt

---

BAKLAVA
(Use 9 x 13-inch pan)

Syrup:	1 lb. filo dough
2 cups sugar	1 1/2 cups melted butter
1 cup water	1 1/2 lbs. ground walnuts
1 teaspoon lemon juice	1 cup sugar
1 tablespoon rosewater	1 tablespoon rosewater

Butter the pan. Boil sugar and water together until syrupy and add lemon juice and rosewater. Set aside. Cut filo sheet to fit the pan. Cover unused half with damp cloth to keep moist. Carefully separate the filo sheets, brushing each with butter. Stack the buttered sheets in the pan until half are used. Mix walnuts flavoring and sugar and distribute evenly over the stacked and buttered layers. Butter the remaining sheets as before and place on top of the nut filling. Using a sharp knife, cut the baklava into small diamond pieces. Bake at 275 degrees for about 1 1/2 hours until golden brown. Pour the reserved syrup over the baklava while hot.

The Democratic Republic of Sudan is the largest country in Africa, over one-fourth the size of the U.S. The northern part of the country is desert, and in the north is the mountainous Nubian desert. Sudan is the principal world source of gum arabic, with cotton as another main export. Mining of chrome, gold, and copper is also done. North Sudan is the site of the ancient kingdom of Nubia, settled by Egypt in antiquity.

GLAZED STEWED FRUIT

6 cups apples or peaches, peeled and sliced	3 cups sugar
Juice of 1 orange or 1 lemon	1 stick butter
3 cups water	Dash of cinnamon and nutmeg

Put fruit, sugar, water and butter in pan and boil until fruit is tender. Place in casserole, sprinkle with more sugar and spices. Bake until glazed and candied. Wow!

SORGHUM MILK PUNCH

2 cups milk	1/8 teaspoon salt
1/4 cup sorghum or molasses	1/2 teaspoon ginger

Mix and serve.

DATE CHUTNEY

1 lb. pitted, chopped dates	1 tablespoon chopped fresh, candied ginger
2 red hot peppers, crumbled	1 teaspon salt
1 tablespoon garlic, finely chopped	1 tablespoon garlic, minced
1 cup chopped onion	
1 cup red wine vinegar	

Place all ingredients in a deep pan and cover. Put in oven and cook in 300 degree oven about 1 hour. Stir often (excellent served with lamb.)

The Ethnic groups living in this country on the north shore of South America are varied. East Indians, Creoles, Javanese, Europeans and Chinese make the cuisine very exciting. The land is very flat and dikes are used to keep out the sea. The main industry is aluminum. The chief crops are rice, sugar and wonderful fruits. Interesting shops make it a delightful vacation spot. The Netherlands acquired Suriname from Britain in exchange for New York State in 1667. This country received its independence in 1975.

NAPOLEONS

Pastry:
- 1 1/2 cups butter or margarine
- 3 1/4 cups sifted all-purpose flour
- 3/4 cup cold water
- 1/3 cup shortening (except butter, margarine or oil)
- 2 tablespoons lemon juice or water
- 1 egg, beaten

Make pastry at least a day before you plan to serve these rich delicacies. Freeze the butter. Combine water, juice and egg. Add to flour and stir until mixture holds together. (In cold weather, add one or two tablespoons more water.) Knead gently until dough is smooth and cover bowl for 10 minutes. Gently roll out on lightly floured board to rectangle 1/8-inch thick. Divide hardened butter into thirds and shortening also. Starting at narrow end, spread a third of shortening over two-thirds of pastry and coarsely grate one-third of butter on top of shortening. Fold unbuttered third of dough over center third, then fold last third on top of it. (You now have three layers.) Fold opposite ends towards center overlapping again making three layers. (You now have a square.) Wrap in foil paper and chill 1 hour or longer. Again roll out dough to 1/8-inch thick, repeat above process using second thirds of butter and shortening, chill 1/2 hour. Then repeat with remaining thirds of butter and shortening. Roll, fold and chill four more times. Wrap in foil and store for a day or so in refrigerator.
Divide dough into thirds. Roll out one-third of dough to a rectangle 1/8-inch thick. Cut in even strips 3 inches wide. Trim ends so all are equal. Place on ungreased cookie sheets close together as they rise — not spread — and prick with a fork. Repeat with rest of dough. Bake for 10 minutes or until golden brown in a 425 degree oven. Cool. Split and fill with vanilla pudding and ice with chocolate glaze.

Traditionally, Swazis eat their meat barbecued in an open fire, outdoors most of the time. These people are beef lovers. When they cook beef, they simply boil it. No sophisticated spices are used. The only common spice you can find and see being used by a traditional Swazi is hot small red peppers and also onions. Those who live in the city cook more or less as we do here and use all the spices that we have here.

The only custom that most of the Swazi people observe is that the head of the family, the father, is the first to be served. Also he has his own utensils that the children are not allowed to use to serve themselves. The children have their own place to sit and eat during the meal hour. This is changing in the urban areas, but in the rural parts of the country it is traditionally observed. Swazi children always respect anything that belongs to their parents. Their common vegetable dish is spinach or cabbage.

CORNMEAL DUMPLINGS

10 ml. sugar
12.5 ml. flour
1/2 cake yeast

Mix the sugar and yeast. Add flour and a little lukewarm water. Leave in warm place 15 minutes, or until bubbles rise to the surface. Boil 125 ml. water and 250 ml. cornmeal. Cook for 5 to 10 minutes. Add 250 g. flour to this mixture and mix well. Pour in the yeast mixture and 30 g. melted butter. Add warm water and knead. Leave in warm place to rise. Knead again and place in a well-greased basin or bowl. Let rise for 15 minutes.

Place the dumpling mixture in a saucepan of boiling water and allow to steam for 1 hour.

BEEF STEW WITH MACARONI

1/2 kilogram stewing beef
1 1/2 teaspoons salt
4 large carrots, sliced across
2/3 litre water
1 beef stock cube
1/4 teaspoon garlic powder

1/4 teaspoon pepper
Small onion, chopped
1 1/2 tablespoons flour
Cream, optional
1/2 kg. macaroni pieces

Brown meat on all sides. Add garlic, onion, water, stock cube, salt and pepper. Cover and simmer until meat is almost tender. Add carrots, cover and continue cooking for about 25 minutes. Blend a little cold milk with the flour to make a thin paste. Stir into meat-vegetable mixture. Cook about 3 minutes or until thickened. Stir in sour cream, if wanted, and heat, but do not boil.

Boil the macaroni in salted water according to the directions on the package. Drain. Add to the stew and serve nice and hot.

Dill is the characteristic flavoring herb in Sweden. One of the most delicious cake breads is Limpa. Lox, herring, mushrooms, veal, and cabbage are all used abundantly in Sweden. Crayfish are boiled and eaten with dill sauce at their Kraftor or Autumn Festivals.

LIMPA BREAD

1 cup ale
1 cup molasses
1 tablespoon fennel or anise seed
1 1/2 tablespoons grated orange
   rind
1/4 cup butter

1 pkg. dry yeast
1 tablespoons lukewarm water
4 cups white flour
2 teaspoons salt
3 cups rye flour

Bring to a boil, the first 5 ingredients. Cool. Add yeast, softened in warm water and let stand 30 minutes. Beat in flour and salt, let rise until double in size. Add more white flour if necessary. Punch down, and knead well. Shape into oblong loaves. Let rise until double in size. Bake in 350 degree oven 45 minutes. Brush several times with cold water.

KOTTBULLAR
(Swedish Meat Balls)

2 slices white bread, crust removed
1/4 cup cream
1 egg
1 1/2 teaspoons salt
1/2 teaspoon pepper
1/4 teaspoon nutmeg
1 large onion, finely chopped
8 tablespoons butter

1 lb. lean ground beef
1/2 lb. veal or chicken, ground
1/2 lb. pork, ground
1/2 cup fresh dill, minced or
1/4 cup dried dill
1 1/2 cups beef broth
1/2 cup sour cream

Soak bread and cream and egg. Mix to paste with salt, pepper and nutmeg. Sauté onion in 3 tablespoons butter. Add the meats and one-third of bread mixture and the dill. Mix very well. Cool. Wet hands and shape into 1 1/2-inch balls. Heat the remaining butter and sauté meat balls until brown. Add the broth and simmer 15 minutes. Stir sour cream into broth and add rest of dill. Dish up meat balls, and spoon sour cream sauce over all. Serve.

FLAGS OF THE UNITED NATIONS

SYRIA

TURKEY

TANZANIA

UGANDA

THAILAND

UKRAINE

TOGO

U.S.S.R.

**TRINIDAD
AND TOBAGO**

**UNITED ARAB
EMIRATES**

TUNISIA

UNITED KINGDOM

3 tablespoons butter	2 tablespoons sugar
4 tablespoons flour	3 tablespoons vinegar
2 1/2 cups liquid from meat	3 tablespoons dill, finely chopped
1 cup cream	2 tablespoons vermouth, dry
Salt and pepper	

SWEDISH DILL SAUCE

Melt butter in saucepan. Stir in flour. Add meat broth and rest of ingredients, except cream and vermouth. Cook until thick. Stir in cream and vermouth. Serve hot over lamb, veal or Kraut Balls.

———————

	1 cup milk
1/4 lb. ground pork sausage	3 cups firmly packed sauerkraut,
1/4 lb. ground cooked ham	drained and chopped fine
1/4 lb. ground cooked corned beef	3 cups fresh bread crumbs
1/4 cup finely chopped onion	Melted shortening or oil for deep
1/2 teaspoon finely chopped	frying
parsley	Egg Batter:
1 cup all-purpose flour	2 eggs, beaten
1/2 teaspoon salt	2/3 cup water
1/2 teaspoon dry mustard	1 teaspoon salt

SAUERKRAUT BALLS

(Makes approximately 75)

1. Break up pork sausage into small bits and fry in a heavy skillet until lightly browned.
2. Add ground ham and corned beef, chopped onion and parsley; continue to cook, stirring frequently with a fork until hot.
3. Sift flour, salt and dry mustard together once; add to meat mixture, stirring constantly to combine.
4. Add milk and continue to cook over low heat until mixture is thickened. Remove from heat.
5. Stir in chopped sauerkraut and mix well. Chill mixture thoroughly. For rapid chilling, spread in a shallow pan and place in freezer for 30 minutes.
6. Shape mixture into 3/4-inch balls. Roll lightly in flour.
7. Combine beaten eggs, water and salt and blend to make egg batter. Dip floured balls into egg batter, then in fresh bread crumbs.
8. Deep fry in 360 degrees F. fat for 1 1/2 to 2 minutes or until golden brown. Drain on absorbent paper and serve hot.

Arbete befodrar halsa och valstiud
och forhindrar minget tillfol till sydn.
Work promotes health and wealth and prevents
many an opportunity to sin.

Syrians eat three meals a day. Futoor (breakfast), is usually bread in boiled milk, white cheese, figs, and coffee. Gotha is the main meal at noon, usually pilaf, either rice or wheat, and it may include Kibbe. Asha is the light supper meal, usually a soup or salad or bread and cheese.

LAHM AJOUN
(Meat-Bread)

4 slices toast
1/2 lb. ground lamb
1 cup tomatoes canned, peeled
1/4 cup bell pepper, chopped
1/2 cup parsley, chopped

1/2 teaspoon allspice
1/2 teaspoon salt
1/4 teaspoon pepper
Yogurt

Lay the toast in a flat greased baking pan. Mix the rest of the ingredients together. Spread on bread. Bake in 350 degree oven for 1 hour. Serve hot with yogurt.

KURBAN
(Flat Syrian Bread)

2 1/2 lb. flour
1 cake yeast, dissolved in 1/2 cup
  water

1 teaspoon salt
1 teaspoon orange blossom water
2 cups water

Put flour and salt in large mixing bowl. Add yeast and orange water. Moisten dough with enough water to knead. Knead until smooth. Let rise 3 hours. Divide dough into rounds 1/4-inch thick. Let rise 1 hour. Bake in 450 degree oven until light brown. Cover with Saran wrap or cloth to prevent drying out.

Butter Tea from Tibet consists of a churned mixture of tea, butter, salt, soda and parched barley, finely ground.

Use rich yeast dough (see recipe page 123). Add 1 teaspoon mace and 1 teaspoon lemon rind, grated. Let dough rise and bake in tube cake pan. Soak while hot in rum sauce made by boiling together 1/2 cup sugar, 3/4 cup apricot juice, 1/2 cup raisins, 1/2 cup mashed cherries, 1/2 cup water and 1/2 cup rum. Reheat and serve sliced with whipping cream.

Tanzania is an island in the Indian Ocean. Its new central government is called Dares Salaam or Haven of Peace.

CIPATE
(Meat Pie)

1 4-lb. chicken	1/2 lb. mushrooms
2 lbs. pork shoulder	2 teaspoons salt
2 lbs. stewing veal	2 cups diced potatoes
1 lb. stewing beef	1/2 teaspoon pepper
2 cups onion	1/2 teaspoon savory
1 1/2 cups diced celery	2 crust pastry
1 cup thinly sliced carrots	

Roll both pastries to fit a large casserole.

Bone and skin chicken and cut meat in 3/4-inch cubes. Make stock of bones, and skin. Remove fat from pork, dice fine and fry till crisp. Cut pork, veal and beef into 3/4-inch cubes and mix with chicken. Mix vegetables and seasonings. Scatter fried pork fat over bottom of large heavy casserole. Fill dish with alternate layers of meat and vegetables. Make pastry and roll out to fit top of casserole. Seal edges firmly and make several steam vents in top. Refrigerate overnight to blend flavors. Next day, pour enough chicken stock through vents to fill pie. Cover with foil and cook 4 1/2 to 5 hours, till meat is tender. If pie gets dry, add more stock. Uncover for last 30 minutes to brown pastry. Serves 12.

LEMON CRACKERS

2 1/2 cups sugar	1/4 ounce oil of lemon
1 cup shortening	2 tablespoons crushed bakers
2 eggs, well beaten	ammonia
1 pint sweet milk	

Heat milk to nearly boiling and dissolve ammonia in it. Add to beaten eggs, creamed sugar and shortening. Add enough flour for stiff dough. Put on well floured board and beat for 1/2 hour. Keep plenty of flour on board. Roll thin, cut in squares and bake in hot oven.

HOT SPICED COFFEE

1 stick cinnamon	12 lumps sugar
10 whole cloves	4 tablespoons instant coffee
1 teaspoon orange peel	4 cups boiling water

Steep all together for 30 minutes. Serve in demitasses with whipped cream and brandy.

Thailand, on the Indo Chinese and Malayn Peninsulas, is about three-fourths the size of Texas. A plateau dominates the northeastern third of Thailand, dropping to the fertile alluvial valley of the Chao Phraya River. Rice is a major export, and Thailand is also the world's 5th largest producer of tin. Thailand is the only country in southeast Asia which was never taken over by a European power, due to the efforts of King Mogkut and his son, King Chualongkorn, who modernized the country, and signed trade treaties with Britain and France.

Thai foods are hot and spicy!

MUSTARD LAMB CHOPS

2 tablespoons olive oil
8 lamb chops
Salt and pepper
8 potatoes, boiled half-done
2 cups milk

1 teaspoon oregano
4 tablespoons hot mustard
2 tablespoons flour
2 cups water

Brown chops in olive oil. Place in casserole dish with boiled potatoes. Sprinkle with oregano. Mix milk, mustard, flour and water until blended. Pour over potatoes and chops. Bake covered in 300 degree oven for 1 hour. Sprinkle with parsley and serve!

ASPARAGUS

2 tablespoons oil
1/4 cup chicken stock
1/4 cup water

1 tablespoon sherry
2 tablespoons soy sauce
1 tablespoon corn starch

Combine all of the above. Bring to a boil. Add 1 can, drained asparagus spears. Heat just until hot. Serve!

BEAN THREADS AND CHICKEN

Soak 1 package bean threads in water for 30 minutes. Sauté diced cooked chicken in peanut oil with 2 pods of pickled garlic. Stir in 1 beaten egg. Add the noodles and fish sauce (bottled) to taste. Sprinkle with pepper. Add 1 cup green slivered onions and strips of thin egg omelet for garnish. Heat until onions are hot through. Serve.

Iced Jasmine Tea is a favorite drink.

Togo is a thin slice of land on the West African Coast, between Ghana and Dahomey. I am so glad that at last, the world is recognizing the very fine cuisine of Africa: the African jam, palm wine and African methods of cooking. All too often in the big cities, one gets a cosmopolitan meal served to them. In the rural depths of the African countryside, meat is a luxury. Sheep, goats and cattle are a form of currency. Eggs are used for bartering. The average farmer lives on milk products, green vegetables, lots of peas and beans and cereals and sweet potatoes. Sweet potatoes are so large that one can serve a family of eight from one potato. The Baobab tree is treasured for its seeds, fruit and often sustains life in the desert.

RICE CREAM WITH MANDARIN ORANGES

1 tablespoon unflavored gelatin	1 cup cooked rice
1/2 cup water	1 1/2 teaspoons vanilla
3 eggs, separated	1 can (11 ounces) Mandarin orange
1/2 teaspoon salt	segments, drained
2/3 cup sugar	Sweetened whipped cream; chopped
2 cups milk	candied orange peel, optional

Soften gelatin in water. Beat egg yolks with salt and 1/3 cup sugar; gradually beat in milk. Cook over hot water, stirring constantly, until mixture coats a spoon. Remove from heat and add softened gelatin, stirring, until it is dissolved. Add rice and vanilla. Chill. Beat egg whites until they form soft peaks. Gradually add remaining 1/3 cup sugar and beat until stiff. Fold into rice mixture. Arrange 3 or 4 orange segments in individual molds or custard cups. Fill with rice mixture. Chill until firm. To serve, unmold on dessert plates and garnish with sweetened whipped cream and chopped candied orange peel, if desired.
Makes 8 to 10 servings.

FRIED CARDAMOM COOKIES

1/3 cup butter	1 1/2 cups flour
1/2 cup sugar	1/2 teaspoon ground cardamom
1 egg yolk	1 1/2 teaspoons baking powder
2 tablespoons milk	1/4 teaspoon lemon peel

Cream butter and sugar until light and fluffy. Beat in remaining ingredients. Pinch off and fry on buttered grill. Serve warm with ice cream.

African saying: "The sun is but an egg that hatches great things."

TRINIDAD AND TOBAGO

Trinidad and Tobago, off the eastern coast of Venezuela, have a combined territory about the size of Delaware. Three low mountain ranges cross Trinidad, with a well watered plain between the north and central ranges. The islands produce oil products, rum, and cement. Sugar, cocoa, coffee, citrus fruits and bananas are grown. A British possession since 1802, the islands won independence in 1962.

SALTFISH ACCRA

1/2 lb. salted codfish
1 small onion
1 bunch scallions
1 piece hot pepper

1/2 pkg. yeast
1 1/2 cups lukewarm water
1 cup flour

Put salted codfish on to scald in hot water. Pour off water and repeat three times with clean water. Cool and remove bones, flake and mince together with onion, scallions and pepper. Soak yeast in 1/2 cup lukewarm water for 10 minutes. Add remaining water and flour. Beat vigorously, adding remaining ingredients. Blend well. Add salt if necessary. Leave to double in size. Drop by spoonfuls into hot fat and dry until golden brown. Drain and serve. Serves 6.

SWEET BREAD

2 cups sugar
3 teaspoons baking powder
1 teaspoon Angostura aromatic
    bitters
1/2 cup mixed peels
1 teaspoon vanilla
1 tablespoon cooking butter

1 tablespoon shortening
3/4 cup water
3 cups flour
1 cup raisins
1 cup coconut, grated
1 egg

Mix sugar with coconut and a little water. Add egg, mix thoroughly. Add bitters, shortening and butter. Sift dry ingredients together and add to mixture. Add rest of water to make soft dough. Add raisins and mixed peels. Drop by spoonfuls on baking pan. When baked, remove from oven. Mix sugar with a little water for syrup, baste on top of each and place in hot oven for 2 minutes. Makes 8 loaves.

Proverb:
"It is better that a man wait for his meal, than the meal wait for a man."

CALLALOO

1 8-ounce pkg. frozen spinach, chopped
2 8-ounce pkgs. frozen okra
4 scallions, chopped
1 small onion, chopped
1/2 lb. smoked pig knuckles or smoked pig tails cooked for 45 minutes or until tender
2 tablespoons creamed coconut
2 tablespoons butter
3 crabs, halved (optional)
1 hot pepper, whole
Salt to taste
Water to cover, plus 1/2 cup water from smoked pig knuckles or pig tails

In large pot, put spinach, okra, scallions, onions, pig knuckles or pig tails, in water. Let boil for 10 minutes. Then add coconut, butter, pepper and allow to cook for 1/2 hour on medium heat. Add salt as needed. Remove pepper and pig knuckles. Pour mixture into blender and flash blend until mixture is smooth, about 3 seconds. Return mixture to pot, with crabs and pig knuckles and simmer for about 10 minutes. Serve with cooked rice. Serves 6.

WEST INDIAN SOUSED FISH

6 fish filets
1/2 cup lemon juice
1/2 teaspoon Worcestershire sauce
1/2 teaspoon salt
1 egg, beaten
1/2 cup flour

Marinate fish in a mixture of lemon juice, Worcestershire sauce and salt; refrigerate for at least 1 hour. Then dip filets in egg and in flour. Pan fry. Place in a baking dish and cover with the following sauce:

1 cup cider vinegar
1/4 cup finely chopped green pepper
1 1/2 tablespoons minced onion
1 1/2 tablespoons salt
1/2 teaspoon crushed whole allspice
1 teaspoon crushed whole black pepper
1 pinch garlic powder
1/2 hot red pepper, crushed

Combine all ingredients in a saucepan and bring to a boil. Pour over cooked fish filets. Chill for 24 hours. Serve cold. Serves 6.

Tunisia, on the north coast of Africa, is just slightly larger than Florida. The northern part of the country is wooded and fertile, while the central coastal plains are given to grazing and orchards. The south is arid. Industries include food processing, textiles, clothing, leather, oil products and construction materials. Tunisia is on the site of ancient Carthage, and a former Barbary state under the suzerainty of Turkey. The country gained independence in 1956.

LAMB & GARLIC STEW

2 lbs. lean boneless lamb, cut in 1-inch cubes
1 cup whole peeled garlic cloves
1 cup pitted black olives
1/2 cup chopped parsley
1/2 cup chopped celery leaves
2 medium carrots, cut in 1/2-inch rounds

1 bay leaf
1 teaspoon salt
1/4 teaspoon black pepper
1/4 teaspoon thyme
1 cup dry white wine
1 cup dry red wine

Mix all ingredients, except red wine. Place in a heavy casserole baking dish, with a tight cover. Bake 2 hours at 325 degrees. Thicken to make gravy if desired.

TOMATO SALAD

Skin tomatoes and scoop out centers. Season inside with salt, pepper and pinch of dill. Place one canned artichoke in each tomato and chill. Half hour before serving, cover with following dressings:

Curried Mayonnaise:
1 pint mayonnaise
1/2 pint sour cream
1 teaspoon curry powder

Lemon juice
Grated onion
Mix and serve over tomatoes.

YOGURT OR SOUR CREAM DRESSING

Yogurt or Sour Cream Dressing:
1/4 teaspoon mustard
1/4 teaspoon paprika
1 teaspoon salt
1/4 cup milk

2 tablespoons vinegar
Dash of Tabasco
1/2 cup yogurt or sour cream
1 teaspoon onion powder

Mix well and serve over tossed salads. Great over lettuce and tomatoes!

The ancient country of Turkey is in Asia Minor, between the Mediterranean and Black Seas. Central Turkey has wide plateaus with hot, dry summers and cold winters. High mountains ring the interior on all but the west. Turkey produces silk, textiles, steel, shoes, and furniture. It is famous for its special tobacco and is the world's 6th largest producer of this crop. Ancient inhabitants of Turkey were among the world's first agriculturists.

IMAN
BAYILDI
(Stuffed Eggplant)

1 eggplant, medium size, sliced in cold, salted water	1/4 cup chopped mint
	1/4 cup rice
6 large onions	1 cup olive oil
3 bell peppers	3 fresh tomatoes
1/2 cup parsley	1 lemon, sliced thin
5 cloves garlic	Salt and pepper to taste
1/2 cup seedless raisins	1/3 cup hot water
1/2 cup pine nuts	

Chop onion, pepper, parsley, garlic and mint. Add raisins, pine nuts and rice. Make layers of eggplant and mixed chopped vegetables and rice. Slice the tomatoes over top and add sliced lemon. Season to taste. Pour hot water over all and cover and bake in 300 degree oven for 2 hours. Chill and serve. Make a day before and chill in refrigerator overnight.

TURKISH
COFFEE

For each cup:

1 heaping teaspoon pulverized coffee	1 heaping teaspoon sugar
	1 small cup water

Put all ingredients in a small pot. Bring to a boil and remove from heat. Shake. Bring back to boil. Shake 3 times or whip. Pour into cups. The grounds will settle in each cup. Flavor coffee if desired with orange blossom water or cardamon seed.

YOGURT
SHERBET

1 can frozen tangerine juice	1 teaspoon lemon juice
1/2 cup honey	Pinch of salt
1 cup yogurt	2 egg whites, beaten stiff

Mix together and freeze. Remove from freezer and beat smooth. Fold in egg whites, and freeze again until smooth.

"The soul enters by the throat!"
An old Turkish proverb.

Uganda, formerly British, is in East Africa, and is a land of beautiful lakes and high mountains. It is about the size of Oregon. It is the world's 5th largest coffee exporter. Nearly half the population are Christians, mostly Roman Catholics.

SOUR CREAM PUMPKIN SPICE ROLL

Beat together:
2 eggs (3 if small)
1 cup sugar
1 teaspoon soda

1/2 teaspoon cinnamon
3/4 cup flour
2/3 cup pumpkin, squash or carrots
   cooked

Pour onto greased cookie sheet and bake 15 minutes at 350 degrees. Turn out on dish towel that has been sprinkled with powdered sugar. Cool 15 minutes and roll up with towel for several minutes. Unroll and spread filling on entire layer. Sprinkle with chopped pecans or walnuts and roll back up and chill.

Filling:
Mix till smooth:
1 cup sifted powdered sugar
1 teaspoon vanilla
1 teaspoon nutmeg

1 teaspoon cinnamon
1/2 cup sour cream
Then spread on cake.
Sprinkle 1/2 cup chopped nuts on
   filling before rolling up.

Slice and serve with cold applesauce and whipped cream.

COFFEE LIQUEUR

2 ounces instant coffee
3 1/2 cups sugar
2 cups boiling water

1 pint brandy
1 whole vanilla bean

Stir coffee and sugar into boiling water. Stir until sugar is dissolved. Cool, add to brandy with vanilla bean. Let stand 1 month. Wonderful over vanilla, chocolate or coffee ice cream.

ORANGE LIQUEUR

2 cups fresh orange juice
1/4 cup lemon juice
2 cups sugar

1 vanilla beanf
1 litre of gin

Let sugar dissolve in fruit juice. Stir until dissolved, add gin and chopped vanilla bean. Let stand 2 weeks. Shake well. Serve over ice cream.

The Ukraine lies in southwest Russia, north of the Black Sea. It is rich in farmland and mineral deposits. The Ukrainians are Slavic people who know and appreciate excellent cuisine.

UKRAINIAN BORSCHT
("My favorite recipe the world over!")

400 grams meat
400 grams cabbage, finely shredded
400 grams potatoes, diced
250 grams beets, skinned, cut in
   shoestring slices
1/2 cup sour cream
1/2 cup sliced tomatoes
1 sprig parsley
1 carrot, finely minced
1 onion, finely minced
20 grams salt pork

1 tablespoon butter
1 tablespoon vinegar
1 tablespoon sugar
2 cloves garlic
2 peppercorns
1 bay leaf
6 lbs. meat bones for stock (beef,
   lamb, chicken)
   Cook meat bones in 1 gallon
   water, simmering for 24 hours.
   Strain stock.

Boil meat until tender and cut into julienne strips. Cook cabbage for 20 minutes. Cook potatoes for 25 minutes. Cook beets for 15 minutes. After beets have been shoestringed, cook with 1 tablespoon vinegar and the finely chopped onion and cubed pork until tender. Add to soup stock and add rest of ingredients and simmer until vegetables are tender. Serve with julienne strips of meat and sour cream. Sprinkle with dill.

PIROSHKI

1/2 cup chopped onion
1/2 tablespoon butter
1/2 lb. ground beef
Salt and pepper
1 tablespoon minced dill

1 tablespoon flour
2 tablespoons water
1 hard cooked egg, chopped
1 recipe for plain pastry using 2
   cups flour

Sauté onion in butter in skillet; push aside. Add meat and brown. Season to taste. Sprinkle in flour. Mix, add water and cook until done. Cool. Add egg. Drop by tablespoon onto pastry circles (3 1/2-inch). Carefully close edges by folding one and moistening the edges. Press down with fork or fingers. Bake 30 minutes at 400 degrees.

PYSANKY
(Easter Eggs from Ukraine)

2 dozen fresh eggs
Water to cover
3 tablespoons vinegar

Bring to a boil and let boil for 15 minutes. The vinegar softens the shell and allows the dye to penetrate.

See next page.

Color Easter Eggs with natural dyes:
Red Beets turn eggs crimson.
Saffron — brilliant yellow.
Onion skins — deep orange.
Red cabbage — Robin egg blue.

To make designs stick pin in pencil eraser and dip pin head into
melted wax and draw on egg. Then dip egg on dye. Scrap off wax.

BLACK BREAD

Bring to a boil:
2 cups water
1/4 cup cider vinegar
1/4 cup molasses

1/2 cup oil
1 square (1 ounce) unsweetened
chocolate
Cook mixture to lukewarm.

Combine 2 envelopes of dry yeast with 1/2 cup lukewarm water
and add 1 teaspoon sugar. Let stand 10 minutes.
Combine 4 cups rye flour with 3 cups white flour. Toss with fork
until blended. Take 3 cups of the rye flour mixture (reserving rest
to use when kneading bread) and add 2 cups whole bran cereal, 2
tablespoons caraway seed, 1 tablespoon salt, 2 teaspoons of instant coffee, 2 teaspoons freeze-dried minced onion, and one
teaspoon fennel seed. Stir in the cooled water-vinegar-molasses
mixture and add yeast mixture. Beat dough with dough hook or
spoon for about 2 minutes. Add enough of the remaining rye and
white flour to make a soft dough. Make a ball and grease well. Let
rise in a warm place for 1 hour, then knead the dough with the
rest of the flour mixture for about 15 minutes until it is smooth
and resilient.
Shape into 2 loaves (round) and fit into well-greased 8-inch cake
pans. Oil the top of the bread, and let rise for 1 1/2 hours or until
doubled. Bake in 350 degree oven 50 minutes. Serve with butter
sour cream or cheese.
Loaves may be glazed with a cornstarch wash made by bringing to
a boil 1/2 cup water and 1 teaspoon cornstarch. Brush on baked
bread and return to the oven for 5 minutes.
Wrap bread with Saran wrap to retain moisture. This slices beau-
tifully.

The U.S.S.R. consists of 15 union republics. The Byelorussians are also members of the U.N. The Ukraine is the most densely populated. It borders on the Black Sea.

BOUBLIK
(Ring Bun)

4 cups flour	2 3/4 cups water
1 1/2 cups butter	12 eggs

Melt butter, mix with water, bring to a boil. Stir in flour. Cool slightly to 70 degrees. Then beat in eggs, one at a time. Shape into rings and bake at 350 degrees for 15 minutes.

APRICOT SALAD

2 cups fresh, chopped apricots, mix with 3 tablespoons powdered sugar. Marinate in white wine and juice of 1 lemon. Serve on leaf lettuce with sour cream.

SOUR CREAM SOUFFLE

2 cups thick sour cream	
6 eggs, separated	1 teaspoon vanilla
2 tablespoons flour	4 tablespoons sugar

Beat sour cream, add egg yolks, flour, vanilla and sugar. Fold in stiffly beaten egg whites. Bake in 350 degree oven for 45 minutes. Serve with sweetened whipped cream.

A favorite dessert of mine is grated, raw apples, cherries or berries mixed with white wine or rum. Fold in sweetened whip cream and serve immediately.

Yushka — Soups made from cereals, vegetables, legumes, and mushrooms.
Zatirka — Little flour potato balls the size of peas, dropped in hot soup. Generally mashed potatoes, flour, onion and allspice, adding enough cold water to make dough.

DRAGLI
(Whipped Cream Mold)

1 litre whipping cream	3 envelopes of plain gelatin (30
1 teaspoon vanilla	grams)
4 tablespoons powdered sugar	

Beat whipping cream, add vanilla and powdered sugar. Continue to beat until stiff. Soak gelatin in 1/2 cup water. Melt over hot water. Cool. Fold into whipped cream. Turn into molds. Chill. Unmold and serve in raspberry juice or with sliced peaches.

United Arab Emirates on the southern shore of the Persian Gulf is mostly a barren, flat coastal plain. The chief component of the economy is the reserve of crude oil, but the country is also becoming a center of international banking.

ADEECE HOMEED
(Lentils-Spinach)

1 cup lentils	1 tablespoon salt
1 potato, cubed	Pepper to taste
1 small onion, minced	1/8 teaspoon allspice
2 small yellow squash, cubed	1/8 teaspoon cloves
1 lb. spinach, half or fourth each leaf	1 1/2 lemons, squeezed, use juice only
Oil or butter	

Brown onions in oil. Set aside. Fill 1 1/2-quart pan with water. Add washed lentils and salt. Cook over medium heat until lentils are well done, but still whole, approximately 20 minutes. Add browned onions, stir and add potatoes, squash. Simmer slowly until done. Add spinach. When cooked to taste, add lemon juice and simmer 2 minutes.

PICKLED TURNIPS

2 lbs. small white turnips	6 level tablespoons salt
a few celery leaves	3 1/2 cups water
4 cloves of garlic	1 1/4 cups white vinegar
1 raw beet, peeled and cut in medium pieces	

Cut turnips in quarters. Pack in clean glass jars with celery leaves and garlic cloves. Place pieces of raw beets in the layers for color. Dissolve salt in heated water and stir in vinegar. Store at room temperature for 10 days. Then chill and serve. Keep in refrigerator. Eat within 1 month.

There is an old tale of folk lore origin, that the students of wise men of old ate lentils to stay wise and healthy.

Countries in the United Kingdom include Britain, Scotland, and Northern Ireland. Terrain is mostly rolling land rising to the Uplands of southern Scotland. Due to the action of the gulf stream the British Isles have a milder climate than northern Europe. Industries include steel, metals, vehicles and shipbuilding. Major occupations are manufacturing and trade. Metals and metalworking industries comprise more than 50% of the country's exports.

THE REAL TRIFLE

3 small sponge cakes
6 macaroons
1 ounce ratafias (if unobtainable,
  use extra macaroons)
1/4 pint cooking sherry
3 tablespoons brandy
A little grated lemon rind
1 ounce blanched almonds, cut in
  strips

Strawberry jam
1/2 pint egg custard, freshly made
Whip of: ‹
1/4 pint cream
3/4 ounce sugar
1 egg white
1 teaspoon cooking sherry

Place sponge cakes, macaroons and ratafias in a dish. Mix sherry and brandy and pour over them. Over this put the lemon rind, almonds and a layer of jam. When the custard is cool, pour it over the trifle. Make the whip by whisking together cream, sugar and egg white and sherry until the bulk is nearly doubled. Heap the whip lightly over the top and garnish with crystalized fruits.

ROAST BEEF
(With Yorkshire Pudding)

One top or bottom of round, 15-18 pounds, of prime ribs. Salt and black pepper roast. Allow to stand until it reaches room temperature. Roast in 350 degree oven until desired doneness (use meat thermometer). DO NOT cover while roasting and DO NOT add water to pan. When done remove roast from pan. Add 2 cups hot water to pan drippings. Thicken with cornstarch and water.

YORKSHIRE PUDDING

1 cup sifted flour (pastry)
1/2 teaspoon salt
1/2 cup milk

2 eggs, separated
1/2 cup water
Beef drippings or 1/2 cup butter

Sift flour and salt into a bowl. Stir in milk. Beat until foamy. Beat egg yolks until thick and lemon colored. Beat whites until stiff. Fold in egg yolks. Beat eggs into the flour and milk batter. Then add water. Beat until large bubbles rise to the surface. Let stand 1 hour. Beat again. Pour into preheated butter-greased baking pan. Bake in 450 degree oven 45 minutes. Cut in squares. Serve with roast beef and gravy.

HAGGIS

1 sheep's bag (I have to use cooking bag)	Salt and pepper
1/2 lb. liver, sheep or beef	1 cup stock
1 sheep heart and lungs	1/4 lb. beef suet
1 cup oatmeal	2 large onions, minced

Boil liver, lungs and heart for 1 hour. Cool, grate the liver, and chop finely the heart and lungs. Chop the suet. Toast the oatmeal in a shallow pan in the oven. Mix liver, heart, lungs, suet, oatmeal and onions together with the stock. Add seasonings. Put into slightly greased Pyrex bowl. Cover with 2 or 3 layers of foil and steam on a rack in a pan of boiling water for 2 hours. Add boiling water as necessary.
Or:
Turn into roast and baste bag and gently simmer for 2 hours. Serve with mashed "neeps", turnips mashed with butter, and "nips", Scotch whiskey.

SCOTCH EGGS

(A Favorite for Hunting Trips)

6 hard cooked eggs	Salt and pepper to taste
1 lb. sausage	2 beaten eggs
2 tablespoons flour	Bread crumbs

Mix flour with sausage and shape around eggs. Dip in beaten eggs and roll in bread crumbs. Fry in deep fat until brown. Wrap in foil and take to the Highlands. These are delicious cold.

CULLEN SKINK

1 small or 1/2 large smoked haddock	Salt and pepper
1 onion, peeled and chopped	Hot mashed potatoes
1 pint milk	2 ounces butter

Skin fish and place in pan with the onion. Cover with water and simmer gently till tender. Remove fish and flake the flesh. Return bones to the cooking water and simmer for 1 hour. Strain. Add to the milk and flaked fish. Bring to a boil and then simmer for 5 minutes. Whisk in sufficient hot mashed potatoes to give creamy consistency. Check seasonings, add butter and reheat before serving.

FLAGS OF THE UNITED NATIONS

UNITED STATES

YEMEN

UPPER VOLTA

YUGOSLAVIA

URUGUAY

ZAIRE

VENEZUELA

ZAMBIA

VIETNAM

1 1/2 cups salad oil
2 cups sugar
3 eggs
3 cups sifted all-purpose flour
1 teaspoon salt
1 teaspoon baking soda

1 teaspoon cinnamon
1 teaspoon vanilla
2 cups chopped canned Bartlett
  pears, well drained
1 cup chopped pecans

Combine oil, sugar, eggs; beat well. Sift together flour, salt, soda and cinnamon. Add to creamed mixture. Add vanilla. Fold in pears and pecans. Grease and flour a 10-inch Bundt or tube pan. Spoon in batter. Bake at 325 degrees for 1 hour and 20 minutes, or until cake tests done. Let cool in pan for 20 minutes and remove to cake rack for complete cooling. Drizzle white glaze over cake top, letting some run down sides.

1 tablespoon soft butter 1 1/2 cups
  powdered sugar

2 to 3 tablespoons syrup from the
  canned pears

Blend butter and sugar with enough pear syrup to make a smooth, slightly runny frosting.

2 cups sugar
1 cup butter
5 beaten eggs (add to butter
  mixture)
1 cup sour milk
2 cups flour
1 teaspoon soda
1 teaspoon salt

1 teaspoon cinnamon
Grated rind of 1 orange
2 squares chocolate, melted
1 cup raisins, ground
1 cup nuts, chopped
1 cup riced potatoes (do not press
  down)

Cream butter and sugar. Add rest of ingredients in order given.

Bake at 350 degrees for 1 hour or more. This torte is like a European Christmas pudding. Spoon glaze over cooled pudding or cake.

To make Vanilla Glaze: Combine 2 cups sifted powdered sugar and 1 teaspoon vanilla in a small bowl. Stir in enough milk (about 2 tablespoons) to make the glaze of spooning consistency. For Chocolate Glaze add 2 tablespoons cocoa.

Located on the continent of North America, the United States is one of the largest countries in terms of square miles in the world. Terrain is extremely varied, ranging from the temperate climates on the East Coast and the older, lower mountains of the Blue Ridge, to the arid heat of the Southwest, and the heights of the Rocky Mountain range in the West. The country is bisected by the Mississippi River. Crops include grain, corn, soy, alfalfa, citrus fruits and vegatables. The United States has many natural resources including oil, iron, copper, coal, gold, and a small amount of gemstone mining. Cuisine is as varied as the climate and topography, ranging from the more tradition-oriented dishes of the New England area to the rather more spicy and varied dishes of the South, and the hot, Mexican style cooking of the West.

TURKEY IN A BAG
(Do not use recycled paper.)

Rub your turkey (or any fowl) with salad oil. Place in paper bag (do not use recycled paper) and tie up with a string or skewer. Place on a cooking pan and roast according to chart. Oven temperature 300 degrees.

7-10 lb. — 30 min. per pound	18-20 lb. — 15 min. per pound
10-15 lb. — 20 min. per pound	20-23 lb. — 13 min. per pound
15-18 lb. — 18 min. per pound	

Remove paper and slice and serve.

GOURMET SALAD DRESSING

1 cup crumbled bleu cheese
5 ounces anchovies
4 ounces onion
1/2 cup lemon juice
6 ounces poupon mustard
1 teaspoon basil
2 teaspoons tarragon
1 tablespoon parsley

1 tablespoon chives
1 teaspoon Coleman mustard
1/2 cup tomato catsup
3 quarts oil
1 quart white wine
Vinegar
1 tablespoon salt
1 tablespoon pepper

Mix all ingredients together and blend well. Serve over leaf lettuce.

FROZEN FRUIT SALAD

1 pkg. favorite flavor jello (lemon, lime, orange or berry)
1/2 cup hot fruit juice
2 cups sliced fruit (bananas,

pineapple, oranges, pears, peaches or berries)
1 cup whipped cream
1/2 cup chopped pecans or nuts

Dissolve jello in hot water. Stir into fruit, add nuts. When cool fold in whipped cream. Turn into mold and freeze. Slice and serve on lettuce leaf.

6 cups blueberries or huckleberries
2/3 to 1 cup sugar
8 to 10 seedless grapes, peeled, cut
   into small pieces
2 tablespoons lemon juice
2 tablespoons butter

Pie Crust:
1 1/2 cups flour
1/2 teaspoon salt
1/2 cup shortening or lard

Sift flour, then measure. Mix flour and salt while sifting. With a fork blend in shortening. When blended in well, add 3 tablespoons water. When mixture holds together, roll out. Prepare blueberries in a bowl. Mix in sugar, grapes, lemon juice. Pour into a deep dish and dot the fruit with the butter. Cover with the pie crust and bake at 450 degrees for 10 minutes. Serve hot or cold. Pour a little heavy cream over when serving. Makes a 10-inch pie. *Canned berries may be substituted. Be sure to drain off most of the juices.

FUDGE CAKE

1 1/2 teaspoons vanilla
3 eggs
3 1-ounce squares unsweetened
   chocolate, melted
3 cups sifted cake flour

1 1/2 teaspoons baking soda
3/4 teaspoon salt
1 1/2 cups ice water
3/4 cup butter
2 1/4 cups sugar

Cream butter and sugar until light and fluffy. Beat in vanilla. Add eggs, one at a time, beating well after each addition. Blend in chocolate. Sift together cake flour, baking soda and salt. Add dry ingredients alternately with water to creamed mixture, beating well after each addition. Pour batter into 3 greased and waxed paper-lined 8-inch round cake pans. Bake in 350 degree oven for 30 to 35 minutes. Cool in pans on racks for 10 minutes. Remove from pans; cool on racks.

DATE CREAM
FILLING

1 cup milk
1/2 cup chopped dates
1 tablespoon flour
1/4 cup sugar

1 egg, beaten
1/2 cup chopped walnuts
1 teaspoon vanilla

Combine milk and dates in top of double boiler. Heat mixture over low heat; combine flour and sugar in small bowl. Add egg; beat until smooth. Stir into hot milk; place over simmering water. Cook, stirring constantly, until thick. Cool. Stir in walnuts and vanilla.

FUDGE FROSTING

2 cups sugar
1/4 teaspoon salt
1 cup light cream

2 tablespoons light corn syrup
2 1-ounce squares unsweetened
   chocolate

Combine all ingredients in 2-quart saucepan. Cook over low heat, stirring constantly, until sugar dissolves. Cover saucepan, cook 2 minutes. Remove cover and cook to soft ball stage. Remove from heat. Beat with wooden spoon to spreading consistency. Add a little hot water if frosting becomes too stiff or confectioner's sugar if it becomes too thin.

GREEN HERB DRESSING

1 cup parsley leaves (fresh
   chopped)
1 cup watercress, chopped
1 cup green onions or shallots,
   chopped
1 1/2 tablespoons dry mustard
1 tablespoon horseradish

1 tablespoon Worcestershire sauce
4 egg yolks
2 cups oil
2/3 cup vinegar
1 tablespoon dried mixed salad
   herbs

Place all in a blender and mix until thick. Serve over vegetables and lettuce salad and cooked egg.

ROQUEFORT CREAM DRESSING

Cut out the root ends of several green onions, dice and then chop very fine, tops and all. You will need 1/3 cup finely chopped Bermuda onions and chives if you don't have fresh green onions. Add to 2 cups mayonnaise; grate 2 cloves garlic into this and add 1/2 cup chopped parsley. Mix 2 tablespoons anchovy paste with 1 cup thick sour cream, and add to mayonnaise. Thin this mixture with 1/2 cup of the best vinegar and 2 tablespoons lemon juice. Crumble 1/2 pound Bleu or Roquefort cheese and beat into dressing. Season to taste with salt and pepper.
Excellent on tomato, aspic, or just a wedge of lettuce, or as a dip with potato chips. Serves 12.

CARROTS IN WINE VINEGAR

2 lbs. slightly cooked carrots,
   peeled, cut in 1/4-inch strips
2 cups finely chopped celery
1 thinly sliced bell pepper
1 large red onion, sliced

Marinade:
1 can condensed tomato soup
1 cup sugar
1/2 cup red wine vinegar
1 teaspoon dry mustard
1 teaspoon Worcestershire Sauce
1/2 cup oil

Combine all ingredients. Pour over vegetables. Let stand 24 hours. Keeps well in refrigerator.

4 eggs
2 cups sugar
1 can sweetened condensed milk
1 jar marshmallow creme

1 quart half and half
2 tablespoons vanilla
Enough milk to finish filling
    freezer 2/3 full

VANILLA ICE CREAM
(1 gallon)

Beat eggs and sugar. Combine rest of ingredients. Pour into freezer.

Freeze using 3 parts ice to 1 part salt.

--- ❋ ---

Crust:
1 stick butter

3 oz. cream cheese
1 cup flour

BITE SIZE PECAN PIES
(Makes 24)

Mix well and refrigerate. Make into 24 balls and press into small muffin tins.

Filling:
1 1/2 cups light brown sugar
2 eggs

2 tablespoons butter, melted
2 teaspoons vanilla

Mix well.

Drop few pecans on crust and spoon in filling. Bake at 325 degrees for 25 minutes.

--- ❋ ---

1 lb. New York State sharp
   Cheddar cheese
1 stick butter

1/2 teaspoon salt
1/2 teaspoon cayenne pepper
2 1/4 cups flour

CHEESE STRAWS

Grate cheese, put in Pyrex bowl; add butter and put in 150 degree oven to soften and slightly melt. Add salt and cayenne. Slowly add sifted flour, mix well. Force through a press into strips, or make in 1-inch roll; chill and cut in thin rounds. Bake in 300 degree oven for 30 minutes.

--- ❋ ---

8 ounces tomato juice
3 ounces vodka
Juice of 2 lemons
1 egg white

1/2 teaspoon salt
Fresh ground pepper
Dash of Worcestershire Sauce
1 cup cracked ice

FROZEN BLOODY MARYS

Blend all ingredients and freeze. Garnish with tarragon. Serves 4.

BAKED OYSTERS
(From West Coast)

1/4 cup butter	1 1/2 tablespoons Worcestershire
1 cup chopped celery	Sauce
1/2 cup chopped shallots	1/4 teaspoon Tabasco
1 teaspoon chopped parsley	1 teaspoon seasoning salt
Sauté until tender. Add 16 to 18	1/2 teaspoon salt
oysters, cut in half.	1/4 teaspoon pepper
8 ounces chopped mushrooms	3 eggs
1 teaspoon soy sauce	1 cup bread crumbs

Cook until thick. Combine with oyster mixture. Cover, with bread crumbs. Bake 20 minutes at 350 degrees.

SOFT SUGAR COOKIES

1/2 cup shortening	1/2 cup thick sour cream
1 cup sugar	2 1/4 cups flour
1 egg	1 teaspoon soda
1 teaspoon vanilla	1/2 teaspoon salt
3/4 teaspoon nutmeg	

Cream shortening, sugar, egg and vanilla and nutmeg. Add sour cream and blend well. Roll out 1/4 inch thick. Cut and sprinkle with sugar and bake in 325 degree oven for 12 minutes.

CRISP SUGAR COOKIES

1 cup shortening	1/8 teaspoon salt
3/4 cup sugar	1/4 teaspoon baking powder
1 egg, unbeaten	1 teaspoon almond extract
2 1/4 cups sifted all-purpose flour	

Cream shortening adding sugar gradually. Add rest of ingredients. Mix well. Fill cookie press. Form cookie on ungreased aluminum cookie sheet. Bake 7-10 minutes at 400 degrees.

FILET MIGNON WITH PEPPER SAUCE AND BRANDY

8 Filet Steaks (6 ounces each)	1 ounce brandy
1 cup Black Pepper Sauce*	1 tablespoon Hollandaise Sauce
1 ounce butter	2 tablespoons stock
Half clove garlic, finely chopped	Freshly ground pepper
2 tablespoons diced onion	

Grill steaks to slightly under degree of doneness required. Keep warm in serving dish together with vegetables. Next melt butter in a skillet over low flame, then add the garlic and onion, and fry until brown. Add steaks to the skillet. Brown both sides for one minute. Sprinkle both sides with pepper to taste. Add stock to cool down skillet, then pour in the brandy, and flame. Remove steaks to serving dish. Add the Black Pepper Sauce to skillet.

Bring to a boil, stirring occasionally. Lower heat, and add Hollandaise Sauce. Stir with spoon to blend. Pour contents of skillet over steaks. Serve immediately.

---

1 cup of Brown Sauce
Half clove garlic, finely chopped
1 tablespoon onion, finely chopped
1 teaspoon chopped parsley

1 1/2 ounces crushed black
  peppercorn
2 ounces dry red wine
1 ounce butter

Melt butter in a skillet, add garlic and then onion to brown. Add crushed peppercorn to fry. Stir constantly to prevent burning, and fry over low heat until peppercorn gets roasted thoroughly. Add red wine. Then add cup of Brown Sauce. Bring to a boil and then simmer until sauce reaches consistency of heavy cream. Add chopped parsley. Set aside for later use.

---

1 box brown sugar
1/2 cup sugar
1/2 lb. butter
1 cup pecans, chopped
4 eggs

2 cups flour, sifted
1 teaspoon baking powder
1/4 teaspoon salt
1 teaspoon vanilla

Cream brown sugar, sugar, butter. Mix in the rest of the ingredients. Bake in 300 degree oven for 30 to 40 minutes.

Crumb Base:
2 cups crisp cookie crumbs
1/4 cup sugar

1 tablespoon ground cinnamon
1/4 cup melted butter

Mix all ingredients and press into a springform pan. Then —

Chocolate Cream Cheese Filling:
2 lbs. cream cheese
1 1/2 cups sugar

1/3 cup cocoa
4 whole eggs
1/3 cup orange liqueur

Let cream cheese stay at room temperature for 1 hour; cream and beat with the rest of the ingredients until smooth. Pour into the crumb-lined pan and bake at 350 degrees for 35 to 40 minutes. While still hot put on this Sour Cream Topping:

Topping:
1 cup sour cream

1 tablespoon vanilla
1/4 cup sugar

Mix well and put on cheese cake. Turn on broiler, and broil fo 5 minutes. Chill cheese cake overnight, and serve with whipped cream, chocolate shavings, and cherries.

The Republic of Upper Volta is approximately the size of Colorado, located in West Africa south of the Sahara Desert. Chief crops include cotton, rice, peanuts, karite, grain, and corn. Menerals include manganese, gold, and diamonds. It is in the savanah region of West Africa. Upper Volta became independent in 1960.

LAMB AND POTATO BALLS

1 1/2 lbs. ground lamb	1/8 teaspoon pepper
4 medium sized potatoes, cooked and chopped	1 egg beaten
1/2 cup onions, grated	1/4 cup butter
1 1/2 teaspoons salt	1 1/4 cups sour cream

Mix together lamb, potatoes, onions, seasonings and egg. Shape into round balls to fry in butter until well browned. Add 3/4 cups sour cream and simmer, covered for 15 minutes.

Serve with Sour Cream Sauce:

SOUR CREAM SAUCE

(For Vegetables)

1 tablespoon butter	1 1/4 cups sour cream
1 1/2 tablespoons grated onion	Salt and pepper
1/2 cup dry white wine	

Melt butter and sauté the onion until it is soft but not browned, stirring constantly. Add the wine and simmer until liquid evaporates. Stir in the sour cream; stir and heat thoroughly. Add salt and pepper to taste. This is a great sauce over any boiled vegetable.

WHOLE CALF'S LIVER

1 large calf's liver (2 lbs. or more)	Gravy:
1/4 lb. salt pork, cut in strips	2 tablespoons flour
Salt and pepper to taste	2 cups pan juice
2 tablespoons butter	Salt and pepper
1 cup bouillon	
1 cup cream	
2 tablespoons grated cheese	

Trim and wash the liver. Wipe well. Cut little strips of the salt pork, roll in salt and pepper; and with a sharp knife, force the lardons into the liver. Rub the liver with the salt and pepper. Roll and tie the liver to condense the size. Fry in butter, turning with a wooden spoon, until evenly browned. Remove to heavy roasting pan. Add stock. Cover and cook slowly for 50 minutes in 325 degree oven. Baste occasionally with pan juices and cream. Remove liver to heated serving platter. Slice thin. Serve with gravy made by browning the flour in butter; add the pan juices. Cook and stir until thick.

Uruguay is a land of rolling, grassy plains and hills, well watered by rivers flowing west. It is located in southern South America on the Atlantic Ocean. Chief industries include meat packing, metals, textiles, wine, cement, and oil products. The country was originally settled by the Portuguese from Brazil, but was later attached to the Spanish Viceroyalty. Independence came in 1825.

ZUCCHINI BREAD

3 eggs
1 cup salad oil
2 cups sugar
2 cups raw zucchini, peeled and
    grated
2 teaspoons vanilla

2 teaspoons cinnamon
1 teaspoon salt
1 teaspoon baking soda
2 teaspoons baking powder
3 cups flour

Combine all ingredients in a large bowl. Mix until blended. Grease and flour two loaf pans, fill with batter, and bake 1 hour at 350 degrees.

AVOCADO BREAD

1 egg at room temperature
1/2 cup mashed ripe avocado
1/2 cup buttermilk or sour milk
1 cup chopped pecans
2 cups all-purpose flour, sifted

1/2 teaspoon baking soda
1/2 teaspoon baking powder
3/4 cup sugar
1/4 teaspoon salt

In medium bowl, combine egg, avocado, buttermilk, and pecans. Set aside. Sift together flour, sugar, soda, baking powder and salt. Pour into avocado mixture, mixing only until all the flour is moistened. Pour mixture into 8 1/2 x 4 1/2-inch loaf pan, greased and lined with waxed paper, and greased again. Bake for 1 hour at 350 degrees. Turn out of pan, peel off paper and allow to cool on wire rack. Slice and spread with whipped cream cheese.

OATMEAL BREAD

1 pkg. active dry yeast
2 tablespoons honey
1 cup potato water, heated to 110
    degrees
    (water you have boiled potatoes
    in)

1 cup milk, scalded
1 3/4 cups Old-Fashioned Quaker
    Oats
1/4 cup butter, melted
1 tablespoon salt
5 to 6 cups flour

Don't use the quick-cooking oats. Add yeast and honey to warm potato water in a cup or bowl and stir until completely dissolved. Let proof, mixture will be bubbly and rise a bit. Combine milk with oats, butter and salt in a large bowl. Stir and let stand 5 to 10 minutes. When cooled, slightly, add yeast mixture and stir in flour, 1 cup at a time. Continue stirring in flour until dough is firm and not too sticky. Place dough on a floured board and knead about 5 minutes or until dough is smooth and no longer sticky. Add more flour as necessary. Place dough in a buttered bowl and lightly butter top and sides of dough. Bake in 350 degree oven in loaf pan for 1 hour or until it tests done.

KEEPING FLOWERS FRESH

Sweetpeas Tulips	Plunge stems into boiling water then into cold water.
Violets	Tie in bunches and submerge in water; then shake off all water.
Zinnia	Stripped of lower leaves, place in 2 quarts of water containing 2 tablespoons of rock salt.
Snapdragons	Place stems, stripped of lower leaves, in two quarts water containing 3 tablespoons of baking soda.
Cat Tails	Cut with few leaves about August 25th. Place in vase upright, no water.
Pansies	Place stems in 1 pint of water containing 5 drops of wood alcohol.
Peonies	Crush stem ends up 3 to 4 inches and place in two quarts of water containing 2 teaspoonsful of sugar.
Poppies	Char stem tips 2 to 3 inches over a hot flame and plunge into cold water.
Ranunculas	Add vinegar to the water, at the rate of 1/2 cup vinegar to 2 cups water.
Roses	Slit the stem up 2 inches and place in 2 quarts of water containing 5 drops of wood alcohol.

Venezuela is a predominately Roman catholic country in South America about twice the size of California. Its population is Spanish, Portuguese, Italian, Negro and Indian. Its terrain is made up of plains and mountains. It has a strong economy. Among the most prominent industries are steel, oil products, textiles and tobacco. Much coffee is grown as well as cocoa, sugar cane and fruits.

GUACAMOLE

2 ripe avocados
1/2 teaspoon lime juice
1 small hot pepper
1 tablespoon grated onion

2 teaspoons salt
Pepper to taste
1 large ripe tomato, skinned and
   strained

Mash and blend all ingredients well. Serve with toasted cassavitos or tortillas.

MOLASSES COOKIES

2 eggs
3/4 cup molasses
3/4 cup brown sugar
3/4 cup lard
3/4 cup sour cream

1 tablespoon soda
1 tablespoon salt
1/2 tablespoon ginger
Flour to make soft dough

Blend lard and sugar together; add molasses, eggs which have been well beaten and sour cream. Alternate with dry ingredients. Chill. Roll out 1/2-inch thick. Bake on greased baking sheet for 10 minutes in 350 degree oven.

COFFEE MOUSSE

6 egg yolks, beaten
3/4 cup sugar
1/2 cup milk
2 tablespoons instant coffee,
   dissolved in 1/2 cup water

1 pint cream, whipped
1 teaspoon vanilla
1 tablespoon gelatin

Soak gelatin in a little cold water, dissolve over boiling water. Heat milk, pour slowly over beaten egg yolks which have been whipped with sugar. Cook in double boiler until thick. Add gelatin to coffee and chill; add to custard and blend well. Add vanilla and whipped cream. Pour into greased mold and congeal. Serve with whipped cream, sprinkled with chocolate bits.

187

Vietnam, roughly the size of New Mexico, is on the east coast of the Indochinese Peninsula. Vietnamese cuisine is becoming popular in this country as a result of an influx of many refugees. Food processing, textiles, and paper are among the country's industries, and rice, sugar cane, corn, sweet potatoes, coffee, and tea are among its crops.

SKEWERED PORK

1/4 cup soy sauce
1/4 cup creamy peanut butter
1 tablespoon firmly packed light
   brown sugar
1 tablespoon curry powder
2 tablespoons lemon juice

1/2 teaspoon crushed red pepper
1 clove garlic, crushed
2 lbs. cubed boneless pork loin
6 skewers
4 cups hot cooked rice

In a large bowl, gradually blend soy sauce into creamy peanut butter. Stir in brown sugar, curry powder, lemon juice, red pepper and garlic. Add pork; toss well to coat all sides. Cover bowl tightly; chill 4 hours or overnight.

About 1 hour before cooking pork, prepare Dipping Sauce (below).

Thread marinated pork cubes onto skewers. Broil slowly, turning often, until pork is cooked, about 20 to 25 minutes. Serve on hot cooked rice with prepared sauce. Makes 6 servings.

Dipping Sauce: Combine 1 tablespoon firmly packed light brown sugar, 2 tablespoons creamy peanut butter, 1/2 teaspoon crushed red pepper and 1 clove garlic, crushed. Gradually stir in 1/2 cup soy sauce. Let stand 1 hour. Strain before serving.

"When you go shopping for wisdom, visit every tent in the Bazaar."

The Yemen Arab Republic is on the southern Red Sea coast of the Arabian Peninsula. It is bordered by Saudi Arabia on the northeast, South Yemen on the south. The coast is sandy, but there are well-watered fertile mountains in the interior. Yemen's territory was once part of the ancient kingdom of Sheba, or Saba. A Biblical reference speaks of gold, spices, and precious stones as gifts by the Queen of Sheba to King Solomon. Today, the country produces textiles and cement, and grows crops of coffee, cotton, grain, etc. Yemen won independence in 1918.

EGGPLANT HORS d'OEUVRES

1 medium size eggplant
4 tablespoons olive oil
1/4 cup chopped green peppers
1/4 cup diced celery
1 cup chopped onions
2 cloves garlic, chopped
1/4 teaspoon dried oregano

1/2 teaspoon curry powder
1/4 cup cider vinegar
1 cup tomato pureé
1 1/2 teaspoons salt
1/4 teaspoon pepper
2 tablespoons parsley, chopped

Trim ends from eggplant, do not pare, cut in 3/4-inch cubes. Heat 3 tablespoons oil in large skillet; add eggplant and sauté until just tender. Remove from skillet; drain on paper towels. Add 1 tablespoon oil to skillet. Sauté green pepper, celery, onion and garlic for 3 minutes until tender. Return eggplant to skillet; add oregano, curry powder, vinegar, tomato pureé, salt and pepper. Cover, simmer for 5 minutes. Cool. Chill mixture thoroughly. Spoon into serving bowls and sprinkle with parsley. Serve with lettuce leaves, as a salad, and saltines.

MARINATED SPROUTS

Cook brussel sprouts until tender. Stir in 1/2 cup low calorie Italian dressing. Add 1 small clove garlic (minced), 1/2 teaspoon dried dill weed, 2 tablespoons chopped onion, and 1 teaspoon dried parsley flakes. Marinate overnight!

MARINATED MUSHROOMS

1 lb. fresh mushrooms
1/8 teaspoon thyme
1/8 teaspoon fennel
1 piece bay leaf
1/2 teaspoon parsley
1/2 teaspoon garlic powder
Dash of pepper

1 teaspoon onion powder
3 tablespoons red wine vinegar
2 tablespoons oil
1/4 teaspoon lemon juice
1 tablespoon seasoning salt

Combine all ingredients and cook until mushrooms are tender. Refrigerate overnight!

DATE BARS

3/4 cup shortening (part butter)
1 cup brown sugar
1 3/4 cups flour

1/2 teaspoon soda
1 teaspoon salt
1 1/2 cups quick rolled oats

Cream shortening and sugar. Sift together flour, soda and salt and add to creamed mixture. Fold in rolled oats. Press half of this mixture firmly into a greased and floured 9 x 13-inch pan. Spread with cooled filling and cover with remaining half of mixture. Bake 25 to 30 minutes in 375 degree oven until golden brown. Cut into bars while warm.

Filling:
3 cups dates, cut up

1/4 cup sugar
1 1/2 cups water

Cook over low heat, stirring constantly, until thickened. Cool.

KOURABIEDES

2 cups melted butter
3/4 cup powdered sugar
1 egg yolk

1 jigger brandy
4 1/2 cups flour

Mix all ingredients with hands. Shape into balls. Stick a clove in the top of each cookie. Bake 15 minutes at 300 degrees. Roll in powdered sugar.

The life that shall flourish will be the life that adapts to its environment and its changes.

Yugoslavia is about the size of Wyoming, and is on the Adriatic coast of the Balkan Peninsula in southeast Europe. Industries include steel, chemicals, wood products and cement. The Dinaric Alps run parallel to the Adriatic coast, which is lined by offshore islands. The area was formerly known as Serbia, which had been a vassal principality of Turkey. It was established as an independent kingdom in 1878 and was named as Montenegro. The name was later changed to Yugoslavia.

DJUVETCH
(An Oven Stew)

10 medium sized onions	1 large eggplant
10 fresh tomatoes, sliced	6 green bell peppers
1/2 cup rice, uncooked	1 cup okra
10 medium potatoes, sliced	Salt and pepper
5 lamb chops	2 tablespoons butter
5 pork chops	

Chop onions fine and cover bottom of roasting pan. Arrange slices of tomatoes on onions, then sprinkle with 1/2 cup rice. Next add a layer of potato slices; then the chops. Peel and dice the eggplant. Then cover the chops with eggplant and sliced bell pepper. Add another layer of sliced tomatoes and top with sliced okra. Sprinkle with salt and pepper and dot with butter. Cover pan and bake 1 hour at 450 degrees. Remove cover and continue to bake 30 minutes more reducing heat to 350 degrees.

STUFFED ONIONS

Stuff onions with eggplant, squash or tomato. Cut off top of 8 onions about size of orange. Remove inside leaving a good onion shell. Grind or chop fine the onions with 1 medium peeled eggplant or favorite vegetable. Mix lightly with 1/2 cup butter and 1 cup bread cubes. Season with black pepper. Divide into 8 portions and stuff lightly into onion cases. Cover and bake 20 minutes at 400 degree (200 degree C.). Lower heat and bake at 350 degrees (180 degree C.) for 25 minutes longer. If necessary add a little water.

191

Zaire, located in Central Africa, is about one-fourth the size of the U.S. Zaire includes the bulk of the Zaire (Congo) River Basin. The vast central region is a low-lying plateau covered by rain forest. Mountainous terraces in the west savannas cover the south and southeast, the north has grasslands, and there are high mountains on the east. Crops include coffee, cotton, rice, sugar cane, bananas and plantains. Zaire provides two-thirds of the world's supply of cobalt.

EGGS IN A HOLE

5 large onions, chopped
5 large tomatoes, chopped
5 sweet peppers, bell

1 small hot pepper
1/2 cup oil

Simmer all ingredients until reduced to a pulp. Divide into individual pottery casseroles. Make a well in the pulp. Break 1 egg into each well. Bake in 300 degree oven until egg is set.

YOGURT RICE PUDDING

In a large bowl mix 1 ounce gelatin with 3/4 cup sugar. Use one #10 can (6 lbs. 12 ounces) of peaches. Add reserved juice heated to boiling and stir until gelatin is dissolved. Add 1 quart vanilla yogurt, 2 teaspoons ground cinnamon, 1/2 teaspoon ground nutmeg, 2 quarts cooked rice, 1 cup seedless raisins. Pour into baking pan and chill. To serve cut into 2-inch squares.

MOLASSES GINGER PUNCH

(Very Refreshing)

Into 1 gallon jug put
1 cup molasses
1 cup cider vinegar

1 tablespoon ground ginger
Pinch of salt

Fill jug with water. Shake and serve over cracked ice.

The banana was discovered along the Indus River three centuries before Christ. A diet consisting solely of this fruit will sustain life for a long period. Consequently, it is one of the major foods of the world.

Zambia is located in South Central Africa. It is a very high plateau, surrounded entirely by land, and a very rich farming and cattle country. Victoria Falls on the Zambezi River is more than 3 times the width and twice as high as Niagara Falls.

FRIKKADELS

2 lbs. ground lamb	1 teaspoon coriander
1/2 cup soft bread crumbs	2 teaspoons salt
1 large onion, chopped fine	Fresh ground black pepper
2 eggs	1/4 cup peanut oil
1/4 teaspoon nutmeg	

Combine first 8 ingredients in a bowl and knead until well blended. Make 12 equal portions and shape into patties. Heat the oil until very hot. Brown the patties, 4 at a time, until richly brown. Keep warm.

Make a sauce by using some of the pan drippings: approximately 1 cup with 1 cup hot water. Bring to a boil and thicken and season to taste!

PEPPER AND SPICE COOKIES

1 1/2 cups flour	1/2 teaspoon cloves
2/3 cups brown sugar	1/2 teaspoon ginger
1/2 teaspoon salt	1 egg
1/8 teaspoon black pepper, cracked	1/4 cup butter

Combine dry ingredients. Make well in center, add soft butter and egg. Work in flour, and shape into a big ball. Break off pieces and shape into cookie. Bake in 325 degree oven about 18 minutes.

WILD GAME IN YOGURT SAUCE

3 lbs. lean game	2 carrots, grated
2 slices of bacon, chopped	1 onion, chopped
1 tablespoon oil	1 clove garlic, minced

Sauté vegetables with oil and bacon. Brown pieces of wild game (after marinating in milk overnight) in pan. Remove meat to baking pan. Add 1 cup beef stock and 1 cup yogurt to pan drippings. Season to taste with thyme, bay leaf, salt and pepper. Pour over game and cover and bake in 325 degree oven for 4 hours. Add more liquid if necessary. Thicken pan juices and serve over game.

Wild hare, birds, camel, venison, elk and wild boar are excellent prepared in this manner.

193

SAHADI IMPORTING CO. INC.
187 Atlantic Ave.
Brooklyn, New York

BARZIZZA BROTHERS
351-353 S. Front St.
Memphis, Tennessee

ATHENS IMPORTED FOOD
103 N. Alakama St.
Indianapolis, Indiana

KAUFCO SALES
1072 First Ave.
New York, New York 10022

Products:
Venison, Buffalo, Boor, Lion,
Elephant, Hippopotamous, Llama,
Raccoon, Possum, Whale Steaks,
Turtle, Rattlesnake, Quail,
Pheasant, Wild Hares

**HEALTH WATERS OF THE
WORLD, INC.**
1440 Broadway
New York, New York 10018
(212) LW 4-3377
Products: Mineral Waters
Brands: Evian, Vichy, Perrier, Badoit,
Contrexeville Mineral Waters from
France; Apollinaris from Germany;
Fiuggi from Italy; Mountain Valley
Water from Hot Springs, Arkansas

HOLLY WORLD FOODS, INC.
310 Townsend St.
San Franciso, California 94107
(415) 392-6520
Products: Artichokes, caviar, cookies,
crackers, biscuits, candy, cereal, coffee, chocolate, chutney, cheese, fish
and seafood, fruit, jams, jellies, marmalade, marrons, meat, mushrooms,
mustard, olives, Jewish foods, Japanese foods, dates, vegetables, soups,
seasonigns, tea, truffles, snails,
sauces, onions (wholesalers and im-
porters)

ORIENTAL BAZAAR
262 E. Paces Ferry Road
Atlanta, Georgia 30305

Aromatic herbs may be ordered from
Kalustyan Orient Expert Trading
Corp., 123 Lexington Avenue, New
York, New York 10016.

SOURCES FOR BEANS
Nichols Garden Nursery
1190 North Pacific Hwy.
Albany, Oregon 97321

The Natural Development Co.
Bainbridge, Pennsylvania 17502

Joseph Harris Co. Inc.
Moreton Farm
Buffalo Road, Rt. 33
Rochester, New York 14624

LIBERTY IMPORT CORP.
A Div. Of Lankor International
66 Broad St.
Carlstadt, New Jersey 07072
(201) 935-4500
Products: Biscuits, bread, nuts, con-
fections, cocktail accessories, cocktail
mixes, fish products, game and meat
specialties, condiments, jams, snack
items, non-alcoholic beverages.

ISRAEL PRODUCTS INC.
11 W. 25th St.
New York, New York 10010
(212) 243-8020
Products: Soup mixes, puddings,
jells, sauce mixes, casseroles, soup almonds, pancake mix, couscous, ta-
hina, hummus, halva, preserves, mar-
malades, honey, gefilte fish, syrups,
chocolate, candies, wafers, dragees,
cocoa, chocolates.

WEISEL & CO., INC.
2113 North Humboldt Ave.
Milwaukee, Wisconsin 53201
(414) 264-5060
Products: Gourmet sausage products
Brands: Weisel's — Milwaukee's
Finest Sausage

Dry Measure:
1 teaspoon — 4 grams
1 tablespoon — 10 grams
1/4 cup — 33 grams
1/2 cup — 66 grams
1 cup — 130 grams

Meat:
1 lb. 3 ounces — 500 grams
1 kilogram — 1000 grams

Liquid:
4 1/4 cups — 1 liter
2 1/8 cups — 5 deceliters
1/2 cup — 1 deceliter

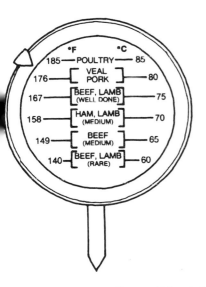

°F		°C
185	POULTRY	85
176	VEAL PORK	80
167	BEEF, LAMB (WELL DONE)	75
158	HAM, LAMB (MEDIUM)	70
149	BEEF (MEDIUM)	65
140	BEEF, LAMB (RARE)	60

Convert Fahrenheit to Celsius by
subtracting 32 and dividing by 2

OVEN TEMPERATURES

Description	Fahrenheit	Celsius
Cool	200	90
Very Slow	250	120
Slow	300-325	150-160
Moderately Slow	325-350	160-180
Moderate	350-375	180-190
Moderately Hot	375-400	190-200
Hot	400-450	200-230
Very Hot	450-500	230-260

Metric measures are much like customary types, even in quanities. Smallest (1 mL) spoon holds about 1/4 teaspoon; top line on big cup marks 500 mL, or about 2 cups.

METRIC CHOCOLATE CHIP COOKIES

METRIC CHOCOLATE CHIP COOKIES

550 mL unsifted flour
5 mL baking soda
5 mL salt
250 mL butter or margarine, softened
175 mL granulated sugar
175 mL firmly packed brown sugar
5 mL vanilla extract
2 eggs
2 168-gram packages semi-sweet
chocolate chips (500 mL)
250 mL chopped nuts

Preheat the oven to 190°C. In small bowl, combine flour, baking soda, and salt; set aside. In large bowl, combine butter, sugar, brown sugar, and vanilla; beat until creamy. Beat in eggs. Gradually add flour mixture; mix well. Stir in chocolate chips and nuts. Using 5 mL measure, drop by rounded measures onto ungreased cookie sheet. Bake 8 to 10 minutes. Makes 100 5-cm cookies.

France — Creme de Cerise — Cherry Liquor
Mexico — Chokalu — Delicious coffee creme liquor
Dutch West Indies — Curacao — Orange and spicy liquor
Scotland — Drambiue — Made form Scotch whiskey, herbs and heather honey
Columbia — Fleur de Mocha — Delightful coffee liquor
Italian — Galliano Liquor — Mellow smooth anise flavored
Austrian —— Enzian — Made from the blue mountain flower
Swiss — Pear Liquor — William Schnapps
Ireland — Irish Mist — A smooth drink. Irish whiskey and honey
Japan — Ocha — Made from green tea
France — Parfait Amour — Made from Violets
Turkey — Pasha — Turkish coffee liquor
Peppermint Schnapps — Not so sweet mint flavored
Jamaica — Pimento Dram — Rum hot with pepper
South Pacific — de Pina Licor — Pineapple flavor
Middle East — Raki — Anisi flavored
Banana flavored
Sloe Gin — Not gin — Liquor made from plums
East Indian — Swedish Punch — Made from tea, citrus fruit and spice
Jamacia — Tia Maria — Coffee and spice flavor
Triple Sec — Orange liquor
Italian — Tusca — Milk brandy flavored with orange and coconut
Africa — Von der Hum — Made from tangerines and spices
Polish — Wisniowka — Made from wild cherries

Spirits can be distilled from anything which can be induced to ferment. Apples, cactus, coconuts, dates, all fruits and grains, milk, molasses, potatoes and rice are used in making spirits around the world.

Benedictine is possibly the oldest and best known of the liqueurs. It was developed by the Benedictine Monks of Fecamp, Normandy, in the year 1510.

SOME OF THE WORLDS GREAT CHEESES

*Swiss
Appenzeller — Firm, tangy. Good table cheese. Melts well.

*Italian
Bel Paese — Smooth and waxy. Mild. Keeps 3 months. Good with light wine and cheese.

Ireland
Blarney — Firm with holes. Mild. Keeps 6 months. Spread at room temperature.

France
Bonbel — Very mild. 9 months. Great with Sherry.
Boursault — Triple creme. Keeps 4 weeks. Good dessert cheese.
Brie — Soft. Mild earthy flavor. 4 weeks. Good all around.
Camembert — Soft. Mild, distinctive. 4 weeks. Good with wine and cheese and fruit.
Coulommiers — Soft and creamy. 4 weeks. Spreads well.
Neufchatel — Soft and creamy. 4 weeks. Table and dessert cheese.
Petit — Swiss — Soft uncured. Eat at once. Great with berries.
Pont l 'Eveque — Soft, fairly strong. 4 weeks. Good with wine and bread.
Port du Salut — Mellow and robust. 7 weeks. Dessert and table cheese.
Reblochon — Mild and nutty. 7 weeks. Dessert cheese.
Roquefort — Sharp and piquant. 3 months. Dessert, salad, robust wine.

Sweden
Bondost — Firm, dome shaped. 5 months. Good with beer and crackers. Farmers cheese.

Hungary
Brindza — Soft pickled cheese, buttery, sharp and salty. 8 weeks. Good eating cheese.

Germany
Butter Kaese — Semi-soft to hard. Mild, unusual flavor. 6 months. Good with beer and robust wine.
Muenster — Semi-soft, mellow, delightful. 5 weeks. Good table cheese.
Tilsiter — Firm with holes. Hearty flavor. 1 year. Slices well.
Hard cheese — Soft, very strong. 6 months. Good with pumpernickel. Sprinkle with caraway seeds.

Denmark
Danablu — Semi-soft, blue mold, rich and spicy. 6 months. Excellent with salads, fruit and dips.
Danbo — Firm to hard, tangy. 1 year. Good on smorgasbord.
Esrom — Soft with holes. Mild and mellow. 4 months. Spread at room temperature.
Havarti — Soft firm, mild and sweet. 4 months. Light wine and beer.
Kuminost — Firm with cumin and caraway. 4 months. Good table cheese.
Samsoe — Swiss type with holes. Nutty, sweet. 1 year. Good with fondues.

England
Derby — Firm and smooth. Mild. Good, keeps 8 months. Table cheese.
Cheddar — Firm to hard. Mild to sharp. 1 year. Good grating cheese for cooking and snacks.
Cheshire — Semi-soft, moist. Slightly salty. 3 months. Good for Welch Rarebit.
Gloucester — Firm, some holes. Pungent. Keeps 3 months. Good with pies.
Lancashire — Moist and crumbly. Strong. 3 months. Excellent melting cheese.
Stilton — Crumbly, blue mold. Mild. 6 months. Served with unsalted crackers.

Egypt
Domiati — Soft. Pickled or Soft, pickled like Feta. White to dark color. Strong and acid. 1 year. For eating.

Turkey

Zomma — Firm to hard. Mellow to sharp. Keeps 1 year. 5 lb. wheels. Smooth and table cheese.

Scotland
Dunlop — Firm Cheddar type. Black wax rind. Keeps over 1 year. Delightful for cooking and table.
Highland — Semi-soft. Mild and pleasant. 3 months. Spreads at room temperature.
Orkney — Plain or smoked Cheddar type. Mild. 3 months. Melts well.

Holland
Edam — Semi-firm, irregular tiny holes. Red wax rind. Mild, nutty flavor. 6 months. Good table cheese.
Gouda — Semi-firm. Like Edam.
Leyden — Semi-soft with caraway or cumin. Blend. 3 months. Good for sandwiches.

*Switzerland
Emmentaler — Hard, smooth wheels. 180-lb. Keeps over 2 years. The original Swiss cheese. Mild sweet, nutlike flavor. Great all around cheese.
Gruyere — Firm to hard like Emmetaler.
Sap Sago — Very hard grating cheese. Keeps indefinitely. Flavored with clover. Light green in color. Sharp flavor.

*Italy
Caciacavallo — Hard goat or cow cheese. Sharp and salty. 10 pin shape. Over 2 years. Table and snack cheese.
Fontina — Semi-soft wheels. 14-30 lb. Nutty flavor. Keeps 6 months. Melts well for fondue.

Gorgonzola — Semi-soft. Pasty blue mold. Piquant and spicy. Keeps 9 months. Great with robust wine.

Mozarella — Semi-soft, unripened, mild. Good pizza cheese. Melts easily.
Parmesan — Hard to very hard. 50-70-lb. wedges. Sharp. Piquant. Keeps 3 years. Good grating cheese.
Provolone — Hard, flaky cheese. Pear, salami and sausage shape. (2-200 lb.) Keeps 3 years. Good on spaghetti.
Taleggio — Soft and pasty cheese. 4-lb. square. Keeps 6 weeks. Dessert cheese great with fruits and nuts.
Romano — Hard, mild to sharp cheese. Smooth cheese and grating.

United States
Beer Cheese — Soft limburger type. Excellent with beer and dark bread.
Brick — Semi-soft with holes. Mild and pungent. Melts well.
Colby — Firm, mild cheese. Keeps 1-3 months and smooth. Excellent for sandwich.
Coon Cheese — Firm cheddar type. 10-oz. sticks. Great for sandwiches.
Cream Cheese — Smooth and buttery. Mild. Great on sandwich spreads.

Liederkranz — Soft, creamy, strong aroma. Keeps 4 weeks. Like a mild limburger.
Longhorn — Firm, mild cheddar type. A great American favorite.
Monterey Jack — Smooth open texture, mild flavor. Keeps 9 months. When young, a table cheese; good for grating after aging.

Wales
Caerphilly — Soft, granular, moist cheese. Has an acid, buttermilk flavor. Excellent for sandwiches and fondue.

Greece
Feta — Semi-soft and crumbly, sharp and salty cheese. Great with olives and wine and crackers.

Norway
Gammelost — Semi-soft, blue mold, brownish yellow. Very strong cheese. Keeps 1 year. Blend with cream cheese.
Gjetost — Hard, firm buttery brown sweet cheese. Keeps 1 year. Eat on crackers.
Jarlsberg — Firm Swiss type cheese, mild and nutty. 20-lb. which keeps 1 year. Good all purpose cheese.

Romania
Kaskaval — Firm sheep milk, mild, slightly smokey. Good table cheese.

Finland
Lappi — Firm, semi-soft, mild pleasant cheese. Keeps 6 months.

Belguim
Limburger — Soft creamy, very strong cheese.

large cardboard square (see diagram
  below)
1 box cake mix

1 egg
1/2 cup oil

Out of cardboard cut two rectangles 4 x 6 inches for front and
back of house. Cut two rectangles 3 1/2 x 7 inches for roof and
two 4 1/2 x 6-inch pieces for sides that are cut into a point for
gables. Cut two 2 1/2-inch pieces for chimney, shaping bottom to
fit over pitch of roof.

For cookie dough blend cake mix, egg and oil with fingers to form
smooth dough. Using fingertips, spread dough onto patterns 1/4-
inch thick, allowing 1/4-inch margin. (This allows dough to rise
while baking.)

Use spice can to cut out windows and doors.

Bake the cookie house on cardboard in 300 degree oven for 10-15
minutes. You may put cardboard on pan if desired. Allow cookies
to cool and dry before removing from cardboard.

Now assemble house together using this delicious icing for mortar:

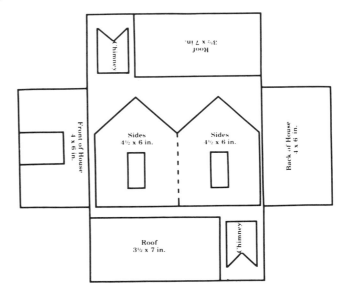

Icing:
1 box powdered sugar
2 tablespoons cocoa

1/4 cup vegetable shortening
1 teaspoon vanilla
1/4 cup milk

Blend thoroughly with mixer all the ingredients. Carefully spread
around edges of cookie house. Stand up front and back and sides,
sticking together. (I construct my cookie houses on heavy cardboard so they can be moved around.).

Be patient! After your sides and front and back stand for about 30 minutes, place on roof and chimney. Use Drip Icing to stick on both extra cookies made from the leftover dough and pieces of hard candy. Drip Icing is made with 1 cup powdered sugar and 2 tablespoons hot water. This may be tinted and dribbled all over finished house. Use hard candies for the walkway.

---

2 cups sugar
1 cup butter
2 cups flour
2/3 cup cocoa
4 eggs
1 teaspoon vanilla

Cream sugar and butter, add rest of ingredients. Press into greased 9 x 14-inch baking pan. Bake 25 minutes at 300 degrees. Then spread with 1 package colored minature marshmallows. Bake 5 minutes longer. Cool cake for 1 hour then frost.

1/3 cup canned milk
1 stick butter
6 ounces chocolate chips, semi-
 sweet
1 cup sugar
1 teaspoon vanilla

Mix all ingredients, bring to boil. Boil 1 minute. Beat slightly and pour over marshmallow brownies. Cool before cutting.

209

210